Also in the series:

Agaves, Yuccas, and Their Kin: Seven Genera of the Southwest
Jon L. Hawker

Between Two Rivers: Photographs and Poems Between the Brazos and the Rio Grande
Jerod Foster and John Poch

Cacti of Texas: A Field Guide
A. Michael Powell, James F. Weedin, and Shirley A. Powell

Cacti of the Trans-Pecos and Adjacent Areas
A. Michael Powell and James F. Weedin

Cowboy Park: Steer-Roping Contests on the Border
John O. Baxter

Dance All Night: Those Other Southwestern Swing Bands, Past and Present
Jean A. Boyd

Dancin' in Anson: A History of the Texas Cowboys' Christmas Ball
Paul H. Carlson

Deep Time and the Texas High Plains: History and Geology
Paul H. Carlson

"Don't Count the Tortillas": The Art of Texas Mexican Cooking
Adán Medrano

Equal Opportunity Hero: T. J. Patterson's Service to West Texas
Phil Price

Finding the Great Western Trail
Sylvia Gann Mahoney

Grasses of South Texas: A Guide to Identification and Value
James H. Everitt, D. Lynn Drawe, Christopher R. Little, and Robert I. Lonard

A Haven in the Sun: Five Stories of Bird Life and Its Future on the Texas Coast
B. C. Robison

In the Shadow of the Carmens: Afield with a Naturalist in the Northern Mexican Mountains
Bonnie Reynolds McKinney

Javelinas: Collared Peccaries of the Southwest
Jane Manaster

A Kineño's Journey: On Learning, Family, and Public Service
Lauro F. Cavazos, with Gene B. Preuss

Kit Carson and the First Battle of Adobe Walls: A Tale of Two Journeys
Alvin R. Lynn

Land of Enchantment Wildflowers: A Guide to the Plants of New Mexico
LaShara J. Nieland and Willa F. Finley

Little Big Bend: Common, Uncommon, and Rare Plants of Big Bend National Park
Roy Morey

Lone Star Wildflowers: A Guide to Texas Flowering Plants
LaShara J. Nieland and Willa F. Finley

My Wild Life: A Memoir of Adventures within America's National Parks
Roland H. Wauer

Myth, Memory, and Massacre: The Pease River Capture of Cynthia Ann Parker
Paul H. Carlson and Tom Crum

Opus in Brick and Stone: The Architectural and Planning Heritage of Texas Tech University
Brian H. Griggs

Pecans: The Story in a Nutshell
Jane Manaster

Plants of Central Texas Wetlands
Scott B. Fleenor and Stephen Welton Taber

Seat of Empire: The Embattled Birth of Austin, Texas
Jeffrey Stuart Kerr

Texas Natural History in the 21st Century
David J. Schmidly, Robert D. Bradley, and Lisa C. Bradley

Truly Texas Mexican: A Native Culinary Heritage in Recipes
Adán Medrano

The Wineslinger Chronicles: Texas on the Vine
Russell D. Kane

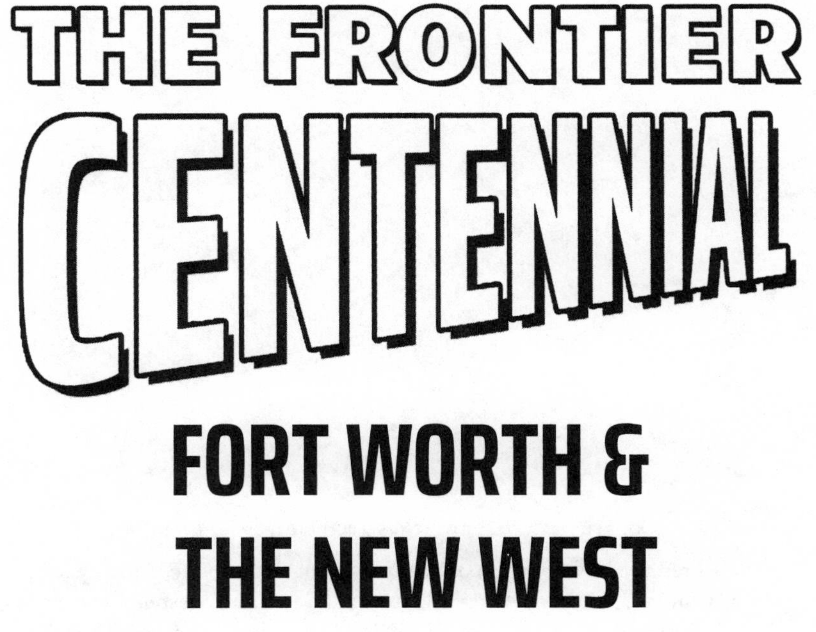

FORT WORTH & THE NEW WEST

JACOB W. OLMSTEAD

TEXAS TECH UNIVERSITY PRESS

This book is typeset in EB Garamond. The paper used in this book meets the minimum requirements of ANSI/NISO Z39.48-1992 (R1997). ∞

Designed by Hannah Gaskamp

Cover design by Hannah Gaskamp

Library of Congress Control Number: 2020950821

ISBN 978-1-68283-083-3 (cloth)

ISBN 978-1-68283-084-0 (ebook)

Printed in the United States of America

20 21 22 23 24 25 26 27 28 / 9 8 7 6 5 4 3 2 1

Texas Tech University Press

Box 41037

Lubbock, Texas 79409-1037 USA

800.832.4042

ttup@ttu.edu

www.ttupress.org

For my three Texas girls
& my three new Utah girls

CONTENTS

ILLUSTRATIONS

ACKNOWLEDGMENTS

When I came to Fort Worth as a graduate student, I thought I had a good understanding of what it meant to be "western." I spent my youth in the forests and on the beaches of Oregon and in the deserts and mountains of Utah—both west places thousands of miles further west than Texas. But Fort Worth was like a different world. I was taken aback by the stunning Moderne architecture downtown but equally thrilled with the stockyards, the longhorns, the steakhouses, and the cowboy culture on display all around me. It was a fascinating landscape. I can't quite remember what I thought Fort Worth would be like when I decided to attend Texas Christian University (TCU). But when I arrived, I was ill-equipped to understand what I experienced. This book is my effort to explain, at least in part, why Fort Worth is the way it is. My first acknowledgment is to thank the City of Fort Worth for the wonderful years my family and I spent in North Texas. In a short time, it became home.

The manuscript for this book was an outgrowth of research I completed while attending TCU. I am grateful for the opportunity to pause and share my overwhelming feelings of gratitude for those who guided and, in some cases, nudged me down the road to publication. Few, I believe, have had mentors as devoted to their students as I had while at TCU. The chairman of my dissertation committee and friend Dr. Todd M. Kerstetter went beyond the requirements of his position many times on my behalf. His door was always open. He willingly and patiently listened to my frustrations and half-baked ideas, responding with timely candor and sage advice. Above all, he continually expressed confidence in my ability to succeed. Following the completion of my graduate work, Todd continued to encourage my efforts to publish this book. To the other members of my committee: Drs. Gregg Cantrell, Rebecca Sharpless, and Peter Szok, I appreciated your thorough reading of this book when it was in dissertation form, saving me from more than a few embarrassing mistakes. Your critical insight made the completed product much better than it otherwise would have been.

The earliest drafts of this book benefitted from the review and feedback from my fellow graduate students. I would especially like to thank Jahue Anderson, Robert Butts, Glen Ely, and Peter Pratt. To David Grua I want to extend a special "thank you." As a former fellow student turned colleague, he provided an example and encouragement for moving my dissertation to a book manuscript.

I wish to extend my appreciation for the guidance and help provided by the staff at the Mary Couts Burnett Library, Special Collections at Texas Christian University; the staff at the Fort Worth Public Library Archives; the staff at City Secretary's Office of the City of Fort Worth; the staff at the Amon Carter Museum Library; the Woman's Club of Fort Worth; Evelyn Barker, Sara Pezzoni, and the staff at the University of Texas at Arlington, Central Library, Special Collections; the staff at the University Archives at University of North Texas; Susan Richards at the Dallas Historic Society; the staff at the Texas State Archives; the staff at the Barker Center for American History; and the staff at the Southwest Collection/Special Collections at Texas Tech University. Susan Pritchett, the former archivist at the Tarrant County Archives, gets credit for suggesting the Frontier Centennial as a subject demanding further research and for tutoring me in Fort Worth's fascinating history.

Several institutions and organizations provided generous financial assistance in the completion of this manuscript. I would like to thank the late Donald E. Worcester, Professor Emeritus Paul F. Boller, and the Department of History and Geography at

TCU for the generous financial support that made travel possible to several archives and special collections. The Tarrant County Historical Society and the TCU Institute on Women and Gender also provided essential funding for travel to historical repositories. The Church History Department of The Church of Jesus Christ of Latter-day Saints also provided timely funding to acquire permissions for the photographs appearing in this book and to hire an indexer.

It has been a joy to work with Texas Tech University Press (TTUP) in the publication of this book. The staff and editors have demonstrated exceptional patience with me and provided invaluable advice for refining and tightening the manuscript. They also deferred to my opinions and suggestions about the final cover design. For this I give TTUP my sincerest appreciation and respect.

Most of all, I want to thank my family. My parents have been a constant source of support and listened while I discussed my research *ad nauseam*. I also appreciated my father's careful reading of every draft chapter of my dissertation. To my children, Portland, Elle, and Mayer, I express my love and gratitude for your patience while I worked on my dissertation and years later as I worked on the book. You have been a great source of joy and strength and daily provided me with a much-needed diversion from my work. And to Carie, thank you for your constant support and encouragement as I labored to complete the revision of this manuscript. I love you.

INTRODUCTION

It is a truism that the more exciting and colorful the story, the wider the audience.
ROBERT G. ATHEARN, *THE MYTHIC WEST*

In the afternoon on July 18, 1936, President Franklin Delano Roosevelt, aboard his yacht floating off the coast of Maine, pressed a button sending a signal via radio waves and Western Union telegraph lines to the front gate of Fort Worth's celebration of the Texas state centennial. With thousands of onlookers cheering, the signal sent a knife slicing through a ribbon attached to a lasso stretched across the entrance to the centennial grounds. The event marked the beginning of the "Frontier Centennial," Fort Worth's four-month celebration of the Texas livestock industry and the city's past as a frontier settlement on Trinity River. The rough-hewn script above the turnstiles reminded visitors that Fort Worth was "Wher the Wezt Begins [*sic*]."[1]

But the Frontier Centennial did not really speak to those commemorative objectives. Consciously distancing the event from anything as banal as historic commemoration, planners hoped to draw millions of visitors from around the state and nation with a celebration based on popular frontier mythology. Fort Worth called to Americans laden with fears about what the future of their nation would bring and the current woes of the depressed economy to escape into the thrilling days of the Old West. Removing allusions to traditional commemorative fare such as pageants or historical exhibits, promotional literature for the

Frontier Centennial boasted "a living, breathing recreation of the Old West" fashioned purely for the fun and entertainment of fair-goers. "Go Elsewhere for Education," the slogan went, jabbing at the neighboring Texas State Centennial Exposition in Dallas, and "Come to Fort Worth for Entertainment."

Rather than highlighting the distinctive western history of Fort Worth or West Texas, the Frontier Centennial presented a more homogenous mythic West. The celebration featured standard western favorites such as a horse show, rodeo, and Wild West show including live bison, whooping Indians, sharpshooting cavalrymen, and trick-riding cowboys. Frontier Centennial planners further wrapped these attractions in a western-themed environment with recreated buildings typifying the frontier including a stockade, Old West Main Street, train station, and Native American village. Less a composition of historic fact, the "recreation of the Old West" exhibited an easily consumable western experience. With broad strokes, centennial planners fashioned a landscape priming America's imagination with widely understood western symbolism.

Centennial planners always intended to host a celebration with a dominant western message, although their initial conception of the event oriented more toward honoring Fort Worth's history and its contribution to the Texas livestock industry. Celebrating Fort Worth's western past appealed to civic leaders and politicians because it paired Fort Worth with the distinctly American ideals of progress, independence, and self-reliance. The West provided a past to match Fort Worth's projected image as a thriving and progressive metropolis. Furthermore, civic leaders and centennial planners wanted to host a profitable event to help boost Fort Worth's sluggish economy in the midst of the Great Depression. Fearing a largely commemorative celebration would fail to attract enough visitors to Fort Worth's celebration, Frontier Centennial planners belatedly turned to Broadway producer Billy Rose. While he dismissed much of the planned commemorative features of the celebration as boring, Rose embraced the western theme for its universal appeal and its great potential for sensationalism and spectacle. Rose relished the opportunity to dramatize hostile Indians raiding stagecoaches and other violent conflicts between cowboys and Indians, although in fact Fort Worth's early history mostly lacked such conflicts. He kept some concepts initiated by centennial planners such as the recreation of a frontier village, but by dropping other features he sanitized the event of local flavor in favor of presenting a more entertaining and widely recognized conception of the American West.

Still, the celebration was not entirely bereft of commemorative offerings. Prior to Rose's arrival, the Women's Division of the Frontier Centennial Exposition Commission, composed primarily of Fort Worth club women, played a leading role in the shaping of the celebration. Seeking to imbue the occasion with some references to Fort Worth's western heritage and the Texas livestock industry in the face of Rose's alterations, the Women's Division fought for the inclusion of historical and cultural attractions. In the long run, however, the sensationalized expressions of the mythic West muted the celebration's location-specific commemorative message.

At the time of the Frontier Centennial, Fort Worth—like much of Texas—had a foot in two worlds environmentally and culturally.[2] On the one hand, Fort Worth, and Texas in general, inherited a southern past. Southern states supplied the city with most of its early Anglo pioneers who brought with them slaves, cotton, and southern ranching culture.[3] Although home to few large plantations or slaveholders, Tarrant County (which includes Fort Worth) voted in favor of secession to preserve the institution of slavery. Following the war, former Confederates fleeing the Deep South for a better future settled in Fort Worth and Tarrant County and played a singular role in their development and the maintenance of the cultural attitudes of the Jim Crow South.[4]

On the other hand, situated just east of the 98th meridian, Fort Worth stood on the environmental precipice of the West. Moving west from Fort Worth, precipitation declines, vegetation changes dramatically, and the topography flattens into the southern Great Plains. Such environmental changes created a uniquely western culture.[5] As a military outpost on the Trinity River supporting forts further west in the 1850s, Fort Worth played a part in the westward movement of the line dividing settled from unsettled lands and later served as a major terminal for ranchers and cowpunchers driving cattle from Texas to northern markets.

If Fort Worth was a product of both southern and western parentage, the city initially favored its southern parent more than its western one. In his analysis of Texas identity, Texas historian Glen Ely showed that Texas communities situated between the 98th and 100th meridians exhibited characteristics from both the West and South. In what he calls the "shatterbelt" region, the collision of environmental and cultural traits of the two larger regions created cities with mixed identities. Cities such as El Paso and Lubbock, located west of this region, have much more in common with the American West than do cities to the east of the belt, where characteristics of the Old South are dominant. Fort Worth, located to the east of the 98th meridian and the "shatterbelt," was among the more distinctively southern communities of Texas.[6]

To understand the diversity, complexity, and creation of Texas's identity, scholars have also turned to the study of historical memory.[7] Collective identity has been shown to flow from how groups such as families, societies, and nations collectively remember their pasts.[8] And collective memories, often intentionally shaped, played a central role in the evolution of Texas's identity. In his landmark study, "The Bones of Stephen F. Austin," historian Gregg Cantrell convincingly demonstrated that politicians during the Progressive Era worked to shape "a new public view of Texas history that emphasized Texas as both a *Western* and a quintessentially *American* state whose identity sprang from the hardy pioneers who tamed the wilderness and defeated the Mexicans in the Texas Revolution."[9] Through the removal of the remains of Stephen F. Austin to the state's capital, the commissioning of monuments honoring Texas pioneers, and the restoration and veneration of the Alamo, progressive politicians turned their back on the poverty and defeat of the South and its devotion to the

Lost Cause by creating a more usable memory pointing toward a progressive Texas future.

The new memory of Texas as western and American became so ingrained in public consciousness that it influenced the perspective and writings of Texas history.[10] It also helped shape the theme of progress promoted by the Texas State Centennial in 1936. Historian Walter L. Buenger concluded that the presentation of Texas as progress and western during the centennial celebration "culminated a two-decade-old process—the conscious and unconscious distancing of a people from the South of defeat and poor expectations."[11] It is within this larger shift in Texas memory that Fort Worth began to reshape its own memory and identity.

The doubling down of civic leaders and boosters in 1936 on Fort Worth's western past while omitting its southern roots was the outgrowth of a process that had started forty years earlier. These decades witnessed exponential growth for the city and marked its birth as a modern metropolis. The arrival of the Armour and Swift companies in 1903 brought meatpacking jobs and growth in the local livestock industry. Following the discovery of oil in West Texas, petroleum money inundated Fort Worth. The construction of refineries brought additional jobs, and Fort Worth became a center for the oil industry in the state and region. City boosters worked to secure an Army camp and several airfields during World War I, resulting in the city's fledgling aviation industry. Finally, between 1909 and 1929, Fort Worth led the state in percentage increase of manufacturing. As a result of the city's economic growth, its population grew exponentially.[12]

In developing a coherent strategy for economic growth, city boosters, civic leaders, and cultural elites found the progressive message of the American West more appealing than the South's legacy of defeat and concomitant devotion to the Lost Cause.[13] Similar to most Americans, Fort Worth boosters "associated the American West with the future, one of independence and self-reliance."[14] The reshaping of its historical memory came through the publication of popular histories casting Fort Worth as a town typical of the Old West, celebrations commemorating the city's pioneer heritage, and Fort Worth's annual hosting of the Southwestern Exposition and Fat Stock Show.

The 1923 celebration of the city's 75th anniversary provided city officials with another opportunity to fortify Fort Worth's western memory. Diamond Jubilee planners selected an Old West theme to commemorate the event. With promotion materials promising "the greatest frolic of fun that was ever held in the Grand Old West," the festivities included, among other things, a historical pageant with a cast of 2,500 and stagecoach and Pony Express races.[15]

Fort Worth's annual hosting of the Southwestern Exposition and Fat Stock Show was perhaps the most important element in solidifying its burgeoning western identity. Meant to support the city's livestock exchange and attract meatpacking interests to the city, beginning in the late nineteenth century the stock show welcomed ranchers and cowboys to conduct business in the city. During the first three decades of the twentieth-century stock show, owners worked to widen the appeal of the event to locals who possessed little or no knowledge of the livestock industry by adding entertainment venues such as carnival rides, sporting events, and rodeos. At the same time, stock show officials shed features commemorating the Confederacy such as raising the Confederate flag or Confederate military drills conducted by Confederate commemorative groups in favor of offerings with a western theme. By ritualizing Fort Worth's frontier past, the stock show, as an expression of cultural memory, bound the city to the West.[16] Through attendance of and participation in the stock show, Fort Worth citizens both accepted and fortified the western identity chosen by civic leaders and economic boosters.[17] In turn, the city's western image was simply a part of the identity presented for outside consumption.[18]

Fort Worth's embrace of a more useful identity and public image is not unique, particularly in the West. Like Fort Worth, public memory and image hid often conflicting and unflattering features of the past. In San Antonio, for example, boosters preferred to romanticize the Mexican influences on the city for tourism in the annual celebration of Fiesta, even while the southern practice of Jim Crow displaced Mexicanos. To boost tourism, Santa Fe, New Mexico, harmonized historic racial conflicts between Anglos, Mexicans, and Native Americans through the adoption of romantic adobe architectural styles.[19] Likewise, boosters in southern California drew upon Spanish forms of architecture to romanticize the region's Spanish past and promote the city as an appealing place to live and play.[20] In the city of Red Lodge, Montana, boosters opted to promote a memory of cowboys and ranching over its roots as a mining town. To spur tourism, civic leaders remodeled the town's appearance after prevailing ideas about the look of the Old West.[21]

Not just interested in fabricating a tourist gambit, leaders in Fort Worth looked to a western past as a useful reflection of current economic aspirations. For many Americans of the Progressive Era, the West became a powerful symbol. Like many progressives such as Theodore Roosevelt, Fort Worth civic leaders sought to reap the benefits of industrialism while at the same time holding to individual freedoms associated with the frontier. Although the stock show increasingly appealed to tourists with images of cowboys, chuck wagons, and cattle drives, boosters and civic leaders developed a more nuanced image for the city's promotion. They exhibited no interest in reshaping its physical landscape after romantic depictions of the Southwest. Rather, boosters preferred to cast Fort Worth as a futuristic and growing metropolis tapping the vast resources of its hinterlands in West Texas. Chamber of Commerce literature often pictured downtown Fort Worth with towering skyscrapers bustling with commerce and industry and trains, planes, and automobiles moving swiftly to the west in the foreground. Other images evoked Fort Worth's western heritage with pioneers looking into the future and dreaming of a fortress-like city enshrouded in clouds.[22]

The images that boosters conjured began to take physical form in the 1920s and '30s as dozens of private and public buildings designed in the Moderne style in vogue filled Fort Worth's skyline. Fort Worth eventually became a western bastion of Art Deco.[23]

Although messages and images of progress and modernity always graced its covers and front pages, the city's promotional materials also depicted its bygone days as a frontier settlement as not in the too-distant past. Civic leaders in Fort Worth wanted the best of both worlds. They sought to depict their city as possessing the characteristics of modernity while maintaining its wide-open agricultural spaces and the hospitable feel of a small western cow town.

The dichotomy between modern and western is exhibited in the city's slogan: "Where the West Begins." Promoted by Amon Carter and printed on the masthead of his newspaper the *Fort Worth Star-Telegram* since the 1920s, the phrase evokes images of both past and present. Americans viewed the frontier as not only the dividing line between east and west but the verge of settled and unsettled, civilized and savage, and metropolis and wilderness.[24] Fort Worth civic leaders and boosters identified their city as the very point of regeneration.

The continued struggle for boosters and civic leaders to maintain a balanced image of past and present stemmed from Fort Worth's proximity to Dallas. Geography placed Fort Worth in a dangerous position, and its identity and public image played an important role in the town's cultural and economic survival. Claiming a western heritage prevented Fort Worth from becoming derivative in the shadow of its growing doppelgänger. The casting of Fort Worth as a progressive western city with a modern look made it a viable candidate for manufacturers and merchants interested in the region. Boosters regularly fine-tuned Fort Worth's image to meet its contemporary needs. At no time was the need greater for civic leaders and boosters to maintain the city's image of modern western municipality than during the Great Depression.

In Texas memory and historiography, the Frontier Centennial is most often characterized as the "rival" centennial exposition of 1936, a ploy concocted by the Dallas-hating Carter and others to "siphon off" visitors from the Central Centennial Exposition and steal the "national spotlight" from Dallas.[25] Reducing the Frontier

Centennial to a simple scheme of one-upmanship robs the celebration of a more meaningful significance to the history of Fort Worth, Texas, and the imagined West of the 1930s. Yes, Frontier Centennial planners did exploit the storied rivalry between the two cities to promote the celebration. And yes, Frontier Centennial planners shaped their centennial offerings around those planned for the Dallas-based exposition. Far more important, however, the Frontier Centennial was a high-water mark in the decades-old process of reshaping Fort Worth's identity.

The Frontier Centennial is compelling because it illustrates the interplay of civic memory, identity, and image. Fort Worth civic leaders and boosters viewed the state's centennial year as a means to further bolster the city's image as a western metropolis through a celebration of the livestock industry. They hoped to build modern stock show facilities and remove it to a more advantageous and prosperous part of town. In this way the public face of an industry, so vital to both the city's identity and economy, would also reflect the city's images of progress and modernity. In the achievement of these goals, civic leaders and boosters found a willing partner in the Fort Worth citizenry and in the federal government. They successfully procured millions of dollars from New Dealers in Washington who embraced the notions of progress, civic pride, and local development. By seeking federal funding to help alleviate economic conditions, Fort Worth and Texas in general behaved more like new western municipalities than southern ones, who resisted federal aid during the Great Depression.[26] But not all efforts to project an image of western modernity were embraced locally. The overt sexualization of women to promote the celebration was hotly contested by some Fort Worthians.

The Frontier Centennial also provides a poignant view into how civic memories are crafted through celebration. In the case of Fort Worth, club women played an integral role in forming the exposition's initial messaging. After creating commemorative features based on Fort Worth's history, the Women's Division presented the information to the Board of Control. This board, composed of men, then determined which venues would be included and which would not. In the process, planners circumscribed the celebration's western messaging, thus cleansing the civic memory of inconsistencies and unwanted pasts, often at the expense of non-whites. The commemorative venues produced for the Frontier Centennial ultimately reveal how civic leaders and boosters preferred citizens and visitors remember their city's history.

In the shaping of content for the celebration that would fortify Fort Worth's western memory and identity, planners drew upon "mythic West" narratives and symbols that had become embedded in the American psyche.[27] The progressive messaging of the mythic West proved particularly palatable as Americans grasped for meaning and hope during the economic downturn of the Great Depression. Since the early republic, Americans endowed the frontier with ideological and symbolic significance. As outlined by historian Richard Slotkin, as a colony of European nations, from its inception, America's development necessitated "repeated cycles of separation and regression" whereby fortunes and life improved. On the frontier, Americans freed themselves from the constraints of eastern privilege and authoritarian regimes by conquering an untamed wilderness. This path of economic and cultural renewal often involved the displacement of Native Americans and the subjugation of Africans.[28] The myth of the frontier justified these processes as a triumph of "progress" through violent means and ultimately defined the essence of America.

During the nineteenth century, such processes became codified in the American psyche. Stories from the life of Daniel Boone, frontiersman and early archetypal American, served as a foundation for the myth of the frontier. Boone worked out man's struggle between the natural and the civilized on the wild frontier, where he cleared the path for civilization. James Fenimore Cooper later created a series of literary figures based on Boone in his novels.[29] Building on the frontiersmen characters established by Cooper, dime novelists produced thousands of western tales illustrating the tension between social order and anarchy on the frontier.[30]

Toward the end of the nineteenth century, many Americans became acquainted with the mythic West through frontiersman and scout Colonel William F. Cody (Buffalo Bill). In his shows, using symbolic props such as the rifle and the stagecoach, Cody exploited a frontier mythology that cast westward expansion as a process in which the untamed and uncivilized West was subdued and civilized.[31] Cody's narrative hinged on a central facet of the frontier mythology: the characterization of Native Americans as brutal and aggressive.[32] Ultimately, Cody's characterization of westward expansion intentionally promoted an image of American progress.[33]

In the face of growing eastern cities and industrialization in the 1890s, anxiety over the closing of the frontier revitalized America's interest in the West.[34] The "frontier thesis" as posited by historian Frederick Jackson Turner drew upon the basic progressive message of frontier mythology.[35] Turner suggested that as European settlers eked out an existence on the frontier, they became Americans, embracing democracy and developing the traits of independence and self-reliance. Turner's ideas would shape the historical interpretations of the American West for the next four decades. At the same time, three easterners also popularized the mythic West after transformative western experiences. Born into privileged families and constituting the products of Ivy League educations, Theodore Roosevelt, Frederic Remington, and Owen Wister suggested that only the West could preserve essential traits of the nation's ideals of democratic freedom, courage, and common sense in the face of sweeping industrialization. Roosevelt expounded his thoughts on the significance of the West in several works, which later shaped his political views. In the West, Remington rediscovered his love for painting and began a career preserving scenes from the American West on canvas. Drawing upon his experiences in the West, Wister wrote *The Virginian*, a western-themed novel that became a foundational work for the modern Western and later influenced pulp novelists such as Zane Grey.[36]

The growth of the modern Western coincided with the emergence of the cowboy as the hero of the mythic West. Partly the result of a shift in westward settlement to the Great Plains and the Far West and the need for greater historical accuracy, by the 1890s authors began placing the cowboy at the center of the Western.[37] Mythmakers such as Buffalo Bill, who exhibited cowboy skills for the public in his Wild West shows, and Roosevelt, Remington, and Wister, also played a role in popularizing the mythic cowboy.[38] The cowboy, more than any other hero of the western, would become iconic, not only of the West but of America.[39] Writers of the new Westerns as published in pulp novels and weeklies surrounded the cowboy with a cast of stereotypical, if not colorful, characters. Westerns depicted Native American peoples as either noble helpers or savage foils. The use of formulaic plots employing immediately recognizable stereotypical characters contributed to the appeal of the Western as a literary genre.[40]

Recognizing the Old West as "a rich collection of usable myths and symbols," moviemakers began exploiting the western in film early in the twentieth century. The deserts of southern California provided directors with authentic-looking landscapes in which to set their films. Pairing the western myth with the medium of film created powerful visual images of the American West. Drawing on the patterns established in western novels, western films by the 1920s became the most popular type of film in the United States.[41] As with pulp novels, these films cast the cowboy as "a paragon of American qualities that included physical prowess, courage, and a sense of moral rectitude."[42]

The popularity of western novels and film played a singular role in the development of the Frontier Centennial. In their initial planning of the celebration, Fort Worth's civic leadership recognized, as had other leaders of western municipalities, the bankability of the Old West theme to attract tourists.[43] While politicians and scholars debated the usefulness of the frontier to American society in the midst of the Great Depression, the Western remained a valuable source of revenue for Hollywood, which continued to produce hundreds of B-westerns throughout the decade.[44] Moreover, among cowboys, the Texas cowboy reigned supreme and the Texas landscape figured prominently in western films.[45] Centennial planners reasoned that when Americans thought of the Old West they thought of Texas. They further concluded that when Americans pictured the Texas livestock industry and the cowboy, they thought of Fort Worth. Based upon these assumptions, planners developed a radical scheme of celebration. They sought to celebrate the Old West through a recreation of the frontier as it existed in western films—a concept Walt Disney later used in 1955 when creating Disneyland's tribute to the West, Frontierland.[46]

Still, during the early planning stages, local history including the history of West Texas and perceptions of authenticity influenced the celebration's structure more than did the mythic West as portrayed in literature and film. Frontier Centennial planners sought simply to create a film set that reflected Fort Worth and West Texas but sanitized of southern or Spanish influence. Eventually, planners arrived at the conclusion that a celebration commemorating only local and state history could not appeal to a nationwide audience. A movie set filled with participants garbed in western attire and featuring commemorative exhibits neither represented the grandness of the West nor offered sufficient entertainment venue, both of which Frontier Centennial planners aspired to present.

Unacquainted with Fort Worth's heritage or its role in the Texas livestock industry, Billy Rose, after his arrival in Fort Worth, remade the celebration around the immediately recognizable symbolism of the mythic West. Like Buffalo Bill, authors of dime and pulp novels, and movie producers, Rose used the nationally imagined West to appeal to Americans. In his translation of the mythic West into physical space, Rose introduced a new genre, the western theme park. To be sure, the crafting of themed spaces originated more than 300 years earlier with the creation of plush European gardens. More recently, world's fairs formed themed environments in the presentation of cultures, industry, and entertainment. Amusement parks such as Coney Island and Luna Park also attracted customers with themed attractions.[47] These venues in the nineteenth and twentieth centuries fostered sanitized, simplified, widely accepted mythic forms and places.[48] Builders of themed landscapes also conflate opposing myths with a sense of nostalgia. Thus, historically themed environments thrive upon vagueness, comingle eras, and are unbound by chronology. To observers, themed landscape becomes timeless and thus "alleviate[s] the anxieties in [the consumers'] lives and the crises in their societies."[49] Like the myths upon which they are often based, themed spaces appeal to their audiences through allusions to authenticity or fact.

Like film and literature, themed space has become an important medium through which Americans and others experience the mythic West.[50] By the 1930s, destinations such as Indian villages, dude ranches, and at least one drugstore created western-themed spaces for tourists.[51] Several Depression Era world's fairs also included limited space portraying the mythic West, most notably the Gold Gulch of the San Diego International Exposition in 1935–1936.[52] Using western films and pulp novels as a guide, Rose conflated a number of mythic Wests into a singular themed environment. Anticipating Walt Disney's approach, Rose used the mythic West to communicate with audiences in an "attempt to stimulate and direct consumption."[53] The early use of theming as an expression of the mythic West at the Frontier Centennial makes it an important precursor to subsequent theme parks with significant western components such as Disneyland, Knott's Berry Farm, and Six Flags Over Texas.

This book traces the evolution of the Frontier Centennial from its inception as a commemorative fair to themed park enshrining the mythic West to show the various ways centennial planners, boosters, and civic leaders sought to use the celebration as a means to bolster Fort Worth's identity and image as a modern American city with roots in the mythic west.[54] Because the messaging and nature of the Frontier Centennial changed radically after the arrival of Billy Rose, the chapters are divided into two parts. The chapters in part 1 narrate the early planning efforts to create a commemorative celebration of Fort Worth's livestock industry and history as part of the Texas frontier. During these early months, centennial planners put forward a bid to host a memorial celebration to the livestock industry as part of Texas's centennial festivities in 1936. City boosters and centennial planners also labored to use the celebration as an opportunity to repackage the city's livestock industry and promulgate its images as a modern metropolis. Simultaneously, West Texas's gradual disenchantment with the planning and funding of the state's centennial festivities resulted in their regional support for and participation in Fort Worth's celebration. The early efforts of Frontier Centennial planners to develop "authentic" western attractions is also described, as is the prominent role played by Fort Worth's club women in refining the celebration's commemorative message. In part 2, the circumstances that brought about the hiring of Billy Rose and his pitch to revamp the Frontier Centennial are outlined. Rose's efforts to sexualize the celebration are also explored, including the paradoxical role played by women during the Frontier Centennial. Finally, part 2 includes a discussion of Rose's use of prevailing symbols of the mythic West in the creation of a "themed space" in the physical layout of the Frontier Centennial fairgrounds.

As a city, Fort Worth predated the Civil War and for decades showed strong ties to the South and to the nation's westward expansion. The realities of secession and reconstruction saw those dual ties / heritages continued, but the rise of the cattle drives and improved transportation links connecting Fort Worth to West Texas pointed Fort Worth's identity and reality in a new direction. That identity crystallized in the minds of Fort Worthians during the Progressive Era. To Fort Worth boosters and civic leaders, the centennial year presented an unprecedented opportunity. Hoping to do more than simply commemorate one hundred years of the livestock industry in Texas, centennial planners ultimately chose to use the celebration not only to boost the city's economy but also to proclaim Fort Worth's presence on the landscape of the modern American West.

THE FRONTIER CENTENNIAL

PART 1

COMMEMORATING REGIONAL HISTORY

CHAPTER 1

AMON'S "COWSHED"

FORT WORTH'S CENTENNIAL MEMORIAL TO THE TEXAS LIVESTOCK INDUSTRY AND REPACKAGING ITS WESTERN IDENTITY

The impetus for celebrating the Texas state centennial began, ironically, at the urging of a New Yorker. On November 5, 1923, the Tenth District Convention of the Associated Advertising Clubs of America—an organization devoted to boosting the State of Texas—held its annual meeting. Theodore H. Price, the editor of *Commerce and Finance*, told the crowd they had thus far failed to cultivate a reputation equal to the unlimited potential and wealth of the state. Beyond the agricultural and industrial opportunities, Price reminded listeners, the state possessed a singular past, "a gloriously romantic history," which, if exploited properly, could focus the nation's attention on Texas. Price suggested that in 1936, Texas celebrate "a centenary so important and so auspicious by [hosting] an exposition that will attract the attention and presence of the world."[1] His reasoning for staging a Texas exposition echoed the objectives of the world's fairs held in New Orleans, Atlanta, and Nashville at the end of the nineteenth century. Each of these expositions attempted to move past old sectional rivalries and poverty of the past and, through the emphasizing of images of progress and patriotism, place the South in the vanguard of national and international economic growth.[2] Price's remarks set the wheels in motion for what would become Texas's centennial celebration.

Meanwhile, in Fort Worth, leaders worked hard to develop the city's image as a progressive metropolis in the decades before the centennial year. The twentieth century brought economic and population growth based upon oil, military spending, and manufacturing. These developments made Fort Worth Texas's fourth largest city. Although the growth and diversification of its economy marginalized the importance of the cattle industry to the city's economy, ties between the city and its historic livestock business remained strong. Symbolically, the annual hosting of the Southwestern Exhibition and Fat Stock Show represented the primary link between the city and its western heritage. As attendance of the stock show escalated so, too, did the concerns that the deteriorating North Side stockyards that hosted the annual event no longer reflected the image of modernity and progress that civic leaders and city boosters worked to create for their city.

In the year preceding the state's centennial, civic leaders and boosters embarked on an odyssey that would culminate in the building of new stock show facilities removed from their historic home in the Fort Worth stockyards. Using the city's stock show as a foundation, Fort Worth proposed to host a centennial celebration commemorating the Texas livestock industry—a prospect that would reinforce and proclaim the city's western identity. Through the procurement of city, state, and federal funds, Fort Worth civic leaders and centennial planners hoped to build modern livestock facilities for the stock show and in the process provide greater financial unity between the stock show and its host city. After receiving sufficient funding, Amon G. Carter and other civic boosters and members of the city council began a campaign to remove the stock show to a location more consistent with the city's modern identity.

Planning for the state's centennial celebration began in earnest more than a decade after Price's initial suggestion. During the intervening years, the economic climate of the state and nation changed dramatically. The euphoric economic prosperity of the 1920s had given way to poverty and want. Material growth and progress had become so central to American ideology and expectations that the impact of the Great Depression on the American mind was profound.[3] The inabilities of politicians and economists to navigate the nation out of the depression led many Americans to question the value of the American political and economic systems. In Texas, the depression destroyed the foundation of the state's economy as the value of livestock, cotton, and oil fell precipitously. Manufacturing jobs also declined sharply during the decade. Drought in the western half of the state further contributed to the economic plight of Texans hoping to eke out an agricultural living.[4]

Texas legislators believed the state's centennial year could prove useful to help counter rampant feelings of economic defeat and the chaos of the Great Depression. The state legislature passed legislation in February 1934 authorizing a centennial celebration and creating a commission to begin preparing for the state's centennial year.[5] Later that year, the commission developed a plan calling for an event Texanic in size and "international in scope" honoring the heroism of Texas history and celebrating the industrial growth of the state and the contribution of Texans to the arts. The planning committee envisioned a celebration staged on two fronts. First, it called for a series of celebrations around the state carried out on a local level and devoted to commemorating the history of individual Texas communities. Second, it recommended the state sponsor a "mammoth Central Exposition" celebrating the "material, educational, artistic, cultural and religious development of the people of Texas."

The plan for the state centennial demonstrates a desire to strike a balance between the commemoration of the state's history and an exhibition of its material and cultural progress. The dual emphasis on history and progress followed a pattern set by other Depression Era world's fairs. These expositions, particularly Chicago's Century of Progress, "stressed America's historical progress toward becoming a promised land of abundance."[6] Hoping to distract fairgoers from the troubles of the depression and instill images of a future American utopia, fair planners presented displays of American scientific and cultural ingenuity. Using other Depression Era world's fairs as example, Texas politicians looked to the centennial exposition to provide state officials a platform from which to instill confidence in the state's political and economic leadership.

Centennial planners soon discovered that striking an acceptable balance between the celebration of commercial developments and the commemoration of historical ones in the pursuit of their goals became a recurring point of conflict for politicians, cities, and entire regions of the state. The planning committee's proposal offered little direction for financing the various centennial programs. It suggested that funding for the centennial should come from the state. However, the Texas Legislature had yet to allocate any funds for the celebration. It also suggested that the centennial plans as laid out by their proposal necessitated a bankroll of at least $15 million. The figure would eventually generate considerable consternation among prospective host cities, primarily because centennial legislation suggested the honor of being host city would most likely go to the highest bidder.[7]

The Centennial Commission immediately moved forward with the selection of the central exposition host city. By midsummer, the commissioners approved a list of requirements prospective cities would have to meet in their bids to host the central celebration. Substantive requirements included providing 200 acres of land serviced by electric, gas, water, sewage, and drainage facilities. Each city had to submit the dollar amount it could contribute for the financing of the celebration. Proposals would be accepted only if submitted with full support of the mayor, the city council, the chamber of commerce, and prominent citizens including the heads of the major financial institutions and luncheon clubs. Finally, the commission required all bid proposals be submitted to the headquarters of the Texas Centennial Commission in Austin by September 1, 1934.[8] Any interested city could submit a proposal, but Commission Secretary Will H. Mayes sent copies of the proposal form to the mayors of Houston, San Antonio, Dallas, and Fort Worth.[9]

As the four major Texas cities began to craft their bids for the Central Exposition, the impending deadline and size of the financial commitment caused considerable consternation. Houston called for a delay so that questions about the state's financial commitment to the celebration could be answered.[10] Civic leaders in Dallas did not welcome Houston's plea for an extension. Dallas's bid to host the centennial already enjoyed broad public support. Putting off the deadline could only weaken its chances for claiming victory by allowing other cities to strengthen their bids. Officials in San Antonio also balked at Houston's request. Although they chafed at the legislation suggesting financial and not historical considerations would largely determine the location of the Central Exposition, the San Antonio Chamber of Commerce and Centennial Committee prepared a bid, emphasizing San Antonio's historical significance, which met the commission's deadline requirement.[11]

Fort Worth also worked to develop a bid.[12] Even before the Centennial Commission's announcement of the requirements for the host city, momentum gathered for either a Fort Worth bid or a bid to place the Centennial Exposition between Dallas and Fort Worth. Of interest, the development of Fort Worth's bid proceeded without the support of Amon G. Carter, who believed either San Antonio or Houston should host the centennial based on their historical significance.[13] The Tarrant County Advisory Board to the Texas Centennial Commission assumed the central leadership role in the city's earliest centennial planning. Initially, the board wanted to explore the possibility of co-hosting the central exhibition with its neighbor to the east, but officials in Dallas did not respond to the invitation.[14] The Fort Worth Centennial Committee made its first recommendations concerning the content of a bid to the Chamber of Commerce only days before the deadline.[15] But little is known of that proposed plan. Moreover, the subject of a bond issue for a centennial bid never came before the Fort Worth City Council.[16] It seems likely that Fort Worth simply failed to formulate a bid before the deadline.

On the day of deadline, the commission received three proposals. As expected, they came from Dallas, Houston, and San Antonio.[17] A week later, the commission traveled to each of the prospective host cities to hear oral presentations of the cities' plans and examine the proposed sites for the Central Exposition, beginning with Dallas. Unlike Houston and San Antonio, Dallas's bid proposed it host the central centennial exposition because of its ability to highlight the economic development of the state. Regardless of state funding, R. L. Thornton, President of the Dallas Chamber of Commerce, promised the Centennial Commission that Dallas would provide nearly $8 million to support the celebration.[18] Houston's bid touted the city's significance to the history of the state as justification for hosting the central celebration. Officials also promised to invest more than $6.5 million in the celebration, so long as the state provided an additional $3 million.[19] As the "cradle of Texas liberty," San Antonio officials argued their city was the logical choice for a celebration of the centennial year.[20] San Antonio's bid promised to offer just shy of $5 million to secure the appointment as host city.[21] They also required the state to provide at least $1 million.[22]

Returning to Austin, the commission began its deliberations. In a unanimous decision, based largely upon size of Dallas's pecuniary bid, Chairman Cullen F. Thomas emerged from the meeting with the announcement that Dallas had won the race for host city.[23] Although officials in Houston accepted defeat graciously and invited all Texans to support the Central Exposition in Dallas, those in San Antonio chafed at the selection. They argued that most of the members of the commission came from the northern portion of the state, so that the vote for the host city skewed north.[24]

Much has been made of the Dallas host-city selection sparking a plot in Fort Worth to host a "rival" exposition at the expense of Dallas in 1936. Evidence suggests, however, that Fort Worth leaders reacted positively to Dallas's selection. Expressing support for the newly named host city, Mrs. C. C. Peters, vice president of the Tarrant County Advisory Board to the Texas Centennial Commission, urged all Texas cities "to stand behind the chosen city and make the celebration as big as the State." Peters also viewed the proximity of the Central Exposition as a potential economic boon for Fort Worth. "Everyone who visits the exposition," she claimed, "will come to Fort Worth and the Southwestern Exposition and Fat Stock Show likely will draw many."[25]

On learning of Dallas's victory, Amon Carter reportedly "set a record for consecutive gawddamns."[26] However, knowing that the state used a "highest bidder system," Carter must have believed that either San Antonio or Houston would place the highest bid for the Dallas victory to surprise him. Expletives aside, a few days following the announcement, Carter's newspaper, the *Fort Worth Star-Telegram*, published an editorial taking the selection in stride. The editorial claimed that Dallas "fairly earned the distinction of being the Texas Centennial City," and "Fort Worth is happy to bask in reflected glory." As had Peters, the editorial claimed Fort Worth would benefit as the "nearest piece of metropolitanism to what we hope will be the center of Texas interest during the next two years."[27] No evidence suggests Carter or any of the civic leadership in Fort Worth conspired to exact revenge on its neighbor for claiming the Central Exposition. As in other Texas cities and counties, in the spring of 1935, Fort Worth began to develop a proposal for its own offering to the state's centennial celebration.

On May 7, 1935, Governor James Allred signed legislation appropriating $3 million for the state's centennial, of which Dallas received the lion's share, to host the Central Exposition. With the exception of Houston and San Antonio, which each received $250,000 for monuments at San Jacinto and the Alamo, respectively, and Austin, which received $225,000 for a museum, the legislature set aside $575,000 for the construction of historical markers and monuments around the state.[28] To aid the newly established Commission of Control for the Texas Centennial

Celebration in distributing these funds to cities and counties across the state, the legislature created a three-member Advisory Board of Texas Historians. In addition to making recommendations for places and events to receive a commemorative memorial or marker, they granted an audience to delegations lobbying on behalf of cities and counties seeking funds for the construction of memorials.[29] Interestingly, the Advisory Board of Texas Historians included no professionally trained historians. Louis Wiltz Kemp, a former president of several historical societies including the Texas State Historical Association and author of several books on the Republic of Texas, chaired the board. Reverend Paul J. Foik, a Roman Catholic priest and chair of the language department at St. Edward's University, and J. Frank Dobie, a national literary figure and Texas folklorist, joined Kemp on the board.[30]

Meanwhile, in Fort Worth, city fathers began crafting a proposal for a centennial memorial to the Texas livestock industry. Fort Worth's annual Southwestern Exposition and Fat Stock Show provided a ready platform from which to launch a centennial celebration. By the 1930s, the stock show had become an important tradition in Fort Worth and central to its shifting identity from a southern to a western city. Coincidentally, the year 1936 also marked the event's fortieth anniversary, and stock show and city officials hoped to develop a proposal that commemorated the livestock industry in Texas and simultaneously preserved the stock show as one of the premier livestock shows in the nation.

In the late nineteenth century, when Fort Worth resembled only a way station for cattle en route to northern markets in Kansas City or Chicago, Texas stockman Charles McFarland and public relations director of the Fort Worth Stockyards Company Charles C. French believed a stock show represented a means of breathing new life into the city's livestock enterprise.[31] They reasoned that a properly orchestrated stock show would help establish a permanent livestock exchange in Fort Worth and attract the nation's larger meatpacking corporations to establish operations near the stockyards.[32] Organizers planned the first Fort Worth stock show to coincide with the annual meeting of the Texas Cattle Raisers

Armour and Company Building, Fort Worth Stockyards, Fort Worth, Texas, circa 1900. Courtesy, W. D. Smith Commercial Photography, Inc. Collection, Special Collections, The University of Texas at Arlington Libraries.

Association (TCRA) in March 1896. As the stock show grew in significance to the industry, the TCRA held its annual meeting more often than not in Fort Worth. As predicted by McFarland and French, the industry took notice, and the meatpacking giants Swift & Company and Armour & Company built facilities adjacent to the Fort Worth stockyards in 1903.[33]

The earliest shows ran for one day and focused primarily on cattle. In the interest of broadening the show's appeal, officials began admitting auxiliary exhibits including poultry and horses. Show officials later added hog, sheep, and mule exhibits.[34] As the stock show became a vital part of the Texas livestock industry, officials worked to expand the importance of the show throughout the Southwest. Soon stockmen from Oklahoma, Louisiana, and New Mexico began attending the exposition. After a decade of stock show growth, the Fort Worth stockyard facilities had

Stockyards Coliseum, now known as Cowtown Coliseum, Fort Worth Stockyards, Fort Worth, Texas, circa 1908. Courtesy, Jack White Photograph Collection, Special Collections, The University of Texas at Arlington Libraries.

become inadequate. The Swift and Armour companies agreed to help fund construction of a new livestock pavilion in return for the creation of a permanent and incorporated company to oversee and ensure the continuation of the annual event. With additional investments on the part of local businessmen, the Stock Show Association emerged, led by Texas cattleman.[35] The association also oversaw the construction of a new pavilion. At the time of its 1908 completion, the Stockyards Coliseum was hailed as the "largest, most elegant, and perfectly appointed livestock auditorium in the South, and one without superior in the United States."[36] During the first three decades of the twentieth century, the exposition continued to cultivate new national markets and adapt to the changes in the livestock industry. The new facilities housed stock from Iowa, Arkansas, New Mexico, Oklahoma, Missouri, Nebraska, and Tennessee. Indicating the show's renown, former "cowboy-president" Theodore Roosevelt attended and spoke at the 1911 show.[37]

The growth and changing dynamic of the city's economy, particularly the importance of oil following World War I, dramatically altered the purpose and significance of the stock show to Fort Worth. With railroads already in place, the oil discovered in West Texas and elsewhere naturally flowed to Fort Worth; by 1922 the city boasted nine refineries. During World War I, the federal government placed Camp Bowie and several airfields on the outskirts of the city. As a result of local manufacturing and industrial development, Fort Worth's population grew dramatically. From 1910 to 1920, the population increased from 73,312 to 106,482 and from 1920 to 1930 increased to 163,447.[38] The livestock industry and meatpacking companies also continued to fit prominently into the city's economy. By the 1920s, more than two million head of cattle arrived in the city annually, with more than five thousand workers drawing a salary from the stockyards and packing interests.[39]

With the growing influence of oil in the Fort Worth economy, the power the meatpacking companies once wielded in Fort Worth began to wane. A loss of city-approved abatements signaled a shift in influence from the meatpacking companies to oil and other industrial interests.[40] Concomitantly, business and oil men with little connection with the livestock industry assumed leadership roles in the Stock Show Association. Without strong, interested corporations to back the exposition, civic leaders and organizations such as the Fort Worth Chamber of Commerce and Board of Trade stepped in to help underwrite the show. Intriguingly, as Fort Worth boosters and civic leaders worked to promote the city as a modern metropolis, they did not marginalize the stock show or the underlying livestock industry. Rather, in addition to viewing the show as the principal event in maintaining the city's importance to the Texas livestock industry, the new leadership began to mold the stock show into a venue for promoting Fort Worth's western identity.[41]

Beginning in the 1920s, the stock show enjoyed a closer relationship with Fort Worth's civic leadership and even greater ties with its citizenry. Van Zandt Jarvis took the helm of the Stock Show Association in 1924. His appointment as president represented the beginning of a strengthening of the ties between the exposition and the city. An experienced rancher and breeder with a long association with the show, Jarvis also maintained important political connections. Eventually, Jarvis drew upon his broad appeal on both sides of the Trinity River to capture the mayor's office in 1932.[42] Other businessmen such as Amon Carter filled important roles in the association. Since 1918, Carter worked to cultivate a West Texas market drawing upon the newly created West Texas Chamber of Commerce to promote the stock show in the region. Even as leaders like Jarvis and Carter worked to maintain the centrality of the show to the livestock industry in Texas and the greater Southwest, they began to make the show more appealing to locals. While stock show officials continued to enlarge the offerings of the exposition including the acquisition of new land and renovating and building new facilities, they also added attractions and exhibitions that would appeal to Fort Worth citizens to make the show economically self-sufficient.[43]

From the very beginning, organizers sought to make the show a diverse experience. Although the main attractions focused on livestock, the exposition included entertainment geared to interest the family members who accompanied members of the TCRA. In an effort to generate greater ties between the city and the show, organizers hoped to appeal to Fort Worth citizens. As a result, the entertainment accompanying the stock show evolved into a Fort Worth tradition. Over the years, attractions supplementing the livestock exhibitions grew and became more lavish. Early attractions included vaudeville acts and Wild West performances. Eventually, a carnival atmosphere began to accompany the show as a midway formed featuring typical carnival fare including "acrobats, sword swallowers, fakirs, freak shows, 'hoochie girls,' and other 'exotic entertainments.'"[44] Motorized rides and fun houses also adorned the show, providing entertainment typical of the midway at Coney Island.[45]

A reflection of Fort Worth's southern roots, the stock show initially exhibited a southern rather than western orientation. For example, in 1908 the exposition included a reenactment of the Battle of Gettysburg. Dubbed the "Battle of the Cow Pens,"[46] the exercise mocked the Union with a Confederate victory after which the victor raised the Confederate flag over the coliseum.[47]

The following year, local groups of Confederate veterans opened the show with an "Old Confederate Drill" in which the veterans successfully defended a position near the Marine Creek Bridge against an attack led by the Carlisle Cadets of Arlington. After the demonstration, the Confederates again raised their flag over the coliseum. The appearance of the Confederate standard flying over the coliseum became a ritual and a visual indicator of the show's annual commencement. Moreover, accompanying the demonstrations of loyalty to the Confederacy, convention also dictated that a band playing "Dixie" lead a procession into the coliseum at the beginning of the show.[48]

The stock show's southern orientation can also be attributed, at least in part, to the southern roots of the Texas ranching culture. Open-range cattle ranching practiced in Texas originated in South Carolina and later blended with the techniques of Hispanic frontiersmen to produce a "hybrid ranching system that spread through much of the Great Plains."[49] Although the early stock shows included traditionally western fare such as cowboys with six-shooters, trick ropers and riders, and bucking contests, these demonstrations always formed a part of the auxiliary exhibits.[50] Apparently considered alien to the southern livestock tradition, such activities including horse exhibitions and the cutting horse competition (in which a rider and horse demonstrate cattle-handling ability) were designated as part of a "western demonstration."[51] However, by the early twentieth century, exhibitions and entertainment with a western flavor had become wildly popular and more central to the exposition. The show featured purveyors of Wild West entertainment such as Buffalo Bill and his "Congress of Rough Riders" and Native American showman Quanah Parker. In 1908, the Horse Show became an official part of the exhibition, with the "Wild West and Range Country Life and Expert Riding Demonstration" concluding the event.[52]

Gradually, offerings of a western character entirely replaced the southern orientation of the exposition. Revenue was an important reason for the transition. The extreme popularity of western entertainment had the potential to generate larger audiences composed of Fort Worth citizens and others. Western entertainment owed its appeal at least in part to the growing popularity of western films. During the first three decades of the twentieth century, the western had become the most popular film genre in America.[53] Eager to produce greater returns, stock show officials continued to cloak the event in a western garb. In 1916, officials booked Joe Miller and the Miller Brothers Wild West Show. They also invited Lucille Mulhall, renowned as the "first cowgirl," accompanied by showman Will Rogers and Western film star Tom Mix. Continued cultivation of the western theme included the institution of an official competition for cowboys. During the early decades of the twentieth century, rodeo surpassed Wild West shows in popularity and lured away the most talented performers, making it "a competitive spectator sport in its own right."[54] In 1918, the stock show introduced an annual rodeo. Attracting large audiences, the rodeo quickly evolved into the premier event of the entire show and, perhaps more important, its principal revenue producer.[55]

Beyond growing ticket sales, stock show officials, the media, and local businesses promoted Fort Worth's western heritage in connection with the stock show in other ways. Accounting for the growth of a larger audience with little direct knowledge of the livestock industry or ranching lifestyle, show planners worked to educate crowds in the vernacular of ranching life. Stock show programs included dictionaries with titles such as "Your Cowboy Dictionary" and "Dictionary of the West" to aid visitors in understanding standard cowboy, ranching, and rodeo terminology.[56] Show officials also used the programs to emphasize Fort Worth's western identity. "Out of the West came the Rodeo," Frank G. Evans, director of publicity, explained in the 1929 program. "It originated from the land of cattle, expert horsemen, ranchers and bucking broncs." As a throwback to the Old West, the rodeo, he claimed, called Fort Worth "home" because it is situated "where the West begins."[57]

In other instances, casting Fort Worth as a modern western metropolis with close ties to West Texas, advertisements for the city noted that "livestock, grain and petroleum are all of more importance to Fort Worth's commercial life than is cotton."[58] In addition to the rhetoric employed by stock show officials, the media and local businesses cultivated the western identity in connection with the show. An advertisement for the Fort Worth Gas Company explained, "Since the days of the pioneer the trails of the plains country have centered in Fort Worth."[59] As a result, "Fort Worth has made of itself the store house for the West." Local newspapers also encouraged visitors to embrace the trappings of the ranching lifestyle by wearing western attire to the exposition.[60]

The efforts of Jarvis and others to make the exposition economically self-sufficient played an important role in helping it weather the Great Depression. In 1931, the show failed to turn a profit. The Depression thinned the membership of the Texas and Southwestern Cattle Raisers Association—a major supporter of the show.[61] These developments provided an impetus to strengthen the bond between the show and the city. Arguing for its "educational purposes, civic good, and public benefit," Van Zandt Jarvis gained tax exemption for the stock show. Still, the exposition floundered economically to a point at which in 1935 it could no longer afford to pay the rodeo purses. Lower hotel and rail rates, ticket discounts, and experimentation with new events and attractions increased the turnout. In 1935, more than 250,000 attended the exposition—a record year.[62]

Making the show attractive to the public came with a price, however. The discrepancy between what the stock show had once been with what it had become led stock show secretary-manager John B. Davis to remind exposition goers, the following year, of the "Serious Purpose" of the stock show. "The World's Championship Rodeo and Horse Show and Rainbeau [*sic*] Garden, Midway and carnival attractions," he wrote, "make the stock show the Southwest's greatest amusement attraction, but its livestock departments make it an indispensable economic and educational institution."[63] To succeed, the stock show had become more hat than horse.

The state's centennial year presented stock show officials with an opportunity to provide for the show's continued growth and permanence. More specifically, stock show leaders took a proactive approach to using the centennial as a means to rectify the show's inadequate financial backing and cramped stockyards facilities. They turned to the city as a permanent solution to the problem. Despite the millions of dollars that the livestock interest brought to the city, the show proved anathema to civic leaders because it annually attracted a grubby crowd of visitors to an already seedy part of town. The location of the stockyards and later the railroads made the North Side of Fort Worth a natural location for a stock show. Still catering to cowboys who came in with the cattle, North Fort Worth provided a host of illicit and often illegal activities and establishments including saloons, gambling, and prostitution. As a result, the real estate surrounding the stockyards remained dilapidated and underdeveloped. Investors found little prospect or incentive in the redevelopment of North Fort Worth. As the Chamber of Commerce and city officials worked to cast Fort Worth as a modern metropolitan, North Fort Worth remained an embarrassment to the city. And in the minds of many, the stock show remained inseparable from its location.[64]

To be sure, the twentieth century brought some modern changes to Fort Worth's North Side. Improved roads made transporting livestock to the stockyards via truck possible. By the 1930s, parking meters, gas stations, and telephone and telegraph lines graced the streets adjacent to the stockyards. Stockyard cowboys traded in their traditional overalls and heavy work-boots for more modern fashions of high-crowned felt hats, denim jeans, leather belts, and cowboy boots.[65] The Fort Worth Stockyards Company also spent millions to modernize the stockyards facilities and pave livestock pens. Meant to give the impression of modernity, a 1935 advertisement for the Fort Worth Stockyards Company featured a large aerial photograph of the orderly stockyards and boasted of its "modern, sanitary pens."[66]

Still, Carter and other Fort Worth businessmen believed relocating the stock show to a more amenable location would remove a major stumbling block to forging a closer relationship with the stock show and the city. In addition to strengthening stock show

Aerial view of the Fort Worth Stockyards, Fort Worth, Texas, circa 1930s. Courtesy, *Fort Worth Star-Telegram* Collection, Special Collections, The University of Texas at Arlington Libraries.

ties with the city, moving the show to a new location could provide new opportunities for growth. As the show grew, each year required more and more facilities and space. Perhaps more than anything else the rising use of the automobile represented a particularly challenging issue because the stock show grounds lacked adequate space for parking.

Shortly after Dallas received the bid to host the Central Exposition, a delegation representing the interests of the stock show appeared before the senate subcommittee charged with creating a centennial appropriation bill. The group asked for, but failed to acquire, $700,000 to aid in the expansion and renovation of the stock show facilities in North Fort Worth to celebrate the progress of the livestock industry.[67] Unlike Austin, Houston, and San Antonio, Fort Worth did not receive earmarked funds from the $3 million state appropriation, necessitating the development of a proposal to receive funds from the advisory board.

Amon Carter also sent a letter to Secretary of the Interior Harold L. Ickes, who ran Roosevelt's New Deal programs.

Hoping to obtain a Public Works Administration (PWA) loan, Carter sketched a rough picture of the city's plans for a centennial memorial to the Texas livestock industry. The envisioned memorial consisted of new livestock facilities befitting the size and renown of the stock show on a plot of land nearer to the city center. Initial estimates indicated that such centennial facilities, including a much-needed civic auditorium, could not be built for less than $1 million. Carter explained that of the $3 million appropriated by the Texas legislature for the centennial, Fort Worth planned to ask for $300,000 and hoped to procure a federal loan/grant of $700,000 of which the stock show would repay $490,000. Describing the stock show as a "successful civic institution" with close administrative ties to Fort Worth's municipal leadership, Carter hoped to illustrate for Ickes the civic nature of the show and its ability to amortize the loan. To grease the wheels, Carter sent along a steak from the prize-winning steer from the most recent exposition.[68]

Notwithstanding Carter's meaty bribe, Ickes curtly replied that, based upon the information provided by Carter, the PWA might have the authority to grant a loan for a private corporation, such as the Stock Show Association, if it included safeguards to protect against the loss of a federal investment. Ickes's primary reservation regarding a loan/grant for the Fort Worth memorial, however, was that the loan/grant powers of the National Recovery Act expired on June 16, 1935, and he would have no way of knowing the new provisions for making loan/grants upon the renewal of the act. However, Ickes explained, "[W]e have in the past considered several applications for projects similar to the one in which you are interested but have been able to approve none of them."[69]

Despite Ickes's negative reply to Carter's inquiry, plans for the construction of a memorial to the livestock industry and exposition grounds for the stock show moved forward. The stock show's Executive Committee hired a real estate dealer to scan the city for possible sites with at least 100 acres on which to build the new stock show facilities.[70] Given Carter's statement to Ickes that the city intended to build the memorial "near the city," it seems likely that any investigation of North Fort Worth property represented a perfunctory exercise for the placation of the citizens and businesses in that section of the city.[71] The real estate dealer recommended a 138-acre plot of land on the west side of the city dubbed the Van Zandt tract. After two months of negotiations, the dealer procured an option for the city to purchase the site for $150,000.

With an option on the Van Zandt tract obtained, at the behest of Carter, stock show general manager John B. Davis called together the Executive Committee to discuss removing the show to the new location as part of Fort Worth's centennial celebration. At this meeting, Carter brought a new and compelling argument to the deliberations. Carter insisted that if Fort Worth did not celebrate the centennial of the Texas livestock industry in grand fashion, it did so at the peril of the stock show. "Our friends across the River, with their new buildings, costing from $15,000,000 to $20,000,000," Carter explained, "could and possibly would absorb our great Stock Show." Those present, including representatives of meatpackers Armour and Swift, lamented the loss of the show on the North Side but believed the move necessary to prevent the deterioration and perhaps the collapse of the Fort Worth show. Detailed plans for construction of new livestock show facilities as part of Fort Worth's centennial celebration finally received official approval at a joint meeting of the stock show's Executive Committee and City Council, where the council voted unanimously to include the memorial facilities as part of a larger proposal for a number of public building projects requiring a large PWA grant.[72]

The Advisory Board of Texas Historians began hearing proposals for historical commemoration on June 18. Several dozen Texas counties made proposals quickly exceeding the board's allotted budget for memorials and markers.[73] On July 8, a delegation of twelve influential Fort Worth citizens including Mayor Jarvis, Carter, half a dozen members of the stock show's Executive Committee, several members of the city council, *Fort Worth Press* editor Seward Sheldon, and Texas State Senator Frank Rawlings appeared before the board.[74] Although the proposal identified the delegation as representatives of Fort Worth, those present also served in the interest of the Stock Show Association. Interestingly, the proposal carried the signatures of Jarvis, Carter, and Secretary-Manager Davis on behalf of the stock show rather than as representatives from Tarrant County or Fort Worth.[75]

Amon Carter and Van Zandt Jarvis led the group's presentation.[76] Appealing to the board's interests in recommending funds based on historical merit, the content of the proposal focused on conveying the fundamental importance of the livestock industry to the economic and cultural history of the state. The proposal claimed that livestock represented the first industry in the state even before its formation as a republic, and since that time Texas functioned primarily as a "cattle state." Given the central role the livestock industry represented to the state, the proposal argued it required its own celebration. In addition, the proposal argued that the livestock industry played a primary role in the epic saga of western expansion. Retelling the story of the intrepid Texas pioneers who transformed the West, the proposal predicted, would likely represent the most attractive part of the centennial to out-of-state visitors.[77] The "history and development of the livestock industry in Texas have so been intertwined" with Fort Worth, the proposal argued, "there can be no separation." Moreover, Fort Worth hosted the largest, most significant livestock show in the Southwest.[78]

To host an exposition worthy of the Texas livestock industry, the delegation unabashedly requested, as hinted by Amon Carter to Harold Ickes, $300,000 of the $575,000 discretionary funds available for historical markers and memorials for the construction of an "entirely new livestock exhibition plant."[79] The funds, if granted, would be combined with a larger $1.2 million PWA loan claimed to be already under negotiation. Although Fort Worth already had access to facilities for operating a stock show, the proposal reasoned new facilities on a new 140-acre tract were necessary to do justice to the livestock industry in the centennial year.[80] This included a 6,000-seat coliseum, an auditorium, an exhibition building, an arena for auction sales, and a host of buildings dedicated to housing the various breeds of livestock. With the new plant, the proposal explained, Fort Worth planned to stage in the fall of 1936 a grand livestock exposition, horse show, and rodeo, superior to the standard annual stock show.[81]

Several important themes emerged from the proposal that signaled key conceptualizations for the centennial. The proposal cast the livestock industry as a westering phenomenon central to the expansion of the American West. Descriptive terms used to characterize the livestock industry as western included pioneers, cowboys, ranches, horsemanship, and the West. In defining Fort Worth as inseparable from the Texas livestock heritage, the proposal implied that Fort Worth also lay claim to a western heritage based on its historical relationship to the Texas livestock hinterland: West Texas. Thus, it was not really Fort Worth's specific heritage that centennial planners intended to celebrate. Rather, they hoped to "give adequate recognition of the livestock industry [and] the development of West Texas from cattle to an agricultural empire." In describing the historical importance of the livestock industry and Texas's pioneer heritage, the proposal made no reference to the original Fort Worth or the settlement of North Texas. It also made no distinction between a Fort Worth and a West Texas heritage. From a perspective of attracting visitors, the proposal argued a western theme would ensure the exposition's success.[82] Ultimately, the relationship of West Texas and Fort Worth as depicted in the proposal brings into focus the three-decade-long transition in which stock show officials gradually co-opted the West Texas livestock and pioneer heritage for Fort Worth.

Unwilling to trust the advisory board's appraisal of the virtues of the proposal, the Fort Worth centennial delegation also met with the State Centennial Commission of Control. Hoping to sway those who regulated the distribution of the centennial's discretionary funds, the delegation prepared a second proposal addressed directly to the commission. Fort Worth delegates came away from both meetings feeling very optimistic. Delegates took solace in advisory board member Louis Kemp's willingness to consider Fort Worth's claims prior to the board's October 1 deadline to present its recommendations to the commission. Based largely on the comments of Senator Frank Rawlings, Commission Vice-Chairman and Speaker of the House Coke R. Stevenson claimed he would vote for allocating the funds "right now." Rawlings apparently gave an impassioned speech to both the advisory board and the commission claiming the Texas Legislature's centennial appropriation originally included a major allocation for Fort Worth. Building on the major themes of the proposal, Rawlings exclaimed:

> No one contests that Fort Worth is the logical place for the exhibition. The constitutional amendment calls for observation of the progress as well as the history of Texas, and that is where Fort Worth and West Texas come in. This show will attract more visitors than any other phase of the Centennial for crowds do not go to historical scenes only. Since the inception of the Centennial bill in the Legislature it was conceded that Fort Worth should receive an allocation of sufficient amount for a livestock show, and the bill as first drawn had us down for $300,000 and I now lay claim to it. This will be more than just a show, for it will be of permanent benefit. And none of us should overlook that Fort Worth and West Texas pay their share of the taxes that go into the Centennial fund.[83]

During the early deliberations, the appropriations bill apparently included earmarks for all the major metropolitans including Dallas, San Antonio, Houston, Austin, and Fort Worth. Believing the inclusion of Fort Worth represented a slippery slope under which any town of historical importance might demand funds, Walter Cline of Wichita Falls and William Thornton of Austin asked Fort Worth to withdraw its request for funding. According to James M. North Jr. of Fort Worth, who attended the appropriation deliberations, Senator Rawlings only backed down after receiving assurances from Cline and Thornton that Fort Worth would receive funds from non-earmarked funds within the centennial appropriation after it passed. North characterized the exchange between Rawlings and Cline and Thornton not as a "definite agreement" but an "understanding."[84] Later, several politicians who attended the deliberations disputed the existence of the apparently well-known "understanding."

Following a joint meeting of the Commission of Control, the Advisory Board of Texas Historians, and the Advertising Board, on July 20, Commission chairman Lieutenant Governor Walter F. Woodul made a surprising announcement. Heavily influenced by the argument presented by Senator Rawlings, the commission, with a vote of five to one, decided to supersede the advisory board and grant Fort Worth $250,000 of the $575,000 appropriated for historical markers and memorials.[85] The commission awarded the funds to Fort Worth with some caveats. First, the award rested upon the City of Fort Worth raising $1.25 million to match the state allocation. Second, if the federal government appropriated funds to support the Texas State Centennial including a Fort Worth earmark of $250,000, the commission would rescind its offer of the same amount.[86]

At the time, a federal appropriation appeared imminent. Two months earlier, the House Committee on Foreign Affairs had begun hearings for Joint Resolution 293, which contained among other things a $3 million federal appropriation for the Texas centennial and the creation of the United States Texas Centennial Commission led by Vice President John Nance Garner.[87] Aware of these legislative developments, Fort Worth officials began to lobby for the procurement of funds from a possible federal appropriation bill. On July 12, Amon Carter attempted to persuade the bill's creator, Texas Representative Fritz Lanham, to use his influence to convince Garner and others to earmark funds for Fort Worth from a federal appropriation.[88] Subsequently, Van Zandt Jarvis, Carter, and John B. Davis sent in an official application to the United States Texas Centennial Commission requesting an earmark of $300,000 for Fort Worth's memorial of the Texas livestock industry.[89] In light of the likelihood of federal appropriation, the State Commission's award merely assured Fort Worth officials that they would receive some centennial funding from either a state or federal source. However, to help ensure a federal appropriation for Fort Worth, Chairman Woodul publicly promised to travel to Washington and lobby for a Fort Worth earmark as part of the legislation.[90]

Notwithstanding the probability of a federal appropriation for Fort Worth that would mitigate their decision, the State Commission's actions ignited a firestorm of protest. Immediately, all three members the Advisory Board of Texas Historians registered their objections. Following the meeting, both Kemp and Reverend Foik tendered their resignations to the commission. Although in Dallas at the time of the meeting, J. Frank Dobie threatened to submit his resignation if the federal funds were not granted for the Fort Worth monument. An allocation of $250,000 to Fort Worth, they collectively argued, not only muted the authority of their body but also rendered their job virtually impossible by cutting their already woefully inadequate budget in half. Unwilling to second-guess the actions of the commission, Kemp contended the latter simply placed a higher premium on celebrating commercial development as opposed to historical events.[91] Far less charitable in his assessment of the decision, Dobie, despite the transparency of Woodul's reasoning for the appropriation, accused the commission of skullduggery, arguing the decision was a product of "political trades" and "the ambitions of politicians." Casting additional barbs at the commission, he claimed a monument to the pioneer heritage of Texas would be "much more interesting to the public than $1,000,000 worth of hog, sheep and chicken pens."[92] Despite the advisory board's criticisms of the commission's decision, the commission refused to accept the resignations of the members of the advisory board and continued its deliberations, assuming the federal government would allocate $250,000 to Fort Worth and thus maintaining the commission's coffers.[93]

The objections that followed tended to reflect the criticisms already expressed by the members of the advisory board. The commissioner who cast the sole dissenting vote against the Fort Worth appropriation, J. V. Vandenberge of Victoria, boldly announced he had vigorously opposed the allotment in the joint meeting believing it "sacrilege to subordinate the memory of our heroes to an exposition of our industries."[94] State Senator T. J. Holbrook, who fought for the state appropriation, supported Kemp's resignation and claimed politics influenced the commission's decision.[95] Wichita Falls Senator Ben G. Oneal, who authored the amendment to the appropriation bill providing for an advisory board of historians, charged members of the commission and Fort Worth delegates with back-room politics. He claimed, "I purposely put that amendment in the bill to protect the control commission from those who would attempt to play politics or attempt pork barrel allotments." A number of outraged state senators who followed Oneal's lead challenged Woodul's rationale for granting the Fort Worth allotment. Lufkin Senator John S. Redditt and Senator John W. Hornsby of Austin both denied Rawlings's and Woodul's claim that an understanding accompanied the bill's passage that implied Fort Worth would receive an appropriation.[96]

Until Woodul's announcement of the Fort Worth appropriation, the historic rivalry with Dallas remained dormant as regards the Texas Centennial. With the exception of boisterous language in Fort Worth's proposal to the advisory board meant to extol the great public interest in the cattle industry and the pioneer era in Texas history opposed to the sterile commercial theme of the Central Exposition, Fort Worth leaders, including Amon Carter, recognized the unprofitability of "trying to take the play away from [Dallas]."[97] However, an unintended result of the appropriation debacle constituted the cooling of relations between Fort Worth's and Dallas's major media outlets. In the week following the July 20 announcement, the *Dallas Morning News* broke its standards for journalistic objectivity by publishing several front-page "reports" authored by William M. Thornton, its Austin news correspondent, openly critical of the appropriation. In the July 21 report of the commission's announcement, Thornton pointed out the irony that Fort Worth and its memorial to the livestock industry received $250,000 while two locations of enormous historical significance to Texas only received a pale $50,000. He also argued the allotment of $250,000 to Fort Worth placed it "on parity with San Antonio and its Alamo, and Houston where was fought the Battle of San Jacinto, one of the seven decisive battles of the world and which won independence for Texas."[98]

A few days later, Thornton again took the commission's decision to task on the front page of the *Dallas Morning News*. This time, Thornton argued that the Fort Worth allocation set a dangerous precedent. Thornton warned readers that as a result of the allotment, other Texas cities with industries of significance to the Texas economy might make similar demands of the commission. El Paso with its livestock and mining, Lufkin with its lumber manufacturing, Pecos with its cantaloupes, and Cuero with its turkey market, according to Thornton, all claimed as much a right to centennial funds as Fort Worth. But no Texas region claimed more rights to centennial funds than the oil-producing cities in East Texas such as Tyler, Kilgore, and Longview. "Oil production has become by far the greatest industry in Texas," he claimed, "far exceeding the livestock business in valuation and importance."[99]

Thornton's depiction of the commission's Fort Worth allocation so angered Amon Carter that he delegated the task of registering his indignation over the *Dallas Morning News*'s coverage to James M. North Jr., editor of the *Fort Worth Star-Telegram*, believing he would convey the concerns with a more "Christian spirit." In a letter to Ted Dealey, the vice president of the corporation that published the *Dallas Morning News*, North conveyed Carter's bewilderment with the appearance of Thornton's "reports" on the front page. More specifically, North questioned why, given the *News*'s high standards regarding editorial policies, the paper published a news report "belittling a proposition and, by inference at least, condemning a public board for its action." If the *News* opposed the actions of the commission, he wondered why such a position would not be taken up in an editorial. After chiding the *News*, North reaffirmed the desire of Fort Worth officials to complement the offerings at the central centennial rather than to compete directly with it and explained their perspective on the commission's decision to allot the money to Fort Worth.

Given the manner in which the *News* published its objections, North concluded, they sounded "a little 'sour grapey.'"[100]

North ultimately neglected to discuss the real concern with Thornton's reports: to readers his comparison of Fort Worth's allotment with the money granted to Goliad and Gonzales and Houston, San Antonio, and Austin likely added gravity to the charges expressed by Dobie and others that Fort Worth officials engaged in inappropriate politicking. In addition to the letter to Dealey, Carter published an editorial mocking the reports published in the *Dallas Morning News* titled, "Tender Hearts in Dallas." Challenging Thornton's argument for the singular importance of the events at Goliad and Gonzales to the history of Texas, the editorial argued that development "is the best sort of history" and pointed out that such reasoning not only supported Dallas's claim to hosting the Central Exposition but also Fort Worth's plan for celebrating the livestock industry.[101]

The US Texas Centennial Commission settled the debate on August 17 when it announced an earmark of $250,000 to support Fort Worth's celebration of the livestock industry, ending the Commission of Control's financial obligations to that city.[102] The victory for Fort Worth came only after Amon Carter appeared personally before the assistant commissioners of the United States Texas Centennial Commission in Washington, DC, and delivered a passionate speech in favor of a Fort Worth earmark.[103] No sooner had Fort Worth received the $250,000 than the City Council announced a campaign to win public support for a $687,500 bond issue for the new stock show facilities. In a few short weeks, Fort Worth citizens would cast their votes on a series of bond issues funding a large building program of which the livestock memorial formed only a part. The building program included a library, hospital, tuberculosis sanatorium, and new city hall-jail complex requiring the approval of $1,438,500 in city bonds. The City Council voted for William Monnig, a local businessman and perhaps the most influential member of the council, to lead a committee to oversee the stock show bond issue campaign.[104] Once organized, the committee contained more than thirty prominent

Fort Worth businessmen including Amon Carter, Van Zandt Jarvis, Marvin Leonard, and Frank Rawlings.[105] Monnig also formed several subcommittees including a "Speakers Committee" dedicated to educating Fort Worth citizens on the issues and a "Get-out-the-vote Committee" that worked to ensure a large showing on Election Day.[106]

With a promotional organization in place, the movement sprang into action. Members of the Speakers Committee stumped at dozens of venues across the city. Organizations such as the Fort Worth Chamber of Commerce, the East Fort Worth Lion's Club, and various civic groups and labor unions hosted meetings and rallies.[107] Although some speakers mentioned the wide appeal of the "human interest" angle attached to the livestock and western theme for the centennial show, the City Council at this time primarily justified the stock show bond issue to Fort Worth citizens on economic arguments. First, the bond would take hundreds of Fort Worth laborers off federal relief rolls by providing funds to put them back to work immediately. Second, because the stock show represented a self-sustaining enterprise, the profits from the show would be more than enough to repay the bonds without raising taxes. Thus, the construction of the new livestock facilities, they reasoned, would likely cost the public nothing. Third, with an investment of only $687,500, the city would receive nearly $1 million in grants from the federal and state governments. The city, the speakers reassured citizens, would not likely receive a similar deal ever again. Fourth, if the bond issue did not pass, then Fort Worth would lose the $1 million in grants from the federal and state government, making Fort Worth unable to participate in the centennial or to capitalize on the city's proximity to the Central Exposition in Dallas. Finally, stock show supporters repeatedly asserted that if the show facilities went unimproved, Dallas would likely construct superior livestock facilities as part of the Central Exposition and host a superior livestock show of its own. As a result, Fort Worth would ultimately be displaced as host of one of the leading livestock shows in the nation.[108]

After the campaign began, several labor and civic organizations came out in support of the bond measures. On August 22, the Fort Worth Trades Assembly voted nearly unanimously in support of the issue, believing the bonds would help diminish the surplus of unemployed laborers.[109] The Fort Worth Building Trades Council also voted to support the city's building program.[110] The Fort Worth Chamber of Commerce initiated several speeches in favor of the city bond issue. The Allied Civic Leagues launched a campaign in support of the bonds and sponsored meetings and rallies hosted by local divisions of the organization. Prominent individuals such as Monnig, Hammond, and Carter spoke at these meetings located around the city. Councilman Hammond also delivered a radio address sponsored by the Allied Civic Leagues.[111] Moreover, at the invitation of the Allied Civic Leagues, 125 leaders of dozens of women's organizations gathered to hear an explanation of the various bond issues. Following the presentation of James M. North Jr. and others who spoke in favor of all the bond issues, a majority of those present committed themselves to furthering the campaign within their own groups.[112]

Fort Worth's North Side quickly voiced resistance to the bond measures—particularly the bond for the construction of new stock show facilities. Even though six of the sixteen construction site finalists under the consideration of the City Council were located in the North Side, interest in the Van Zandt tract exhibited by some city officials caused North Side residents to fear the possible economic impact of removal.[113] Believing they could prevent the passage of the bond issue if the City Council selected a non-North Side site, the Central Council of North Side Civic Leagues sent a delegation to the City Council to request they announce the final location of the site prior to the bond election. T. P. Leath, president of the North Side group, told city officials that placing a ballot before the voters without knowledge of the location of the new stock show facilities constituted "poor politics."[114] Believing he convincingly conveyed the intention and ability of the North Side to block the bond issue, after the meeting Leath concluded, "the city officials will name the site before the election."[115]

Upon the refusal of City Council to bow to its demands, the North Side group initiated a campaign of its own to educate voters.[116] Although the North Side group never claimed to tell citizens how to vote, speakers at their rallies challenged the propriety of the stock show bond on a number of counts. First, they questioned whether the show would self-liquidate the bonds. Second, they claimed the large site requirements established by the City Council represented an attempt to prevent North Side sites from coming under consideration. Finally, they asserted that the removal of the show represented a plot orchestrated by some members of the City Council to purchase an overpriced piece of real estate.[117] A Reverend Garrett of a North Side congregation went so far as to accuse the city of attempting to hijack the stock show for the city at the expense of the North Side.[118]

Those in favor of the bond issue quickly fired back. Councilman Monnig discounted charges that the City Council favored a non-North Side location, claiming that he would "bend over backwards in favor of the North Side." Supporting Monnig's position, Councilman Hammond argued, "No site has been selected and the cards are stacked in favor of the North Side because that section of the city has many advantages."[119] The City Council, however, remained unwilling to name the location before the election or place the question on referendum to the bond. Still, Councilman Arthur Brown urged Fort Worth citizens to "bury all ideas of selfishness and stage a show that will be of great value to all of Fort Worth, West Texas and [the] livestock industry."[120]

Carter's *Fort Worth Star-Telegram* also attempted to mollify the concerns exhibited on the North Side. The paper published an endorsement of the stock show bond issue given by Al G. Donovan, the general manager of the Fort Worth Stockyards Company. An editorial pointed out that Donovan, whose company annually rented the livestock facilities to the exposition, had much more to lose if the stock show relocated than any other North Side resident. The editorial further pointed out that Donovan recognized that Fort Worth's centrality to the Southwest livestock industry hung in the balance.[121] Answering the North Side assertion that Van Zandt Jarvis or Amon Carter would benefit from the sale of the Van Zandt site, another editorial in the *Fort Worth Star-Telegram* provided a list of the stockholders of the company that owned the Van Zandt site, of which neither Carter nor Jarvis were a part. The editorial also noted that the only commission or bonus resulting from the sale of the property would go directly to the real estate dealer who discovered and negotiated the option for the site.[122]

On September 3, Fort Worth citizens cast their vote for the bond measures. To limit confusion over the stock show bond measure, the City Council arranged for its placement in the number one spot on the ballot. The day following the election, newspapers reported the results indicating that Fort Worthians voted in favor of the stock show bond by a margin of two to one.[123] The passage of the bond issue for new centennial stock show facilities culminated a process in which boosters and stock show officials worked to financially conjoin the Southwestern Exposition and Fat Stock Show with its host city. Members of the City Council demonstrated their support for making the exposition an official institution of the city by moving forward with the bond issue despite threats coming from the North Side and placing the stock show measure in a place of prominence on the ballot over other bonds measures for badly needed civic buildings. Perhaps more important, through their vote, Fort Worth citizens revealed their belief in the significance of preserving the stock show and building modern facilities, no matter their location, to Fort Worth's future. Their vote also tacitly suggested they accepted the stock show's western orientation as representative of the city's heritage and identity.

With the city bond issue and centennial appropriation obtained, city fathers now focused on securing the last piece of funding for the new stock show facilities: the PWA grant. Coming on the heels of victory, Fort Worth officials learned disconcerting news. Public Works Administrator Harry L. Hopkins rejected 132 Texas projects submitted to and approved by Harold Ickes. These rejections included three prospective Fort Worth projects including the library, city hall, and a technical high school.[124] Perhaps of more concern was the fact that the PWA, attempting to aid as many of the truly destitute as possible, would soon require that all proposed projects reduce wage estimates to $800 per man-year. Moreover, the Allotment Board announced it would reject projects as unnecessary where skilled laborers did not appear on local relief rolls. Both requirements jeopardized the livestock memorial.

An irritated Carter sent a telegram to Hopkins to confirm and clarify the rumored requirements. As always, Fort Worth's centennial plans constituted his greatest concern. Carter questioned the propriety of rejecting a project simply because the regional relief rolls included a minimal number of skilled laborers. In most cases, he argued, the skilled workers in Fort Worth maintained the ability to eke out a scanty living but out of pride did not ask for federal handouts. If the government failed to generate more PWA opportunities for skilled workers, he warned, they would surely add to the numbers on relief rolls. As the initial PWA proposal for the new stock show facilities included $1,100 per man-hour estimates for labor, Carter balked at reducing the figure by $300. At $800, he insisted, the per man-year wage would fail to meet the yearly needs of destitute workers.[125] Failing to evoke a response, Fort Worth moved forward with altering its proposals to meet PWA standards.[126]

After the resubmission of Fort Worth's application for PWA grants, the centennial stock show facilities met with continued resistance from federal administrators. Budgetary constraints prevented PWA officials from granting wholesale approval to all proposed projects. When appraising Fort Worth's proposed PWA projects, Ickes judged the construction of livestock facilities for the centennial stock show as lacking "social desirability." As a result, the stock show facilities failed to receive approval from the PWA. Continually haunted with the imminent approach of the centennial year and unable to contact Ickes by phone, Carter traveled to Washington, DC, to defend the project's social desirability. After arriving in Washington, Carter zealously pinned down a vacation-bound Ickes at the train station. Not surprisingly, Ickes, in no mood to debate the PWA's decision, brusquely dismissed Carter's imposition. Upon his return to Washington, however, Ickes sent a letter to Carter on September 27 begging his pardon for his "illnatured [*sic*]" response. He also explained the reasoning behind the rejection of the stock show facilities project but expressed a belief that the PWA should not make decisions in opposition to local interests. "Other things being equal," Ickes explained, "we want to do what any given community would prefer that we should do." In essence, Ickes offered Carter an opportunity to prove that the rest of the city shared his urgency for the construction of the stock show facilities.[127]

Based upon Ickes's offer, a number of civic organizations and important city and business leaders sent telegrams and letters to Ickes requesting the stock show facilities be given precedence over the other PWA projects in Fort Worth.[128] Perhaps the ultimate expression of the city's support for such a preference came in the form of a resolution passed unanimously by the City Council on October 23. The council declared that the imminent arrival of the centennial celebration in Dallas created an "emergency." Therefore, they requested the PWA act in the "best interests of the city" and place the stock show facilities ahead of the other PWA projects proposed by the city.[129]

Apparently, the efforts of local officials to convince Ickes of the public's interest in gaining the approval for the stock show funds over the other PWA projects fell on deaf ears. Carter again traveled to Washington, this time to circumvent PWA administrators. Carter enlisted the aid of Postmaster General James Farley to intercede. After hearing Carter's pitch describing Fort Worth's need for a PWA grant for the construction of new stock show facilities, Farley then sought Roosevelt's personal approval on the project. According to Carter's biographer Jerry Flemmons, Farley took the opportunity to play a joke on Carter. At the meeting with Roosevelt, Farley purposely left the door ajar to allow an unsuspecting Carter to hear his deliberations with Roosevelt. Speaking loudly, Farley proceeded to describe the proposal as Carter's quest to build a "cowshed" in Fort Worth. Taking the bait, Carter stormed into the room shouting, "Now, gawddamit, it's not a cowshed . . ." Both Roosevelt and Farley erupted in laughter.[130] Although Roosevelt endorsed the project, PWA administrators apparently remained adamant that other projects take precedence. Still, Carter, Jarvis, and others continued to lobby for the PWA's approval. Ickes ultimately acquiesced to Fort Worth's demands and the City Council accepted the PWA grant on January 2, 1936.[131]

Selecting a site for the centennial livestock facilities plagued the City Council through the remaining months of 1935. Following the passage of the bond measures, the council's Centennial Building Site Committee began deliberations to make recommendations.[132] Although the Building Site Committee received at least twenty-three proposals for sites scattered across the city, the site discussion revolved primarily around two locations.[133] In the ensuing debate over the two sites, these localities reveal two opposing views of the potential place of the stock show in the city's identity and image. North Side residents continued to voice their objection to the removal of the stock show, preferring the genuineness and grit of the traditional site. Their opposition suggests some North Side residents contested the vision of urban elites who sought to repackage the city's identity and image through the relocation of the stock show. On the other hand, the City Council received several petitions favoring the Van Zandt tract because of its size, location, and accessibility.[134]

On November 8, 1935, W. D. Smith, representing the legal interests of the Fort Worth Stockyards Company, extended an offer to sell the thirty-eight acres of land and improvements constituting the current stock show facilities to the City of Fort Worth for $150,000. After hearing the proposal, the City Council agreed to entertain a formal proposal for the purchase of the stock show facilities from the Stockyards Company, but at a price not exceeding $100,000.[135] Within days, the Stockyards Company complied with the urgings of the council and amended the sale price to $100,000. They also took the opportunity to reinforce the advantages of retaining the stock show's current location, which mostly centered on the preexisting improvements to the stockyards including loading and unloading pens, railroad facilities, sewage and water lines, and paved roads. Statements from the Armour and Swift companies withdrawing their support for removal of the show also accompanied the brief.[136] At the following meeting, the council finally agreed to build the centennial livestock facilities on the existing stockyards grounds and on November 20, Al G. Donovan accepted the council's decision.[137]

Almost immediately, several problems with the North Side site surfaced, jeopardizing the council's decision. Architects Wyatt C. Hedrick and Elmer G. Withers, retained by the city to design the new facilities, informed the City Council of the infeasibility of passing large crowds across North Main Street, which transected the stock show grounds, necessitating the closure of the street during the centennial.[138] As a result, four members of the council publicly aired their view that the issue of North Main Street validated their belief that the stock show facilities should be built elsewhere. "We have made every effort to locate the Centennial stock show and auditorium on the site now occupied by the Southwestern Exposition and Fat Stock Show," Councilman Thompson, one of the four objectors, declared. "Some of us have acted willingly and some unwilling, but there is nothing left for the council to do but select another site."[139]

Councilman Thompson's comments suggest how divisive their deliberations over the site had been and the struggles within the council to settle on the historic or a new site for the stock show. Momentum against the original stockyards site continued to build when officials with the Stockyards Company failed to promptly deliver a contract delineating the terms of the lease for the proposed city-owned livestock facilities and the Stock Show Association. Councilman Hammond, who apparently always opposed the North Side site, viewed the delay as "evidence of mismanagement" and called for a reexamination of the site question. Only Van Zandt Jarvis's vow to hold an emergency meeting of the board pacified Hammond's demands.[140]

Within days, additional issues with the North Side site emerged. On November 26, Fort Worth attorney Baylor B. Brown submitted a brief comparing the North Side grounds with the Van Zandt site to councilmen Hammond and Murphy.[141] At their behest, Brown presented the data included in the brief to the City Council the following day.[142] The brief contained a side-by-side comparison of the two sites on a number of points including acreage, the suitability of foundations and elevations, parking space, division of the acreage in relation to main streets, purchase price, accessibility of the location, railroad and stock pen facilities, and possible future use of the property. According to the report, in every category the North Side site came up short. Even when considering accessibility of the railroad and stock pen facilities, the brief found these improvements a disadvantage to the North Side site because they required additional transportation from pens to the new coliseum and exhibition buildings.

Much of the data would not have surprised the council. The councilmen already knew most of the pros and cons relating to the sites. However, Brown, who apparently consulted test holes excavated by the City Engineering Office and several contractors, raised serious concerns regarding suitability of the North Side site's landscape for the construction of new stock show facilities. Specifically, because the top fifteen feet of soil on much of the site consisted of "manure and rubbish," standard foundations could not be successfully constructed. The site also contained widely variant elevations requiring extensive leveling. The expense in solving both issues, Brown warned, would prove prohibitive. According to contractors, the use of a floating foundation or pilings could add half a million dollars to construction costs.[143] More than demonstrating the need for floating foundations and piles, the excavations illustrated for the City Council not only the actual depths in which Fort Worth's storied past had been written into the landscape but a reality in the North Side that no longer fit the city's modern image.

The individual who commissioned Brown's comparison of the two sites remains unknown. The pro-Van Zandt tract content makes Amon Carter a likely candidate. Carter, indeed, was the chief supporter of the Van Zandt site, and several comments speak to his influence. Rather than assessing economic factors, the brief focused on the less tangible implications of the North Side geography. More than the "unsightly buildings and negro shacks" nearby or the "unpleasant odor" emitted from the stockyards, the brief argued, the property, because it resided in a valley on Marine Creek, "would leave the impression on visitors and others of a crowded and unattractive condition." Perhaps more important, the brief pointed out, "the view of the surrounding city and county is completely shut off." The Van Zandt site, on the other hand, "is located on high, rolling ground, comparatively level, and from this property the entire city can be viewed in all directions." Perhaps most important, the Van Zandt site included a grand eastern view of the Fort Worth skyline—one teaming with modern buildings.[144]

The contrast of the historic livestock industry, representing the city's western past, and the modern metropolis, representing the city's future, provided a physical reminder of Fort Worth's growth and development to visitors of a theme long cultivated by Carter and the Chamber of Commerce. In other words, the juxtaposition provided an excellent visual reminder of the city's identity as a "progressive city" of the modern West.[145] The Chamber of Commerce, in fact, commissioned artwork to grace their promotional literature in the late 1920s and early 1930s contrasting the booming industry and commerce of modern Fort Worth with oxen dragging a wagon and a pioneer gazing west.[146] Carter and others believed the construction of new livestock facilities for the celebration of the Texas State Centennial in an isolated and dilapidated location with the stench of manure and animal entrails wafting through the air would fail to convey an image of prosperity and progress.

Likely as a result of the Brown brief, the council voted on December 3 to reopen deliberations over the selection of a site. Because of "the many problems that had confronted the Council in the selection of a site, both from an economic and social view point," the chairman of the Centennial Building Site Committee presented a solution to split the show and its facilities. According to the solution, the city would go through with the purchase of the stockyard facilities for the purpose of "handling of exhibit live stock, poultry, etc. . . . where they are to be handled after said exhibition." The council stipulated, however, that not more than $150,000 in improvements be constructed on the site.

The city would also construct centennial stock show facilities on the Van Zandt site, including the new coliseum and auditorium for a "rodeo, horse show, agricultural and merchant exhibits and so on." Essentially, the livestock business portion of the stock show would remain sequestered to the stockyards on the North Side while the new facilities would host the show's more profitable and popular entertainment and commercial features. Fairgoers would enjoy a repackaged and scripted western experience cleansed of the more authentic sights and smells of the western livestock industry. With a vote of seven to two, the City Council voted in support of the Building Site Committee's proposal.[147] Shortly afterward, the council authorized the execution of contracts with the K. M. Van Zandt Land Company for purchase of the Van Zandt tract and the Fort Worth Stockyards Company for purchase of the North Side site and improvements.[148]

Time would erase the debate over the location of the new livestock memorial and the centrality of the Southwestern Exposition and Fat Stock Show to Fort Worth's centennial celebration.[149] As discussed, the show proved integral to both the shaping of Fort Worth's western identity and the origin of Fort Worth's Frontier Centennial. During the first three decades of the twentieth century, Fort Worth's population and economy grew substantially, resulting in a distancing of most Fort Worth citizens from the livestock industry and ranching lifestyle. Show officials astutely surmised that without the participation of locals, the stock show would eventually fall by the wayside. In an effort to attract locals, show planners provided entertainment for those not immediately connected with the livestock trade. Because of the popularity of western-type attractions, they sought to engage characters such as

Buffalo Bill, Tom Mix, and others, while eschewing activities and traditions based on the city's and state's southern heritage. The embrace of all things western culminated with the institutionalization of the Fort Worth rodeo.

Meanwhile, the stock show's post–World War I leadership who built their wealth in oil and other industries rather than in ranching increasingly viewed the show as more symbolic of the city's heritage than central to the city's economy. Although the continued cultivation of local patronage made the show a tradition among Fort Worth residents and was eventually absorbed into the city's identity, the decline of the meatpacking industry in the city jeopardized the financial backing of the show. While the Chamber of Commerce and other civic institutions joined in supporting the show, with the onset of the Great Depression show leaders looked to the city for financial backing. The construction of memorial livestock grounds as part of the Texas State Centennial, partially funded through the taxation of Fort Worth citizens, provided an opportunity to make the show a permanent fixture of the city. That an overwhelming majority of Fort Worth citizens supported the use of city funds to help construct new facilities for the stock show suggests Fort Worthians had also come to identify the stock show as symbolic of the city's western identity.

Simultaneously, Fort Worth sought to project an image of modernity. Despite twentieth-century improvements to the North Side and the investment of millions of dollars by the Fort Worth Stockyards Company, city boosters and civic leaders found the city's livestock industry inconsistent with the city's modern image. In the opinion of civic leaders and boosters, Fort Worth's future lay less in the livestock trade than in manufacturing and industry. Although they wore cowboy boots and hats, most Fort Worthians considered the sights and smells of the stockyards and meatpacking plants that represented Fort Worth's heritage to no longer reflect the city's reality. Fort Worth's western history needed "cleaning" to fit with its modern aspirations. From this perspective, building new stock show facilities and removing the show from the cramped, dilapidated, and historic landscape of the stockyards as part its proposal for a centennial memorial to the livestock industry represented an attempt to repackage Fort Worth's western identity—an image contested by North Side residents.

From existing evidence, Amon Carter and others desired to build the new facilities closer to the city. While the move would make access to the grounds easier from downtown and for most citizens in Fort Worth—and beyond the stench of the stockyards—as expressed in the Brown briefing, relocation provided other less tangible benefits. As a symbol of Fort Worth's heritage and identity, some believed locating the memorial livestock facilities in a rundown portion of town would leave an unprogressive impression in the minds of visitors to the city. Conversely, facing the new facilities toward the burgeoning skyline of Fort Worth would provide symbolic continuity. The juxtaposition of the historic livestock industry and the growing metropolis would, it was hoped, provide a visible reminder of Fort Worth's progressive past, present, and future.

CHAPTER 2

"HOW LONG, O LORD, MUST WE SUBMIT?"

THE MARGINALIZATION OF WEST TEXAS AND THE TEXAS STATE CENTENNIAL

While Amon Carter and the City Council toiled over bringing a centennial celebration of the Texas livestock industry to fruition in the second half of 1935, events transpired in West Texas that would ultimately set the stage for the region's overwhelming support for Fort Worth's centennial celebration rather than the Central Exposition in Dallas. Geographic proximity did not predetermine a Fort Worth/West Texas alignment as Fort Worth began preparations for its celebration. Although often labeled a big brother in the West Texas fraternity of cities, Fort Worth did not completely share in the region's cultural, environmental, and historical homogeneity. As a result, Fort Worth often found itself situated east of the line defining West Texas.[1]

Because a portion of Fort Worth's prosperity and progress rested upon successful production of West Texas resources, the region essentially became a hinterland of Fort Worth. Primarily out of economic self-interest, Fort Worth promoted the region and served as a brokerage house for its material output. Indicative of the symbiotic relationship, the Fort Worth Chamber of Commerce played a major role in the organization of the West Texas Chamber of Commerce.[2] The latter held its first meeting in Fort Worth on February 19, 1918. From that time, Fort Worth businessmen occupied prominent positions in the organization.[3]

Amon G. Carter worked more than any other Fort Worth businessman to champion the causes of West Texas and focus the gaze of its population upon Fort Worth. Carter's *Fort Worth Star-Telegram* regularly covered West Texas developments and enjoyed a wide circulation in the region. Carter insisted that West Texas began with Fort Worth. In fact, the banner of every *Fort Worth-Star Telegram* included the slogan, "Fort Worth, Texas, Where the West Begins."[4] Not surprisingly, when recalling Fort Worth's initial motivation for putting on a centennial celebration, Carter wrote in 1937: "Shortly after the announcement that the main Texas Centennial Exposition would be held in Dallas some of us in Fort Worth felt that unless we made energetic effort and provided some character of celebration in Fort Worth, we would be remiss in our duty to the city and the folks in West Texas."[5] The overtures to West Texas, presented in Fort Worth's proposal for a celebration of the Texas livestock industry and pioneer heritage, no matter how well received by the Advisory Board of Texas Historians, the Commission of Control, or the Texas Centennial Committee, did not necessarily represent the interests and views of West Texans.

Despite their shared economic interests, West Texans did not initially appreciate Fort Worth's centennial advances toward their region. In fact, rather than viewing the state's $250,000 allocation for Fort Worth as a victory for West Texas, they viewed it as yet another indication of the centennial leadership's fixation on East Texas. As the state's plans unfolded, West Texas continually found itself on the periphery. Despite the significance of the region to the history and economy of the state in the years following 1836, West Texans lamented the minuscule allocation of state funds for regional

Amon G. Carter, Blackstone Hotel, Fort Worth, Texas, February 26, 1936. On this date, Carter sent a telegram to Texas Centennial leaders suggesting Gertrude Vanderbilt Whitney's sculpture of Buffalo Bill be removed from the Texas State Centennial grounds and placed in Fort Worth. Courtesy, *Fort Worth Star-Telegram* Collection, Special Collections, The University of Texas at Arlington Libraries.

memorialization of historical events and individuals. Moreover, few West Texans received appointments to centennial leadership positions, limiting the ability of the region to represent its interests.

From the very beginning, West Texas maintained a largely antagonistic position regarding the Texas State Centennial.[6]

In 1932, as momentum began to build for the planning of the centennial, West Texas, and more specifically the West Texas Chamber of Commerce, opposed the campaign to grant the Texas State Legislature the power to allocate state funds for the purpose of celebrating the state's centennial. Without such a mandate from an amendment to the Texas Constitution, it made little sense to continue plans for a centennial celebration, especially one sponsored by the state. In May 1931, advocates for the centennial celebration convinced the legislature to approve a referendum to amend the constitution. Centennial advocates hoped to convince Texans to vote in favor of the amendment in November 1932 during the state's general election.[7] Because planners believed securing state funds to be paramount to putting on a successful Texas-sized centennial, the future of the centennial rested entirely upon the outcome of the vote.

During summer 1932, a coalition including the Texas Press Association, the Associated Advertising Clubs of Texas, the Texas Daily Press League, Progressive Texans Incorporated, and the Outdoor Poster Association, with the support of the Centennial Committee, began a campaign to generate voter support for the constitutional amendment. Often cooperating with local county organizations and media, the coalition sought to rally Texans around a celebration of the state's heroic past.[8] Still, the depressed economic conditions of the time made it difficult to sell Texans on a centennial appropriation using state tax dollars. Many believed voting for the amendment meant choosing an increase in taxes when few Texans could comfortably meet their current tax obligations. As a result, many Texas politicians believed the amendment unpopular and therefore did not support it.[9]

Although many advocates argued that the celebration would stimulate the failing economy, opinions regarding the amendment ultimately fell into opposing camps: those who believed honoring Texas history and progress warranted state spending on a centennial celebration and those who did not.[10] Proponents of a state-funded centennial celebration encountered an unanticipated opponent in the West Texas Chamber of Commerce. In

July, its Central Public Expenditure Committee crafted a statement calling for the ninety-nine local chambers in the region to actively oppose the amendment.[11]

Even while granting that the celebration of the state's centennial year represented a "worthy and patriotic project," the Expenditure Committee chaired by none other than Fort Worth mayor and president of the Southwestern Livestock Exposition and Fat Stock Show Van Zandt Jarvis explained that Texans should vigorously oppose the amendment "in view of the present plight of the taxpayers."[12] In light of the depressed economy, the Expenditure Committee suggested making the centennial self-sufficient through private investment and launching the celebration from institutions and facilities already extant. "Why not develop the idea," the Expenditure Committee asked, "through institutions, buildings and equipment we already have, such as the Fort Worth Stock Show, the Dallas Fair, the Waco Cotton Palace, Arlington Downs, etc.?"[13]

Peter Molyneaux, editor of *The Texas Weekly*, a periodical devoted to Texas politics and economics, led the charge to discredit the West Texas Chamber of Commerce's assault on the amendment.[14] With his editorial titled "Do Texans Really Revere Their Past?", which castigated Texans for failing to pay sufficient homage to their history, Molyneaux had already established himself as a vocal leader of the pro-amendment campaign. In the editorial, he discounted rumors that "a large percentage of the people of Texas are already saying that they are going to vote against the centennial amendment." He reminded readers that, if the amendment did not pass, Texans must "acknowledge reluctantly and with some degree of shame that all the loud talk about Texans being prouder of their glorious traditions than the people of any other State is just so much bombast."[15] In essence, Molyneaux believed that despite the tough economic times, the outcome of this campaign would expose the true feelings of Texans regarding their heritage. Directly responding to the chamber's statement, Molyneaux reminded readers that he always supported the efforts of the West Texas Chamber of Commerce in working to bring economic development to the region, but in this instance the chamber would commit a "blunder" if it succeeded in preventing the passage of the amendment. Such an event, Molyneaux argued, would ultimately bring a lasting shame upon the organization.[16]

As word spread of the position of the West Texas Chamber of Commerce, a number of Texas newspapers joined Molyneaux in vocalizing their support for the centennial amendment. Papers such as the *Dallas Morning News*, the *Austin American*, and the *Houston Post* labeled those who opposed the amendment as "short sighted" because they made judgments regarding the proposed legislation based on current economic conditions that they believed likely to change before the centennial.[17] The traditionally West Texas-friendly *Fort Worth Star-Telegram* supported this view, adding that it made no sense to oppose an amendment because it simply "remove[d] the constitutional prohibition against such and open[ed] the way for an appropriation when the time arrives, if such then be desirable." The paper continued, "Certainly, if times should be no better, if people should be having as hard a time paying their taxes as they are having now, the Legislature would not appropriate any money."[18]

Rather than viewing the appropriation of state funds for the centennial as an economic liability, other papers argued that the celebration represented a possible economic boon for the state. West Texas's own *Brownwood Banner-Bulletin*, published southeast of Abilene, countered the regional chamber, arguing that "No waste or extravagance is involved in the proposal for a State-supported Centennial. To the contrary, it will be the most profitable enterprise any State has ever attempted, and will repay its whole cost many times over."[19] *The San Antonio Express* expected much more from the centennial than simply making a profit. "While paying for itself," the paper boasted, "a world's fair here might usher in a new industrial era. Certainly its spirit and its exhibits alike would point the way to such achievement."[20] Many Texas papers simply reduced the issue to a matter of patriotism: those loyal to honoring the state's heritage supported the centennial amendment, while those who opposed the amendment lacked patriotism. "It appears to us," wrote the editor of the *Riesel Rustler*, "that any red blooded citizen of the Lone Star State would welcome the opportunity of having a part in such an event."[21] The *Corpus Christi Caller* labeled the act of opposing the amendment "a palpable betrayal of the glorious past which we now seek to celebrate."[22]

Although the West Texas Chamber of Commerce emerged as the only organization in the opposition movement, the chamber was hardly alone in its negative appraisal of the amendment. Several papers both within and outside of West Texas opposed the amendment. Like the West Texas Chamber, most based their opposition on the assumption that the amendment would result in an additional tax burden. The *San Saba News* in central Texas lauded the actions of the chamber, claiming, "[I]t is refreshing, to say the least, to find a Chamber of Commerce, or business organization, taking a stand for the reduction of taxes and for economy in expenditure of public money."[23] In the case of the *Wills Point Chronicle*, the owner of the northeast Texas paper so vehemently opposed the amendment that he refused "to give free advertising space to propaganda for the proposal."[24]

Statements implying that West Texans represented a disloyal and unpatriotic bunch sparked several reactions from within the region. W. W. Halcomb of the *Moore County News*, who supported the amendment, objected to "the inference that West Texans do not revere the glorious and romantic history of Texas." He argued that contrary to the assumptions of the daily press, the actions of the West Texas Chamber did not represent the sentiments of all West Texans. Linking West Texas with the state's revolutionary past, he insisted that most West Texans were "loyal to the traditions of Texas, imbued with the pioneering spirit of Houston, Fannin, and Travis," and "seriously object to being classified as pennypinchers and calloused materialists."[25] Halcomb's comments, ironically, seem to suggest that he viewed the chamber's opposition to the amendment as unpatriotic—making many West Texans unpatriotic.

The negative response to the chamber's position sparked a direct reaction from Wilbur Hawk, president of the West Texas

Chamber of Commerce. Hawk sent a rebuttal letter directly to Molyneaux and authored a statement appearing in the official publication of the chamber of commerce, the *West Texas Today*. Referring to Molyneaux's coverage of the amendment, Hawk wrote, "The position of our Central Public Expenditure Committee with reference to the Centennial has not been made clear." Although Hawk provided some evidence of exorbitant tax increases from 1912 to 1930, his "clarification" of the chamber's position, in his letter to Molyneaux, resembled little more than a restatement—the chamber's opposition to the amendment did not equal opposition to the centennial. To the contrary, he again affirmed, a "self-supporting and self-liquidating" centennial "would enlist greater and wider spread of voluntary and patriotic cooperation than a tax supported plan."[26]

The rhetoric of Hawk and the West Texas Chamber of Commerce ultimately neglected to articulate what must have been a leading factor in the chamber's opposition to the amendment: latent fears of regional favoritism toward the heritage and progress of the eastern half of the state. Experiences in the late nineteenth and early twentieth centuries convinced many West Texans that those in the eastern half of the state viewed their region as inconsequential—a colony to be pilfered for the greater benefit of the state. On several occasions in the 1860s, politicians in Austin took steps to sell off vast regions in West Texas to the federal government to fund state programs, believing the land to be of no value to the state. For all the wealth garnered in the eastern half of the state from the sale of West Texas lands, including lands to promote desired railroads, West Texans felt they never received the benefit of the programs their region helped fund. For many West Texans, the effort to build a region-specific agricultural college to advance agricultural techniques for West Texas epitomized the general opinions held by East Texans toward their region. Stonewalling politicians fought West Texans, claiming the state had no funds for such an endeavor. Only after a seven-year struggle did Governor Pat Neff signed legislation in 1923 authorizing the creation of Texas Technological College (now known as Texas Tech University).[27]

If the 1936 centennial followed the previous trend, the chamber certainly believed, West Texans should not be forced, through taxation, to fund a celebration of East Texas. Indications that the State Centennial would become a sectional affair appeared long before the West Texas chamber decided to oppose the centennial amendment. With the creation of the Governing Board of One Hundred in April 1924, the first state-sanctioned centennial planning organization, West Texans must have seen the writing on the wall. Intended to provide democratic representation in matters relating to the centennial, the Board of One Hundred included two elected representative directors from each of the thirty-one senatorial districts, twenty-nine at-large directors selected by the district representative directors, five directors appointed by the governor, and two directors appointed by the lieutenant governor and Speaker of the House respectively.[28]

Unfortunately, the final composition of the board heavily favored the eastern half of the state in terms of total representatives. Of the one hundred directors, the board included only twenty directors originating from cities in West Texas, a ratio of five to one.[29] If the eastward orientation could be justified because of its "representative" composition, resulting from population-based senatorial districts, subsequent organizations could not. With each successive centennial planning organization, the percentage of representative West Texans diminished. The creation of the Temporary Texas Centennial Commission organized by Secretary of State Jane Y. McCallum on December 28, 1931, exhibited the same eastward orientation. Assigned to compile data to aid the 43rd Legislature in determining the character of a possible Texas centennial, the twenty-one-member group included only three members hailing from West Texas cities.[30]

Unable as they were to gain adequate representation in these early centennial leadership organizations based largely upon senatorial districting, it may seem surprising that West Texans would not assert their economic relevance to the state in opposing the 1932 constitutional amendment. Estimates at the time indicate that West Texans paid more than forty percent of the state's taxes—a result of West Texas comprising nearly half the state's real estate.[31] If West Texans provided more than forty percent of the state's tax revenue, logic suggested they would also essentially pay for forty percent of a state-funded centennial. Yet, the West Texas Chamber of Commerce neglected to include these numbers in its statements opposing the amendment. Although there is no evidence explaining why they did not present this argument, it seems likely that, wishing to avoid further charges of disloyalty, the chamber and its president shunned the airing of their sectional concerns, preferring to argue that preventing an increase in taxes represented a move for the common good of the entire state. Thus, the chamber pushed for a privatized celebration with annual events already extant, all of which were held in the eastern half of the state, including the Fort Worth stock show.

On November 8, 1932, Texans voted in favor of amending the constitution to make way for the possibility of a state-funded centennial celebration. Still, the small margin of victory of less than sixty thousand votes suggests that depressed economic conditions in the state outweighed patriotism for many Texans when voting for the amendment.[32] The narrow victory did not remove the blemish upon West Texas patriotism, and the region continued to bear the stigma of opposing the celebration.

The second major piece of centennial legislation, Senate Bill 22, initiated in February 1934, continued the trend of inadequate West Texas representation in the appointment of centennial leadership. Among other things, the bill called for the creation of a Texas Centennial Commission and Executive Committee to direct centennial planning. This thirty-four-person commission included only six West Texas residents. The Executive Committee of ten members, which directed the efforts of the commission, included only two West Texans.[33] The bill also called for the organization of a Texas Centennial Advisory Board composed of the old Governing Board of One Hundred. As mentioned, this group included twenty West Texans; however, the board's leadership contained a chairman, four vice-chairmen, a secretary, and a treasurer among whom were no West Texans.[34] In terms of leadership, the passage of Senate Bill 22 rendered West Texas powerless to affect the direction and planning of the centennial.

In the legislative deliberations over the centennial appropriations, State Senator Walter C. Woodward of Coleman County finally voiced the frustrations of West Texans over blatant centennial sectionalism. Senate Bill No. 4 included a nearly nine-million-dollar centennial appropriation for which many of the state's largest cities, all of which were situated in the eastern half of the state, received earmarks. In defiance of the sectional current of the senatorial deliberations, Senator Woodward submitted Senate Resolution No. 3. In what could only be described as a sarcastic motion meant to open the senate's eyes to the injustices perpetrated on West Texas, it chided the senate for its neglect of the region in developing a centennial appropriation bill. Woodward declared:

> Whereas, The Centennial bill now pending before the Committee of the Whole Senate calls for an appropriation of $8,972,174.00 which money if appropriated must be paid as a result of taxes to be imposed upon and collected from the people of Texas; and, Whereas, Under the terms of said bill not one penny is appropriated for any purpose West of a line extending from Fort Worth to Laredo, Texas; and, Where as, There are approximately 150 counties in Texas, West of said line and for none of which has there been any provision made in said bill for any recognition in connection with the celebration of the Texas Centennial; and, Whereas, The people and properties in said counties will be called upon and required to pay approximately 40% of the $8,972,174.00 so appropriated; and, Whereas, The people living in said counties should be advised of their right to at least attend the Centennial to be held in the northeast, East and southeast portions of Texas; now, therefore be it Resolved by the Senate of Texas that the citizens living west of said line be at least invited to attend said Centennial in the northeast, East and southeast portions of Texas, and that said bill contain some provision extending to those who live in West and southwest Texas an invitation to attend the Centennial in Northeast, East and Southeast Texas.[35]

Where the West Texas Chamber of Commerce objected to the funding of the centennial through taxes in general, Woodward took the next step. In terms of state region allocations, West Texas had been omitted from a celebration for which it would pay 40 percent of the cost through taxation. Whether or not the senators perceived the motion's sarcastic tone—it seems hard to believe they did not—it passed twenty-two to two.[36]

Taking a more practical approach, Benjamin Grady Oneal, state senator from Wichita Falls, introduced several amendments to Senate Bill 4 intended to ensure that "all parts of the State should have some kind of celebration." In Amendment No. 1, Oneal called for an expansion of the term "celebration" used in the bill. By opening the interpretation, Oneal hoped to provide a means for cities, other than Dallas and Fort Worth, who planned elaborate celebrations using state funds to commemorate the centennial. Specifically, the amendment added to the definition the placing of commemorative markers, the restoration of historic structures, and the placement of monuments honoring patriots from Texas's early history. To guarantee funding for historical markers, restorations, and monuments as part of the centennial, Oneal introduced a second amendment. In Amendment No. 3, Oneal suggested the creation of an advisory board composed of three Texas historians to make recommendations to the Texas Centennial Commission on the allocation of state funds for justifiable memorials.[37] The provisions of both amendments introduced by Oneal ultimately formed part of House Bill No. 11. Governor Allred signed this bill into law in March 1935.[38]

For West Texans, the Oneal amendments represented their last resort to receive any state centennial funding. Dallas, Austin, San Antonio, and Houston gobbled up the majority of the bill's $3 million appropriation for the centennial, leaving a scant $575,000 for markers, memorials, and restorations around the state. The Advisory Board of Texas Historians heard proposals with the intention of making recommendations to the Commission of Control for the centennial celebration in fall 1935. Like the other centennial planning committees with an eastward orientation, the advisory board included two members from Austin and one from Houston. Still, with the advisory board's declared intentions to "make an impartial recommendation to the Commission" based upon the historical merits of each proposal, West Texans had every reason to expect an unbiased hearing.[39]

Over the course of the summer, the advisory board heard proposals from representatives of more than sixty Texas counties. About two dozen, nearly one-third, of all the proposals submitted to the advisory board during their hearings in June, July, and August represented West Texas interests. The region as a whole, however, asked for a scant sum of $633,497 to help fund the placement of various historical markers and monuments to individuals; the restorations of a number of forts including Forts Leaton, Belknap, Richardson, and Griffin; and the construction of museums, an exposition building, and a club building for ex-Texas Rangers.[40]

On July 2, Judge R. C. Crane, president of the West Texas Historical Association, appeared before the advisory board on behalf of all West Texas. Crane delivered a lengthy speech hoping to convince the board of the region's significance to the state. In his approach, Crane, a leading expert on the history of West Texas, employed an alternative to the economic argument for the equal participation of West Texas in the Texas Centennial. Challenging those "who will tell you that West Texas has no history," Crane assured the board, "West Texas has a history as heroic and colorful as any other part of the state."[41] Crane then recounted the epic history in which Texans pioneered an inhospitable western land, initially eking out an existence on the parched soil under the continual threat of Indian attack. Aided by the US military, who manned a string of forts that divided the civilized from the uncivilized and battled the Native Americans, and the Texas Rangers who also helped to clear the region of its Native population, the pioneers ultimately subdued the land to make it profitable.

Pointing to provisions in the Texas State Constitution restricting the use of state funds for the promotion of lands for immigration and preventing municipalities from contracting large debts,

Crane pointed out that such impinging limitations failed to limit the region's growth. Following the Civil War, the livestock industry took hold in spite of the economic gamble and risks to cattle ranchers on the Texas Plains. The success of the ranching industry and the concomitant construction of railroads connecting the region's urban oases ushered in a boom in the West Texas population. Subsequent growth of wheat and cotton cultivation and the discovery of large natural gas and petroleum reserves in the region made West Texas, in Crane's estimation, "one of the most prosperous regions in the United States."[42]

Echoing the colonial rhetoric employed by westerners in the early decades of the twentieth century, who chafed at extractive industries and the eastern financiers who profited from draining the West of its resources, Crane bluntly pointed out that throughout the history of the state the eastern half continually enriched itself through the exploitation of West Texas.[43] Under the Republic and in early statehood, the sale of West Texas lands funded East Texas development. By the time West Texans could benefit from the sale of their own lands, a surplus of state-owned lands in the region no longer existed. The trend of West Texas financially propping up the East, Crane argued, continued into the 1930s as the vast majority of West Texas counties paid more taxes than required for their operational needs. Economics aside, Crane concluded, "The winning of this vast region for Texas has been glamorous, and has called for as much determination, suffering and power of endurance on the part of its pioneers as has that of any other part of Texas. . . . It would not be far wrong to say that this has required the blood of martyrs." Challenging the board, Crane asked if the West Texas saga "shall be ignored or damned with faint praise?"[44]

Months before the advisory board planned to make its final recommendations, the actions of the Commission of Control indicated to West Texans they would not receive a centennial appropriation proportionate to the heritage and economic significance of the region. Moreover, to the chagrin of the advisory board, the commission awarded $250,000 to Fort Worth and

$50,000 to both Goliad and Gonzales—cutting, by more than half, the amount allotted for regional memorials. Despite the economic relationship between the two, West Texans did not view the Fort Worth appropriation as a nod to their region. Quite the opposite, in fact: West Texans viewed the actions of the commission as another indicator of the bias centennial officials held toward the East.

The decisions of the Commission of Control also likely contributed to a more vocal anti-centennial sentiment growing in the region. Increasingly, commentary critical of the state's centennial plans began appearing regularly in media outlets. For example, the centennial became a continuing theme in "The Plainsman," a regular editorial feature in Lubbock's *The Evening Journal*. A "Plainsman" editorial chided West Texans for adhering to an ideology of "Texas, Indivisible" in accepting the centennial planners' eastern bias. Contending that the centennial planners did not share the same ideology, the editorial stated, "We 'step-children' aren't even considered for anything so far." What should West Texans do, it asked? "Frankly," the editorial retorted, "The Plainsman is in favor of a West Texas boycott on the Centennial."[45]

Another West Texas protest came in August at the annual meeting of the West Texas Press Association at Big Spring. At the concluding session, Will Cooper of Colorado City introduced a motion to pledge the support of the association for the state centennial. For the first time in the organization's history, the group voted down a resolution. Speaking of the significance of the failed measure, Abilene editor Max Bentley noted, "The vote on the resolution is expressive not only of the attitude of the newspapermen but of the citizenship of West Texas generally who feel that our section has been grossly neglected."[46] Perhaps a speech given by W. A. Jackson, the head of the Department of Government at Texas Technological College, during the meeting shaped the outcome of the vote. Jackson described the centennial inequalities, evident in the overabundance of allotments granted to East Texas cities, as the most recent manifestation of West Texas being "left out of the picture." West Texas liabilities, according to Jackson, included lack of legislative representation and government offices held by West Texans and insufficient regional solidarity. Jackson attributed the failure of West Texans to unify to political immaturity, which reduced the region to a set of rival cities.

The defeat of the measure indicated that the members of the West Texas Press Association took Jackson's message to heart. The actions of the press association ultimately garnered the support of the region's largest and most powerful political organization, the West Texas Chamber of Commerce. In a demonstration of solidarity, the chamber published Jackson's speech under the title "West Texas and the Centennial: They've Snubbed Us, as Usual—How Long, O Lord, Must We Submit?" in its monthly publication *West Texas Today*, which touted Jackson as "a loyal Texan" who had resided in West Texas for more than a decade.[47]

The final recommendations made by the Advisory Board of Texas Historians to the Commission of Control likely dashed any lingering hopes held by West Texans for a proportional allocation of centennial dollars to the region. Differences of opinion within the advisory board regarding the proper approach to memorialization produced a schism within the three-member group. The division ultimately contained some negative implications for allocations to counties in the West Texas region. The rift pitted Chairman Kemp against board member J. Frank Dobie. As a Texas folklorist, Dobie believed historical memorials should spark the imagination of the observer. To Dobie, sculpture provided just such a medium to depict the splendor of Texas's past. Kemp, on the other hand, believed memorials should primarily convey the facts of the past.

And in many cases simple historical markers seemed an adequate memorial. Believing that Kemp's proposal to earmark allotments based upon senatorial districts smacked of political payoffs, Dobie suggested dividing funds corresponding to geographic regions instead. In a letter to Kemp, Dobie insinuated that Kemp's attempt to divide allotments along the lines of senatorial districts represented an attempt to "[help] get certain senators reelected."[48] Finally, Kemp believed the board should concern itself primarily with the memorialization of Texas independence and the Republic period alone. Dobie, on the other hand, desired to memorialize all the formative parts of Texas's past. Because Reverend Foik typically sided with Kemp, Dobie's opinions always represented a minority in the board. Ultimately, Dobie, unable to sway the other members of the board, opted to file a minority report to the Commission of Control.[49]

Not surprisingly, Dobie's minority report granted West Texas a slightly larger portion of the state funds set aside for local centennial commemoration. Particularly, his desire to allot funds by geographical divisions and to honor important historical developments not necessarily centered on the Revolution and the Republic stood to benefit West Texans. Still, Dobie's report granted only $184,500—24 percent of the available funds—to cities and counties considered part of West Texas.[50] If the recommendations of the minority report are organized according to West Texas senatorial districts, however, the West Texas allotment is reduced to $169,000, or 22 percent of the total budget, because some traditionally West Texas counties reside in senatorial districts situated mostly in the eastern half of the state.[51] The majority report produced by Kemp and Foik presented to the Commission of Control stuck to the $675,000 budget but granted only $146,950 to West Texas counties, equaling 22 percent of the total.[52] Ultimately, the $3 million state centennial appropriation makes the $37,550 difference between the minority and majority reports for West Texas allotments inconsequential. Whereas cities in the eastern portion of the state such as Dallas, San Antonio, Austin, and Houston received large allotments, the entire region of West Texas could expect to receive, based upon the recommendations of the advisory board, about 5 percent of the $3 million state appropriation.

The recommendations of the advisory board left many West Texas counties feeling bereft. In several of those counties, the advisory board discarded sites, events, and proposals to memorialize distinguished individuals. The wanton disregard for the interests of the region resulted in campaigns to press the region's proposals on the Commission of Control. The two largest proposals authored by West Texas counties provide the best examples. These include requests for allotments to El Paso and Lubbock Counties.

An El Paso County delegation led by Judge Joseph McGill presented a plan to the advisory board similar to that of Fort Worth, but smaller in scale. El Paso desired $150,000 for the construction of a memorial museum and permanent livestock buildings to support the city's annual livestock exposition. The delegation informed the board that in addition to the state's allotment, El Paso County raised $100,000 to contribute to the project. The city also donated a plot of land in historic Washington Park, the reputed location of Cabeza de Vaca's first steps on American soil, for the buildings. Hoping to capitalize on the city's proximity to Mexico, El Paso planned to fund a historical pageant that would include a ceremonial meeting of the president of the United States with the president of Mexico.[53]

To the dismay of El Pasoans, the advisory board flatly rejected the delegation's proposal. Although Dobie allotted the county a relatively generous sum of $30,000, he recommended funds for a monument to Texas Ranger Jack Hays. Perhaps more insulting to Texas's fifth largest city, the majority report earmarked only $1,000 for a historical monument honoring the history of its county.[54] More disappointing, recent changes in the Commission of Control suggested El Paso likely stood a better chance at securing the approval of that body if the advisory board recommended funding the city's proposal. Wallace Perry, prominent El Pasoan and editor of the *El Paso Herald-Post*, had recently assumed one of the nine positions on the commission—one of two seats held by West Texans.[55]

Interestingly, in his effort to garner the favor of the commission, Perry turned to none other than Amon Carter. Perry sent Carter a letter requesting the latter's assistance, hoping Carter might influence the powers that be, the way he had on behalf of Fort Worth. In the letter, Perry described the recent recommendations of the advisory board as "unfair discrimination against Texas's fifth largest city." Knowing Carter's reputation for West Texas boosterism, he hoped Carter would help El Paso. More specifically, Perry hoped Carter would persuade fellow Fort Worthian and member of the commission General John A. Hulen not only to attend the commission's deliberations over the recommendations of the advisory board but also to "vote to give El Paso a substantial allocation."[56]

The Commission of Control began its deliberations for the formulation of allocations based on the advisory board's recommendations on October 17, 1935. Accompanied by Mayor R. E. Sherman and several prominent El Paso citizens, Wallace Perry stood before the other members of the commission to make a case for a greater allotment for El Paso. Denouncing the recommendation of the advisory board, Perry snidely suggested that instead of a $1,000 allotment, El Paso County preferred $100 for a monument honoring El Paso as "Texas' forgotten city." Although intent on eliciting a larger allotment for El Paso, Perry also took aim at the advisory board's recommendations regarding the entire region of West Texas, leveling the same accusation Dobie made against Kemp's apparent political pandering in the dispersion of allocations according to senatorial districts. When no history justified an allotment, he argued, the advisory board simply "made history." What other reasoning could justify awarding New Braunfels $10,000 to commemorate a German colony while the state's fifth largest city and the first location of a European colony established in Texas received only $1,000? Moreover, he noted, "Two hundred dollar markers are repeatedly recommended for oil wells, grist mills, early trading posts or hot dog stands in East Texas—but not a dime for Texas' first mission which was established 225 years ago below El Paso."[57] Whether based on Carter pulling strings behind the scenes or Perry's rousing the sympathies of the commission, the group ultimately reconsidered and granted El Paso County a state appropriation of $50,000 for the construction of the El Paso Memorial Museum (now known as the Centennial Museum and Chihuahuan Desert Gardens).[58]

Lubbock County's experience followed a similar course. Believing the centennial to be a good opportunity to obtain state support for the funding of a museum, the West Texas Museum

Association played a leading role in the formation of Lubbock County's proposal. A group of Lubbock residents including William Holden and Lubbock booster Alaric Brandt "A. B." Davis presented Lubbock's proposal to the advisory board. The group requested $100,000 for construction of a memorial museum on the campus of Texas Technological College exhibiting materials relating to the region's geological, paleontological, archaeological, and historical treasures.[59] Shortly following the submission of the original proposal, the Lubbock Chamber of Commerce joined the quest for an appropriation for a West Texas museum. Believing a more unified West Texas might elicit a greater consideration from the advisory board, the chamber began recruiting West Texas counties to support Lubbock's proposal.

A second Lubbock delegation led by A. B. Davis, manager of the Lubbock Chamber of Commerce, reappeared before the advisory board to amend the county's proposal a few weeks later. Rehearsing the same economic argument made by Crane and Woodward, Davis argued that since West Texas paid 42 percent of the state's taxes, the region should receive a substantial allocation. The delegation produced a document titled "WILL WEST TEXAS HAVE ANY PART IN THE CENTENNIAL?" With a large outline of the State of Texas in the center, the document included a visual depiction of the bias against West Texas perpetrated by centennial planners. With a line cutting across the state from the southwest to the northeast signifying the division between East and West Texas, the map included markers noting the location of the previous allocations of the Commission of Control and the residences of the members of the Commission of Control and the Advisory Board of Texas Historians. With the exception of Speaker of the House Coke Stevenson, who lived in Junction, all the appropriations of the Commission of Control and the residences of its members along with the members of the advisory board were situated to the east of the line. The map also included the outline of an area composing nearly half of West Texas titled "West Texas Regional Application."[60] The Chamber of Commerce successfully procured the signatures of the local Centennial Advisory Committees of sixty-seven West Texas counties representing four-and-a-half West Texas senatorial districts effectually announcing the deferment of their share of any appropriation for local commemoration over to Lubbock County's proposal for a West Texas museum. The Lubbock proposal had become a "regional application."[61]

Following the second meeting with the advisory board, the Chamber of Commerce continued the campaign to gain support for a regional West Texas application. Likely after Fort Worth received a federal appropriation of $250,000, Lubbock County increased its official request to the like amount of $250,000 for the museum project.[62] Moreover, working behind the scenes, William Holden attempted to influence the outcome of the advisory board's recommendations. Such lobbying apparently held little sway with the advisory board. Responding to Holden's suggestion that the advisory board adopt a policy of regional equality in recommending allocations, Kemp retorted shortly, "We shall not make the slightest attempt to have the funds distributed equally." In a veiled reference to West Texas, Kemp further explained, "We are not concerned in the least about how any county in the state may have been discriminated against in the past; how great its population; how much taxes it pays or how much cotton, corn or wheat it raises."[63]

Kemp also enthusiastically acknowledged the advisory board's intent to recommend the distribution of funds based upon senatorial districts. Holden apparently learned from Dobie that the advisory board refused to recognize the Lubbock County proposal as representing sixty-seven counties and had apparently earlier raised the issue with Kemp. Kemp responded by claiming that the Centennial Advisory Committees for the sixty-seven counties, which offered their prospective allocations to Lubbock, were not imbued with the power to democratically represent the citizens living within their counties. Only the state senators were in a position to "to know the wishes of his constituents." And to his knowledge, Kemp told Holden, no senators contacted the advisory board to turn over any allotment their districts would receive to Lubbock County. Aware of what he referred to as the "militant campaign" of Lubbock's chamber to garner additional support for the county's proposal, Kemp concluded by explaining to Holden that "we . . . are going to make our recommendations honestly and fearlessly, irrespective of whom it may please or displease."[64]

Given Holden's heated exchanges with Kemp, the recommendations of the advisory board regarding Lubbock County came as no surprise.[65] The board's majority report recommended for Lubbock County an allotment of $14,000 for a monument to Thomas S. Lubbock and the minority report granted the county $20,000 for a monument to the Santa Fe Expedition—both paltry recommendations compared with the $250,000 request. Undaunted, Holden and the West Texas Museum Association "decided to carry the campaign to the last ditch."[66] Learning that the Commission of Control planned to deliberate the recommendations of the advisory board toward the end of the month, Holden began assembling a panel of prominent West Texans to meet with the commission during these meetings.[67]

Meanwhile, the coalition of West Texas counties began to weaken, making Kemp's assertion that only senators could accurately gauge the interest of their districts seem prophetic. The advisory board awarded Young County $14,000 to restore some of the original buildings at Fort Belknap. Kemp likely relished the opportunity of informing Senator Oneal, a strong supporter of Fort Belknap's restoration, that, because each of the County Centennial Advisory Committees in his senatorial district signed over their funding rights to Lubbock County's proposal, his district stood to lose its allocation if Lubbock County successfully lobbied its case before the Commission of Control. Oneal contacted the County Advisory Committees in his district only to discover that those members who signed the petition did not believe they signed away their county's rights to any allocation. Withdrawing their support from Lubbock's regional application, "The people of the Twenty-third Senatorial District stood firm for Fort Belknap."[68]

In mid-October, a host of Lubbock County delegates, including representatives of the Lubbock Chamber of Commerce, the

West Texas Museum Association, and the sixty-seven West Texas counties and a number of prominent West Texans, stood before the Commission of Control.[69] Asking the commission to discard the recommendations of the advisory board, the coalition asked for an allotment of $50,000 for the construction of a West Texas museum at Texas Technological College. Apparently, the delegation drew from the same arguments raised *ad nauseam* during the past three years by West Texans. With a parade of statistics and data, the delegation argued that according to the size of its population, the expanse of its geographical boundaries, and the large quantity of its tax obligations, West Texas deserved a substantially larger portion of the state centennial allocation. Size of the allotment aside, they also argued that the advisory board's recommendation to build a monument simply failed to represent the greatness of the region's history and progress. "We don't want a cold stone monument," claimed Tahoka senator G. H. Nelson. "It should be a living monument to commemorate a new kind of country and a new type of history."[70]

The commission's response to the Lubbock delegation seemed mixed. Coke Stevenson, one of the members of the commission from West Texas, indicated he would rather allocate funds for a historical memorial because funds might later be awarded for a museum through a legislative appropriation. "When this Centennial money is gone," he said, "we can not appropriate funds for historical purposes, but we could continue to make appropriations for Tech, including a museum." Commission chairman Lieutenant Governor Walter Woodul chided West Texans for the attitude engendered toward the commission by "unthinking people." He declared, "The commission is not a bunch of racketeers."[71] Ultimately, on the motion of Woodul, the commission awarded Lubbock County $25,000 to help with the construction of a West Texas museum at Texas Technological College.[72] Although the $25,000 provision fell well below the requested $250,000, Holden and the members of the West Texas Museum Association viewed the allocation as a victory. The allocation would at least provide funds to begin construction on a museum.[73]

The increased allocations and the promise of a new museum each for El Paso and Lubbock, two of the largest projects approved by the Commission of Control, did nothing to alter the negative view of the state centennial prevailing among West Texans.[74] As the celebration's June 6, 1936, opening day approached, the ire of West Texans toward the state centennial only increased. Coming on the heels of the victories in El Paso and Lubbock, the Chamber of Commerce discovered that the planners of the Central Exposition at Dallas developed no means for the presentation of industrial and agricultural contributions of West Texas to the state. In the process of forming plans for such an exhibition of West Texas resources on the central centennial grounds, the chamber learned space would not be made available in the State of Texas Building as they had hoped. The chamber also approached officials developing the $225,000 museum in Austin for space, but to no avail. Finally, chamber officials learned that if the region wanted to display its agricultural and industrial products at the Central Exposition, space could be rented at six dollars per square foot in one of the centennial buildings devoted to transportation, food, or electronics and communication. Furthermore, the state would make no allocation for the preparation, installation, or oversight of such a regional exhibit.[75]

News of the lack of support for the presentation of the region's resources infuriated officials of the West Texas Chamber of Commerce, who published an editorial in *West Texas Today* castigating centennial officials. Failing to focus "the attention of the outside world on our resources and potentialities," the editorial argued, represented a wholesale violation of centennial campaign promises. Perhaps overstating the original impetus for celebrating the centennial, the editorial claimed, "Taxpayers were led to believe that the Centennial . . . would result in launching a new era of agricultural and industrial development and in bringing to Texas many new permanent citizens."[76] Without an exhibition of the state's resources and products how, they wondered, could such a boom take place? Ironically, the editorial blamed historians for blinding politicians and centennial planners with historical bric-a-brac and derailing the true purpose of the centennial. "Surely, there should be told the story of the most remarkable agricultural development in the history of the United States," the editorial argued. West Texas produced 10 percent of the nation's cotton and oil, 25 percent of the nation's grain sorghums, 7 percent of the nation's wheat, and a majority of the country's wool. And with millions of acres still undeveloped, "The story of the only remaining open range in the United States must be told." Hoping to prevent such an oversight from occurring, the editorial called for the governing powers to "do something about portraying the resources, development and potentialities of the State of Texas."[77]

In the case of West Texas versus the Texas Centennial, population, geographical boundaries, and abundant natural resources ultimately did not translate into historical significance. An enduring irony of the state centennial is that centennial planners refused to recognize the region embodying the western heritage they worked to promote during the centennial year. Since the early twentieth century, state officials had been moving the state away from the state's southern roots in an effort to promote a more American and western identity. The state centennial—with its images of cowboys, pioneers, ten-gallon hats, and Texas Rangers—was the culmination of this process.[78] On the eve of the centennial, however, officials failed to embrace the state's quintessentially American and western half. As a result, a rift grew between many West Texans and the official celebration of the state's one hundredth birthday.

Although Fort Worth, through the efforts of Amon Carter and others, supported the West Texas campaign for greater representation in the centennial, the region's inability to make any progress on that front held important ramifications for Fort Worth's centennial plans. The shared heritage of the state's cattle industry represented the central theme of Fort Worth celebration. As it turned out, West Texas's support proved significant to the success of Fort Worth's own centennial ambitions. Staggering from the defeat of its petition for state funding, dejected West Texans turned to Fort Worth, which welcomed the region's participation in the celebration of the Frontier Centennial.

CHAPTER 3

"HOME OF THE COWBOY"

CLUB WOMEN, WEST TEXAS, AND RECREATING THE OLD WEST

A major reconceptualization and expansion of Fort Worth's centennial offering emerged in the early weeks of 1936. Toward the end of 1935, Fort Worth's City Council organized a Board of Control to develop and implement the celebration.[1] Chaired by William Monnig, a member of the Chamber of Commerce, successful department store owner, and early activist in garnering funds for Fort Worth's centennial observance, the board met for the first time on January 3, 1936, in the *Star-Telegram* building's Club Room. The business of the meeting consisted of organizing planning and finance committees and selecting members of a centennial commission—a body to consist of 200 men and 200 women.[2]

At the second meeting of the board, a week later, its planning committee presented an outline for the celebration expanding the bounds of the original proposal presented to the Centennial

William Monnig, president of the Board of Control for the Texas (later Fort Worth) Frontier Centennial, Fort Worth, Texas, February 1936. Courtesy, *Fort Worth Star-Telegram* Collection, Special Collections, The University of Texas at Arlington Libraries.

Advisory Board of Texas Historians and the Centennial Commission of Control when applying for financial support from the state.[3] In addition to the original concept of celebrating one hundred years of progress in the Texas livestock industry through an expanded version of the Southwestern Exhibition and Fat Stock Show and the construction of modern livestock facilities in Fort Worth, the planning committee's outline called for entertainment based upon the frontier or "Old West." The planning committee believed a celebration depicting the "romance, color, and action" of the Old West to be a more attractive and profitable approach to commemorate the livestock industry than a commercial exposition.[4]

The new plans called for museums containing relics of the pioneer era, shows highlighting historical scenes from frontier Texas, and perhaps most notably the reproduction of a pioneer town including a dance hall, saloon, general store, and post office. These early centennial plans also included recreations of Native American and Mexican villages. To strengthen the emphasis on the celebration's frontier theme, the board changed the official title of Fort Worth's centennial event from "Texas Livestock and Frontier Days Centennial Exposition" to "Texas Centennial Livestock and Frontier Days Exposition"—or simply the "Texas Frontier Centennial."[5] With an agreed-upon approach for commemorating the livestock industry, the numerous committees organized under the Centennial Commission sprang into action, developing a detailed plan for the festivities during the early months of 1936.

The motives for expanding Fort Worth's centennial offering to include entertainment in addition to the centennial stock and horse show resided primarily in potential revenues—the siren song heard by all Depression Era cities that hosted a world's fair, including Dallas.[6] The chairman of the Planning Committee, T. J. Harrell, argued that Chicago provided a case in point. He suggested that the 1933 Century of Progress Exposition put the struggling city, unable to pay its schoolteachers and policemen, back on solid fiscal ground.[7] Officials in Dallas had recently announced they expected centennial attendance to exceed twelve million. The Board of Control reasoned that Fort Worth's celebration, if done right, could expect to draw at least one-third of all centennial-goers in Dallas to Fort Worth.[8] If at least 1.5 million to 2 million could be attracted to travel the thirty-five miles west and each spent only ten dollars, Fort Worth stood to gross $10.5 million to $20 million—more than enough to pay off the bonds issued for the show's production.[9] Moreover, Chairman Monnig estimated that the initial construction requirements would generate at least 700 jobs.[10] To take greater advantage of the crowds that planners believed would flood Dallas, the opening date for Fort Worth's centennial offering was eventually moved forward from August 1 to coincide with the June 6 opening of the Dallas exhibition.[11]

The unfolding construction of the Central Exposition grounds in Dallas also generated fears that the centennial might provide a means for its neighbor to usurp Fort Worth's central role in the livestock industry in the Southwest. In October 1935, work began at the Dallas centennial grounds on the first of two buildings devoted to livestock.[12] Buildings one and two of the Hall of Livestock and Animal Husbandry, which formed a part of the $750,000 Farm Center, appeared to surpass the size and quality of the Fort Worth stockyards buildings used for the Southwestern Exhibition and Fat Stock Show.[13] Moreover, W. L. Stangel, head of the Livestock Exhibits Department at the centennial, boasted, "The prospects now are that the livestock show of the Texas Centennial Exposition will be the biggest ever held in the Southwest."[14] More than a simple infringement on Fort Worth's plans to host a celebration of the livestock industry, the construction of livestock buildings in Dallas and Stangel's assertions posed a significant threat not only to Fort Worth's stake in the Southwest's livestock industry but to its identity as a western city. Boosters and civic leaders believed it would only take one successful livestock show in Dallas to jeopardize the standing of the Fort Worth stock show. Amon Carter drew upon these fears when cultivating support for the city's bond issue for new centennial livestock facilities. Referencing the threat that he believed Dallas's centennial stock show aspirations represented if Fort Worth did not host an ambitious centennial stock show of their own, he wrote to US Vice President John Garner, "We are blown up and Dallas will walk off with our fat stock show."[15]

These fears grew more intense after a mid-January 1936 visit by Mayor Jarvis and Chairman Monnig to the Dallas exposition grounds to witness centennial developments. An editorial in the *Fort Worth Star-Telegram* informed readers that upon returning the delegation expressed their amazement at the "scope and progress of the Central Centennial" and the belief that these permanent livestock facilities could become a "future menace to Fort Worth's own Southwestern Exposition and Fat Stock Show." The editorial asserted, "Unless Fort Worth makes proper provision, Dallas will have the best facilities for a livestock show of any city in the Southwest. It, in time, will have the best show in the

Southwest." In light of the size and scope of the Dallas exposition, the editorial supported the Board of Control's assertion that Fort Worth, if it chose to host an exposition of its own, could not go forward half-heartedly. Fort Worth's show had to be big enough to attract visitors and, perhaps more important, it had to be worth the price of admission. Anything less stood to tarnish the reputation of the city.[16]

The theme embraced by the Board of Control featured a Texas frontier lacking specific geographical and chronological parameters. Underscoring the ambiguity of the theme, Frontier Centennial planners used the phrases "Texas frontier," "Old West," and "pioneer days" interchangeably. Precisely what constituted these mythic terms and how they figured into Fort Worth's and Texas's history, as well as how they should be commemorated as part of the centennial, represents a salient narrative in the development of the Texas Frontier Centennial.

In the minds of Fort Worth planners, the frontier they sought to commemorate existed once upon a time on the vast lands of West Texas. Still, failing to define the specific time and place these terms represented eventually created problems in the realization of accurate historical depictions as part of the commemoration of the Texas frontier.

In any case, Frontier Centennial planners believed that "the Texas cowboy and his experiences in Indian warfare and range work" reflected an important figure within the American frontier experience.[17] Given the pecuniary impetus for expanding Fort Worth's celebration, the board appeared to embrace an Old West theme not only because Texas and more specifically Fort Worth maintained a historic association with cowboys, the western frontier, and the open range, but also because of its marketability. Chairman of the Planning Committee T. J. Harrell explained, "America visualizes Fort Worth as the home of the cowboy when he is not on the open range." This image, he argued, was popularly portrayed in motion pictures, folk songs, and novels.[18] To be sure, centennial planners acknowledged that a history of the cattle industry and the Texas pioneer that depicted their importance to the progress and development of Texas would play a central role in the "character" of the celebration. But, more important, they believed a "frontier" celebration exploited a theme that would attract visitors from the Dallas Centennial. "Properly staged," the Board of Control explained, a frontier theme "from the amusement standpoint, will provide the color, romance and action necessary to make the Frontier Centennial the most appealing and entertaining of all Centennial Celebrations."[19]

In the 1930s, creating successful attractions based upon an Old West theme appeared far from straightforward. Throughout the late nineteenth and early twentieth centuries, western-themed shows proved a big success, particularly William F. (Buffalo Bill) Cody's Wild West. The success of his show and the dozens of imitators it spawned rested in the recreation of the western or frontier experience for eastern audiences—capitalizing on the nation's anxiety over the vanishing frontier. Following World War I, several elements conspired to bring about an end to the frontier shows. Purveyors of such entertainment diluted the potency of the show's meaning through the inclusion of circus-type acts. Wild West features became only one genre of the entertainment presented in these shows. By the 1920s, the rodeo, as a popular form of entertainment and sport, had come into its own and exhibited some of the same type of entertainment featured in the Wild West shows. Moreover, the most talented cowboys and cowgirls gravitated toward rodeo competitions.[20]

The emergence of western-themed motion pictures played the most important role in usurping Wild West entertainment. Silent films were far more successful at capitalizing on the "lingering spirit of frontier anxiety" felt by Americans than were the last remnants of Wild West shows.[21] The Board of Control readily recognized that Texas-based characters and landscapes often played leading roles in Western films. Perhaps more crucial, they understood that Westerns romanticized the life of the cowboy—a character closely associated with Texas. In the 1920s and 1930s, Western plots borrowed heavily from dime novels, plays, and the Wild West shows that depicted the Texas cowboy as the personification of individualism and courage as opposed simply to serving as hired cowhands. Ultimately, American audiences embraced the mythologized cowboy as they had Buffalo Bill's frontier.

Given the popularity of the Texas landscape and the cowboy in Western films, the Advertising Club and Board of Control reasoned that if motion pictures inherited the mantle of preserving frontier nostalgia and drew vast audiences allowing them to experience the Old West vicariously, what better way to commemorate Texas's frontier heritage than to let visitors return to the wild days of the Old West via the reconstruction of a movie set resembling a frontier settlement. Moving past the false façades of Hollywood, however, Fort Worth planners sincerely desired to imbue their commemorative recreation with "authenticity."[22]

As the organizational structure for the planning and implementing of the Texas Frontier Centennial emerged, women played a leading role. Even before the organization of the Centennial Commission, the Fort Worth Woman's Club adopted a resolution expressing confidence in and offering its services to the newly organized Board of Control in its centennial efforts.[23] Established in 1923, the Fort Worth Woman's Club represented nearly a dozen white women's organizations composed of the city's privileged women devoted to "the cultural and civic advancement of Fort Worth; and the study of literature, history, science, painting, music and the other fine arts."[24] In addition to advancing these stated objectives, the Woman's Club, like other women's clubs in the state, became actively involved in civic affairs and promoting political reform.[25] Although the committees of the Centennial Commission assigned to see to the planning, financing, and administration of the celebration were composed entirely of men, women accounted for at least half of the Centennial Commission. These women played a more visible role in the centennial's planning than did the male-dominated committees.

On January 24, the Board of Control requested a committee of eight women, including Anna Shelton and Margaret McLean, both notable leaders among the city's club women, to organize a Women's Division of the Centennial Commission to head the efforts of Fort Worth women.[26] The committee invited 500 of the city's most active women, about 90 percent of whom attended the first meeting.[27] The primary business of the meeting included naming committees to carry out the directives assigned to the Women's Division by the Board of Control. Projects assigned to the Women's Division comprised the beautification of Fort Worth (including the cleaning up of alleys and centers of industry) and the placement of street markers. Other initiatives under the purview of the Women's Division included providing centennial hospitality and lodging for visitors exceeding Fort Worth's hotel capacity. Although a male committee developed the official publicity campaign for the Texas Frontier Centennial, a committee under the Women's Division launched a grassroots campaign to advertise the event.[28]

Beyond beautification, hospitality, and publicity, the Women's Division led the effort to imbue the celebration with historicity and culture. Although the Board of Control determined that Texas's frontier heritage would define the centennial celebration, which history would be commemorated and how remained under the discretion of the Women's Division. Thus, at its first meeting, the Women's Division organized committees devoted to historical research, assembling a historical museum, and the creation of genuine frontier entertainment.[29] Eventually, the Women's Division would organize upward of five thousand women into twenty committees, the majority of which were dedicated to developing the means for commemoration of the Texas frontier heritage and instilling the celebration with historical authenticity.[30]

In late January 1936, as the Women's Division began to organize, the Board of Control appealed to the women of Fort Worth and West Texas for suggestions regarding appropriate costuming for women and men during the centennial festivities. Hoping to totally immerse Frontier Centennial-goers in an Old West setting, they called on Fort Worthians to dress the part of pioneer residents of the recreated frontier village. Although the Board of Control sought suggestions for men's costumes, interest in women's wear far exceeded that of men. Offering a prize to the winning costume, the board besought a "practical and effective" mode of dress for women to lend to a western atmosphere.[31] The *Fort Worth Star-Telegram* supported the Board of Control by offering the winner a copy of the very outfit they suggested. The paper also invited men to propose men's costumes.[32]

Helping Fort Worthians visualize the "authentic costumes" of the "Frontier Days," *The Fort Worth Press* printed a series of illustrated articles providing examples of western dress during the 1870s and 1880s. The paper printed photographs engendering images of a violent west including: Rose Dunn, also known as the "Rose of Cimarron," Anna Emmaline McDoulet and Jennie Metcalf, otherwise known as "Cattle Annie" and "Little Britches" of the Doolin Gang, and a posse of cowboys who posed in San Angelo. Dunn posed in a striped frock with a lace-trimmed bonnet holding a .45 Colt, or "thumb-buster," while Annie, in a dress, gripped a Winchester and Little Britches sported leather chaps with a six-shooter at her side.[33]

In the following weeks, nearly two dozen women submitted descriptions of their proposed costumes. Within the pages of the *Fort Worth Star-Telegram*, which published details and photographs of the outfits, a debate unfolded revealing the complexities of Fort Worth's identity and image as a western and modern city in the minds of local women. The submitted proposals reflected a number of approaches to the costume, but most favored costumes featuring elements of progress, modernity, and practicality rather than rigid historical accuracy. Moreover, several women voiced concern regarding the impracticality of historical costumes and claimed they made Fort Worth and Texas women, in general, appear backward and outdated. For example, Dorothy George suggested an anachronistic dress of "bright colored paisley." She justified the inauthentic design by stressing its practicality and style. "I believe the women will wear something stylish quicker," she wrote, "than they will a dress from bygone days. The cowgirl regalia is, of course, picturesque, but I do not believe many women would like to wear it." George believed the message

Mrs. F. D. Boesch models the gown selected as most appropriate for hostesses at the Frontier Centennial, Fort Worth, Texas, July 1936. Courtesy, *Fort Worth Star-Telegram* Collection, Special Collections, The University of Texas at Arlington Libraries.

of progress would benefit Fort Worth much more than would historical accuracy. "If we want to impress the visitors from out of town," she reasoned, "let us impress them with the fact that we have progressed."[34] Mrs. William F. Bryant agreed, fearing that historical costumes would misrepresent Texas womanhood. "Some think [Texas women] go barefoot, never wear corsets, chew gum all the time and dip snuff." She further argued, "Our pioneer mothers could they speak would not want us trailing foot-length beruffled skirts around."[35] Nellie Sue Bliven argued that sunbonnets were more historically accurate but "lack the smartness that women demand."[36]

Other women submitted designs emphasizing the qualities of style, comfort, practicality, and affordability over historical accuracy. Favoring affordability, Mrs. Alma Turner Phelps proposed a simple western-style dress that could be created for less than a dollar. Using an old bedspread, Phelps stitched a frock highlighted on the shoulder with a spray of bluebonnets and recommended an accompanying bluebonnet perfume.[37] Mrs. M. Wright suggested women's dress should promote Texas industry rather than its history in its design. She proposed an outfit consisting of a traditional cowboy hat, a cotton or plaid wool shirt, a woolen skirt trimmed with brown buttons, a bandana neckerchief, tan leather gloves with red fringed trim and belt, a purse, and tanned sports oxfords, "composed as completely as possible of Texas products—leather, wool, cotton and buttons and buckles made of native bone or wood."[38] Mrs. Hugh P. Prince favored comfort and practicality. She suggested a medium-sized cowboy hat with white chin strap, a red bandana, a blue silk shirt, a belt of braded leather or horsehair, a tan light-weight leather skirt, and full-length cowboy boots. Although lacking historical accuracy, Prince believed, this outfit was distinctive, pleasing, and at a price most women could afford. Perhaps more important, she argued, the costume was comfortable and practical for a variety of activities including horse riding.[39]

Some women disagreed as to which style was more historically accurate. Helea Bowles Bowie maintained that her mother, who resided in West Texas since 1882, claimed "no women wore hats on the range. They wore bonnets with splits. The wind would have blown the hats away."[40] Margaret McLean, chair of the Women's Division, held a different perspective. She noted, "Some women of pioneer days wore sunbonnets, just as some women wear today, but all pioneer women were not ridiculous. I am not a pioneer woman, but my mother was and I know that she wore hats and not sunbonnets."[41] Reflecting Fort Worth's historic ties to the South, not all women looked to the West for inspiration for proposed costuming. Mrs. L. E. Hulen suggested an outfit composed of "a white frock, made shirt-waist style with a brilliant kerchief at the neck." She asserted, "This style is becoming to the businesswoman or the housewife, the stout or the slender." For men she recommended a white shirt, white suit, and ten-gallon hat accompanied by a kerchief—attire indicative of the Old South. Hulen wrote, "I can think of nothing that would be more striking than to be entertained in a Southern city where everyone wore white costumes with [a] brilliant scarf advertising our part in the program."[42]

Proposed centennial costuming provides a unique perspective into the contours of Fort Worth's identity and image. Although some still considered Fort Worth a city of the Old South, most women submitted designs adhering to prevailing notions of "western," reflecting Fort Worth's contemporary identity and theme of the Frontier Centennial. Perhaps as important as contributing designs of a western flavor, Fort Worth women emphatically expressed, through the costume designs, their interest in presenting the city's women as modern.

The failure of local women to propose accurate pioneer costuming elicited the chastisement of the *Fort Worth Star-Telegram*. In an editorial, the paper chided that the official centennial outfit "should be as nearly historically correct as possible and should not be treated as caricatures." Furthermore, it maintained, the ceremonies and pageants of the celebration commemorated "real persons and they were as correctly garbed according to the times and the styles as are the Fort Worthians and Texans of today." But the editorial also pointed to an issue that would befuddle the committee charged with adopting an official costume. "There can be no set costume for the 100 years of progress," the editorial charged. "The clothing of the local citizenry," it warned, "when the courthouse was moved from Birdville to Fort Worth wouldn't match the styles of those who turned out to greet the first locomotive."[43] Because the Board of Control chose a frontier theme, reflecting a decades-long process of westward development, the problem of jumbling anachronistic dress, architectural styles, and symbols seemed endemic to the aim of an accurate historical commemoration of the Texas frontier. The very nature of the frontier or Old West defied its commemoration by "authentic" recreation.

On February 27, the Women's Division organized a Suggestions Committee to act as liaison between the public and the Board of Control. The committee's first order of business included deliberations regarding the official costuming of the

Frontier Centennial.[44] After evaluating the many suggestions and conducting hundreds of interviews with Fort Worth women, the committee opted to present no official costume to the Board of Control for consideration. "We are not going to say to the women of Fort Worth," they told the press, "here is something you're going to wear." Although the committee's decision might have been based on the problems of naming an accurate costume for an ambiguous Texas frontier period, it seems their decision stemmed from concerns relating to maintaining Fort Worth's image as a modern city. "There is no use in pretending," stated Mrs. Edwin Phillips, chair of the Women's Division Planning Committee, "that what the women of 1836 wore is the choice of the women today."[45]

In the midst of the debate over women's dress, the committees organized under the Women's Division began in earnest to develop plans for the Frontier Centennial. The surge of women volunteering to aid quickly overshadowed the men's centennial activities. Commenting on the women's efforts, an editorial in the *Fort Worth Star-Telegram* claimed the women's "enthusiastic support . . . introduced sufficient initiative to give the movement a distinct impetus." "The women," the editorial noted, "are setting the pace for public reception of the project. The men's groups should catch the cadence."[46] The *Fort Worth Press* also "wondered how the Control Board, composed entirely of men, could have carried on without the aid of the Women's Division."[47] The flood of support coming from Fort Worth's club women suggests that female planners recognized the centennial as an unparalleled opportunity not only to continue their work cultivating local appreciation for history and culture but also to further extend the position of women in civic affairs.

The shaping of the historical content of the centennial resided primarily with four women's committees: the Historical Research Committee, the Museum Committee, the Fine Arts Committee, and the Planning Committee. Each developed plans intended to play a role in the centennial's historic atmosphere and by extension promote the underlying message of the celebration.

Indicative of the broad heritage contained within the Texas "frontier experience," women's committees introduced features celebrating the frontier history of Fort Worth and West Texas including the commemoration of the Spanish and Mexican frontiers. Notwithstanding the celebration's western orientation, the women's committees also sought to celebrate the region's southern history including the institution of slavery and cotton culture and Texas's participation in the Confederacy and Reconstruction.

The Historical Research Committee began collecting materials documenting the history of the state. The Period Research subcommittee immediately began assembling data on the major periods of Texas history including newspaper clippings, historic correspondence, and books. For each period, the subcommittee collected materials relating to politics, social life, religious life, education; economics and industry, and geography, agriculture, and race.[48] Subsequently, a subcommittee dedicated to gathering historical data on the frontier history of Tarrant County was organized. In collecting materials pertinent to the history of Texas, the Period Research subcommittee called for local women's groups to "search out legends, romantic stories, written and printed documents, and souvenirs."[49] Ultimately, the committee received aid from more than a dozen women's organizations including the National Society of New England Women and the United States Daughters of 1812, which assisted the committee in reaching its objectives.[50]

The Julia Jackson Chapter of the United Daughters of the Confederacy (UDC) and the Frances Cooke Van Zandt Chapter of the Daughters of the Republic of Texas (DRT) played particularly important and public roles aiding the Historical Research Committee. On February 12, the committee announced its intention to restore the dilapidated Van Zandt Cottage. Proposed by Margaret McLean, head of the Women's Division, the committee reasoned the cottage's historical significance warranted commemoration through restoration. The centennial year brought the restoration or reconstruction of numerous structures of historical significance across the state of Texas. The Women's Division

Van Zandt Cottage after its restoration led by the Frontier Centennial's Women's Division, Fort Worth, Texas, August 1936. Courtesy, *Fort Worth Star-Telegram* Collection, Special Collections, The University of Texas at Arlington Libraries.

offered three reasons for the cottage's restoration. First, they argued, the cottage deserved restoration during the centennial year because of its historic connection with the Republic of Texas. Isaac Van Zandt, father of Major Khleber Miller Van Zandt, the builder and original owner of the cottage, served as Minister for the Republic of Texas to the United States during Texas's annexation. Second, they claimed, the cottage represented the oldest home in Fort Worth still on its original foundation. Finally, the Women's Division noted that Major Van Zandt's "connection" with the Confederacy of which Texas formed a part contributed to the cottage's historical value.[51]

The Women's Division's casual connection of Major Van Zandt and his cottage with the Confederacy represented a giant understatement. In a city with virtually no monuments to the Confederacy, the Van Zandt Cottage represented one of the only physical reminders of that body.[52] Van Zandt served the Confederacy as a second lieutenant in the "Bass Grays" militia company in Marshall, Texas, and later as a major in Company D of the 7th Texas Infantry Regiment. After returning from the war, he removed his wife, Minerva Peete, and two daughters, Mary Louise and Florence, from Marshall to Fort Worth to pursue a mercantile business. In the early 1870s, the Van Zandt family moved into the cottage.[53] Most of Van Zandt's family either had served in the war or were active members of Confederate commemorative groups. Because of the cottage's connection with the Republic of Texas and the Confederacy, the Historical Research Committee chose the Julia Jackson Chapter #141 of the UDC and the Frances Cooke Van Zandt Chapter of the DRT to jointly sponsor the restoration.[54] The Research Committee also proposed that the cottage be used as a museum during the Frontier Centennial, after which both organizations would serve as joint custodians.[55]

The restoration of the Van Zandt Cottage became the first in a series of suggestions proffered by the Women's Division that the Board of Control modified or rejected to conform to their evolving vision of the celebration's frontier theme. No documentary evidence remains regarding the Board of Control's deliberations over the proposed restoration of the Van Zandt Cottage, however. It seems likely that the board opted to support the plan due to the cottage's connection with the Republic of Texas rather than that of the Confederacy. In fact, a shift in emphasis from the Confederacy to the Republic of Texas might have been requested by the Board of Control. When the Women's Division proposed the restoration project to the board, Margaret McLean suggested that the UDC take sole charge of the project.[56]

The DRT became involved only after the Women's Division met with the Board of Control. That the cottage sat upon the Van Zandt property purchased by Fort Worth for the centennial grounds and yet resided outside the proposed boundaries for centennial improvements might have played a role. Because the city already owned the plot on which the cottage stood, supporting the restoration required little financial commitment. Moreover, while the restoration of the Van Zandt Cottage represented an additional historic attraction because it stood outside the official centennial grounds, its connection with the Confederacy did not detract from the Centennial's western message. Accordingly, on June 1, the Board of Control awarded $2,000 for the restoration of the cottage and stipulated that the Women's Division oversee the restoration rather than the UDC or DRT.[57]

On February 6, the Museum Committee met for the first time to discuss the creation of exhibits for display in a museum in the frontier village. The group initially designated the major exhibit theme of "Texas Under Six Flags." The committee's objective would be the selection of representative items indicative of the state's frontier experience. Subcommittees established to choose materials for the displays provide insight into the type of exhibits the Museum Committee planned to create. The majority of the subcommittees received assignments to collect items of cultural significance. In addition to subcommittees devoted to old books and rare prints, historical documents and letters, subcommittees on furniture, dolls, old glass, china, costumes, family relics, guns, Indian relics, war relics, telephones, and pioneer Texas relics were organized. Believing that West Texas embodied the frontier experience in the state, the committee enlisted the aid of West Texas women's clubs in the collection of materials and promised that these items would be given prominence in the museum. However, the committee determined that exhibits would include items from all sections of the state.[58] Although the Museum Committee omitted the Civil War as a possible exhibit, the Confederacy would receive a spotlight in the displays relating to costumes and war relics.

In addition to the exhibits proper, decorating and furnishing the recreated frontier buildings fell under the purview of the Museum Committee. Planners of the centennial looked to the latter to provide decorations and furnishings reflecting the time period of the proposed buildings, yielding a sense of historical accuracy. Many of the rooms within the recreated buildings of the frontier village would provide the housing for the museum exhibits. The Museum Committee planned for rooms appointed to contain relics of the cattle industry, old china, and pioneer furnishings. Another room would contain the furnishings of a typical pioneer home.[59] In addition to furnishing the reproduced buildings of the Old West, the Museum Committee received the assignment to furnish the Van Zandt Cottage.[60]

The efforts of the Fine Arts Committee revolved around bringing culture to the "Wild West of the Frontier Centennial Show." In accordance with the ambiguous frontier theme, their selection of material also reflected a wide interpretation of the frontier experience. The "Plinkety-plank of the dance hall piano will have its place," Mrs. Charles Scheuber, the committee chair, noted, but so too would the symphony orchestra.[61] The committee desired a nightly performance of a greatly augmented Fort Worth Symphony Orchestra in the centennial's proposed amphitheater. After hearing the recommendation, the Women's Division concurred but supported the idea for offering one concert a week.

Another proposal of the Fine Arts Committee held a much greater potential to shape the historical message of the Frontier Centennial. The committee suggested that the centennial offer a nightly production of Carl Venth's opera "La Vida de la Misión" ("Life at a Mission").[62] Venth, a German-born violinist and composer, moved to Texas in 1908 and became an influential supporter of the development of the fine arts in the state. At the time of the Texas Centennial, he was head of the music department at Westmoorland College (later known as the University of San Antonio and then Trinity University).[63] Believing nightly productions of "Life at a Mission" would never turn a profit, the Women's Division adopted a plan for one performance every two weeks.[64] Ultimately, the Board of Control declined to produce Venth's work at the Frontier Centennial.[65] Surviving records do not provide insight into the board's deliberations regarding the opera. Whatever the reasoning, by cutting the performance, the Board of Control omitted the Spanish and their interactions with the Native Americans from the Texas frontier heritage, further whitening the commemorative message of the Frontier Centennial.

The Planning Committee of the Women's Division also made suggestions regarding the design of the central attraction of the Frontier Centennial: the reproduction of a frontier township. Although Western films served as the inspiration for the recreation of a frontier settlement, reproductions of historic landscapes and structures had become a standard feature at world's fairs. In fact, the midways of both the Depression Era and Victorian Era world's fairs often included both anthropological and historical curiosities embodied in genuine architectural representations. The Central Exposition in Dallas boasted a number of architectural reproductions. For example, the Texas Rangers exhibit would be housed in "a large rambling structure typical of early Texas Rangers" and the Sheriffs' Association of Texas received permission to build a replica of the famed Roy Bean saloon-courthouse of Langtry, Texas.[66] The 1935–1936 world's fair in San Diego, designed to be "an everlasting symbol of—the West," featured a recreation of a street from a typical forty-niner mining camp known as Gold Gulch. Intended to depict the "colorful towns of that period," the gulch, an off-shoot of the exposition's midway, contained alcohol-dispensing saloons and burlesque shows.[67] For the 1933 Century of Progress exposition in Chicago, planners included a reproduction of the city's earliest settlement, Fort Dearborn.[68] Juxtaposed with the historical reproductions built along the midways in Dallas, San Diego, and Chicago, the frontier village designed for the Texas Frontier Centennial far exceeded the reproductions of the Depression Era expositions in size and scope.

Because the frontier village represented the central entertainment attraction of the Frontier Centennial, the Board of Control carefully deliberated over its design. The composition of the physical layout of the "pleasure grounds" reflected the importance of the cattle industry to the centennial celebration. More specifically, the designs of the proposed buildings were to "depict the homely architecture and life of the frontier cattle towns just as they were in the days when the Longhorn was King of the prairies."[69] Early plans also called for an open-air stockade for the production of pageants and shows with frontier themes. For example, the Board of Control hoped to cast a group of Native American warriors and a troop of US cavalrymen for daily historical reenactments of the Great Plains military conflicts.[70]

The City Council, which oversaw the development of plans and bids for both temporary and permanent structures on the centennial grounds, called upon local architects to develop preliminary plans for proposal to the Council. For this purpose, the council provided a general depiction of what the village should include as a guide from which architectural blueprints could be generated. Council members suggested the village should include replicas of dance halls, an "opery" house, saloons, general stores, and a main street lined with hitching posts. The main street would function as a midway featuring pioneer-themed attractions. The council also noted that an Indian town or village and stockade housing the frontier days show should be situated adjacent to the main street. Admittedly, the council took its cues regarding what the Old West looked like from descriptions presented primarily in motion pictures. As such, they suggested the designs of the buildings should reflect Hollywood movie sets, which they believed captured the atmosphere of the Old West. Moreover, much like movie sets representing the Old West, the construction of the frontier town should be of temporary composition—meaning composed of wood and stucco.[71]

Although motion pictures and novels served as the source of the council's recommendations regarding the pioneer village, centennial planners wanted more than superficial old-looking designs—they desired historical accuracy. According to C. L. Douglas of the *Fort Worth Press*, in reproducing a frontier village, "Fort Worth intends to give its visitors a taste of the real thing—boarded shacks and all."[72] For help, the Board of Control contacted West Texas amateur historian Judge R. C. Crane. They requested that Crane recommend the "most picturesque and the wildest of pioneer West Texas towns for that will be the one we shall wish to reproduce."[73] Crane recommended Colorado City as the "outstanding cow-town in all West Texas."[74] Other old cow towns in West Texas under consideration for use as an architectural model included Mobeetie, Tascosa, Toyah, and Dog Town.[75]

Planners believed that "authenticity" would play a singular role in the financial success of the Frontier Centennial. As J. M. North explained to R. C. Crane, "a historically accurate reproduction will be an attraction worth the money."[76] Several editorials published in both the *Fort Worth Star-Telegram* and the *Fort Worth Press* also championed the importance of creating historically accurate spectacles and attractions to the financial success of the celebration. The *Star-Telegram* urged centennial planners that the gates of the frontier village must generate a powerful first impression. The buildings that followed "must not dissipate that impression . . . just an exaggerated carnival effect will not fill the order." Moreover, the *Star-Telegram* warned that the attractions "must be a . . . prideful reminder in the history of Fort Worth's civic progress."[77] The *Fort Worth Press* noted that "Fort Worth's job is to provide the bait in the way of an authentic, well appointed exposition of frontier days that will typify the factual and legendary picture of the old Southwest."[78]

Prior to the City Council's approval of a set of finalized plans for the frontier village, the Women's Division presented to a group of centennial planners, including city officials and the Board of Control, features they believed should be included on the grounds. The plan, heavily influenced by the suggestions of the Woman's Club of Fort Worth and presented by Margaret McLean, included a number of features already embraced by the Board of Control such as a pioneer settlement and Indian and Mexican villages. McLean also introduced several original ideas. Her group's plan called for a replica of the original Fort Worth complete with a detachment of soldiers from Fort Sam Houston. The fort would house Native American and Civil War relics, including the collection of Cleburne businessman William J. Layland containing an array of firearms, Civil War uniforms, and Native American artifacts. The Women's Division also suggested that the grounds contain a ranch house complete with a chuck wagon and corral accompanied by cowboys playing the banjo and guitar, a miniature Spring Palace, and a "shell" to house presentations of pageants and symphony concerts.[79]

The Women's Division again proposed a number of features intended to commemorate the Confederacy and the Old South. Closely tied to the memory of the Confederacy, the women's division already worked to restore the Van Zandt Cottage. They also proposed filling a recreation of the original Fort Worth with exhibit relics of the Civil War. McLean's plans further called for the inclusion of a reconstructed plantation house accompanied by "belles and beaux of the Old South in costume." Adding flavor to the plantation house, the Women's Division suggested "spirituals sung by negroes."[80] In contrast to the Board of Control, which repeatedly rejected or limited their attempts to inject Fort Worth's southern heritage into the Texas Frontier Centennial, Fort Worth's club women seemed to hold a lingering devotion to the memory of the Old South and Lost Cause, a characteristic common among club women throughout Texas and the South.[81]

In the week following the proposal of the Women's Division's plan for the temporary structures on the centennial grounds, D. L. Bush, a landscape consultant, and architect Joe R. Pelich, both retained by the Centennial Commission, and assistant city manager and engineer L. W. Hoelscher, worked together to draft a layout for the frontier village including cost estimates.[82] After receiving the approval of the City Council on February 12, Hoelscher and City Manager George Fairtrace laid the plans before the Board of Control.[83] The designs presented to the City Council and the Board of Control resembled a simple layout of buildings situated on the east side of the centennial grounds, adjacent to the coliseum and auditorium that composed the new centennial stock show facilities. They also provided some indication of the attractions contained within the centennial grounds. The buildings ran along a midway creating the shape of a triangle—each side commemorating a specific aspect of the frontier experience. Based upon the suggestion of the Women's Division, the scene that would greet centennial visitors was a gate created by two military stockades. A southward path would lead to a quadrangle of military structures representing the old Fort Worth site. Attended by cavalrymen, the fort buildings would house the museum displays developed by the Women's Division's Museum Committee. On the south side, the quadrangle would open to the Cavalry Corral and a trail leading to an Indian encampment including a series of tepees and painted Native American warriors.

The Pioneer Main Street stretched west from the south end of the Cavalry Corral. Pelich's plans proposed to line the street with a general store, dance halls, and a building containing a "Wild West movie thriller." The west end of the Main Street, on the suggestion of the Women's Division, also included a trail leading to a Ranch House providing accommodations for the Frontier Centennial's hospitality hostesses. Taking advantage of a natural slope in the terrain, the plans placed an amphitheater to the south of Main Street's west end.[84] Pelich called for the amphitheater to accommodate at least six thousand persons. The amphitheater design reflected a compromise between the "shell" requested by the Women's Division for symphony orchestra productions and the original conception of a stockade for Wild West-type shows including staged Indian attacks and stagecoach robberies.

The third side of the triangle layout contained a Mexican Village and moved east to west from the entrance to connect with the west end of the Main Street. Organized around a Mexican plaza, the Mexican Village included space for Mexican shops and displays of Mexican crafts. Pelich's plans called for bright serapes and Mexican dancing girls to greet centennial-goers on the west entrance of the Mexican Village.[85] Although the designers of the centennial layout embraced several of the suggestions conveyed by the Women's Division including commemorating Fort Worth's frontier heritage with a reproduction of the original Fort Worth outpost, the plans clearly omitted any references to the Old South or the Confederacy and either erased or limited non-whites from history memorialized during the Frontier Centennial. Planners declined to celebrate the state's Spanish heritage with the production of "Life at a Mission" and reduced Texas's Mexican heritage to the sale of trinkets and dancing girls. Moreover, Fort Worth civic leaders made no room for African Americans in the city's official centennial celebration. As a result, the African American community developed plans for their own centennial celebrating "A Century of Negro Progress" in connection with the annual Juneteenth celebration.[86]

With the general outline approved by the City Council and the Board of Control of the newly organized Centennial Corporation, Pelich, with the aid of Bush and Hoelscher, began preparing draft elevation sketches of the centennial structures. Desiring the appearance of accuracy, the Board of Control stipulated that the architects "consult historical records and pictures" in the developments of the plans.[87] Within days, Pelich, Bush, and Hoelscher presented the Board of Control a set of representative sketches.[88] Sketches published in the *Fort Worth Star-Telegram* and *Fort Worth Press* provided the public with its first glimpse of the proposed recreation of a frontier town. Moreover, the accompanying article provided depictions of additional attractions it would contain. The two stockades and the reproduction of the original Fort Worth appeared to be constructed of roughhewn timbers. The Pioneer Main Street contained a shooting gallery, a dance hall-café, a general store, a penny arcade, a gambling hall, a bank, and a wax museum with false facades constructed of planks typical of Old West construction. The Mexican village, composed of stucco archways, bell towers, and tiled rooftops, included a war museum, a dining room, Mexican shops, a Chinese restaurant, and a chapel. The plaza itself would include shops containing native wares. In the space connecting the Mexican plaza and the old fort, the designers situated a church and accompanying graveyard.[89] Finally, on February 23, the City Council and Centennial Corporation approved the plans for the centennial's temporary buildings with a guarantee they could be completed by the projected June 6 opening. With approval of the plans, the City Council also approved the sale of $500,000 in short-term bonds to finance its construction.[90]

Fort Worth centennial planners looked to West Texas history as the source on which to base not only the construction of an "authentic" frontier village but the celebration itself. Within days of the Board of Control's organization, board member J. M. North Jr. fired off a letter to West Texas historian R. C. Crane. North noted that although the plans were still in the early stage and the "ideas of the organization somewhat nebulous," Fort Worth centennial planners "want to make the central theme pioneer and, along with it, to depict the development of the ranch country, of livestock, and of West Texas." North hoped Crane might "outline a few ideas of the possibilities latent in such a celebration."[91] Looking to West Texas as a latent source for the Frontier Centennial reflected Fort Worth's growing reliance on its historic links with that region, and particularly the cattle industry, as the basis of its western memory and identity. Without the cattle drives that linked the city with the storied frontier history of West Texas, Fort Worth had little to distinguish itself from Dallas or the South. Ultimately, Fort Worth depended on the participation and support of West Texas to lend historical credibility, a major component of the celebration's appeal, to the Frontier Centennial's commemoration of the Texas frontier.

By commemorating the cattle industry and the Old West as experienced in West Texas, Frontier Centennial planners also hoped to appeal to West Texans. As mentioned in chapter 2, the marginalization of the history and industry of the western half of the state in the planning of the state centennial alienated West Texans. In their effort to claim more recognition in the state's centennial planning boards, some West Texans turned to Fort Worth boosters such as Amon Carter for help. Although West Texans did not consider Fort Worth to be a traditional part of West Texas, its emphasis on commemorating West Texas led some to include the Frontier Centennial among the celebrations hosted by other West Texas towns, many of which also celebrated the region's pioneer and western heritage.[92] For example, Mrs. Hulen R. Carroll, a member of the Texas Centennial Commission's press division, proclaimed Fort Worth's celebration the crowning jewel among the thirty-seven other centennial celebrations planned in West Texas.[93] Not surprisingly, Amon Carter's *Fort Worth*

Star-Telegram enthusiastically embraced Carroll's appraisal of the West Texas celebrations and her inclusion of Fort Worth. An editorial exclaimed, "Fort Worth is happy to be a participant in the West Texas enthusiasm over the Centennial."[94]

As Fort Worth's centennial plans moved forward, officials worked to include West Texans. That the Board of Control sought out West Texas historian R. C. Crane is an example of this effort. The Women's Division also supported the effort to cultivate West Texas's participation in the planning of the Frontier Centennial. In their search for the official centennial costumes, members of the Women's Division sought designs from women living in West Texas cities. Working to assemble pioneer artifacts for display, the Museum Committee called on women's clubs throughout West Texas as well as individual women in the region to collect and submit materials.[95] The Women's Division also recruited West Texans in its grassroots advertising campaign. In early March, the Women's Division organized a West Texas All-States Centennial Club. Calling for all first-generation Texans residing in West Texas and Fort Worth to join its efforts, the club began an expansive letter-writing campaign to invite friends and relatives from their home states to attend the Frontier Centennial.[96]

In addition to inviting West Texans to contribute to the planning for the Frontier Centennial, Fort Worth planners also looked to its western hinterlands for revenue—paying customers—for its celebration. As the opening dates of Fort Worth's centennial venues approached and the Southwestern Exposition and Fat Stock Show loomed, various Fort Worth groups sponsored booster tours to travel to West Texas and extended a personal invitation to the festivities. Initiated by the Junior Chamber of Commerce and the Roundup Club, the first of these tours carried approximately one hundred club members for a daylong tour of West Texas towns including stops at a dozen communities.[97] Later, the Fort Worth Advertising Club joined with the Retail Merchants Credit Association to sponsor a two-day booster excursion through West Texas to promote West Texas attendance of the Fort Worth stock show. About seventy boosters stopped at half a dozen West Texas communities while en route to San Angelo. Arriving at their destination, the trippers attended Fort Worth Day of San Angelo's Fat Stock Show and rodeo where a party was thrown in their honor.[98] With West Texas specifically in mind, a group of Fort Worth businessmen also urged the City Council to construct a permanent merchants and manufacturers building on the centennial grounds with floor space for retail and wholesale exhibitions during and after the celebration.

The civic leadership in West Texas also played an important role in boosting Fort Worth's centennial celebration in the region. In addition to promoting the celebration, West Texas officials attempted to subdue any lingering negative sentiment regarding the exorbitant funds initially granted to Fort Worth for their celebration by the state. D. A. Bandeen, the manager of the West Texas Chamber of Commerce, argued that allotments granted to Fort Worth were appropriate because Fort Worth planned to celebrate a century of progress in the livestock industry and labeled the concept a "splendid idea."[99] A member of the State Pension Board, H. T. T. Kimbro of Lubbock urged West Texans to plan a visit to Fort Worth, claiming they "will appreciate the exposition." He also noted that "Fort Worth certainly is the proper place for this exhibition, for it is not only the gateway, but the big brother of the West."[100] Such boosterism not only helped generate goodwill between Fort Worth and West Texas but also helped stimulate interest and participation in the celebration. Early reports indicated that 1936 would represent a record year for West Texas involvement in the Southwestern Exposition and Fat Stock Show, the mid-March prequel to Fort Worth's centennial celebration.[101]

Although Fort Worth courted and received the support of many West Texans, including several important civic leaders within the region, official support from the area came through the West Texas Chamber of Commerce, which viewed the Frontier Centennial as an opportunity to promote the western region of the state. Despite hard feelings in West Texas based on a prevailing notion that state centennial officials dismissed the region as historically insignificant in comparison with the East, West Texas began plans to participate in the state's Central Exposition in Dallas by contributing poster exhibits for display on the centennial grounds. Viewed as an opportunity to advertise the products of the region to the millions of centennial-goers, each of the ten districts represented by the West Texas Chamber of Commerce received a space measuring eight by thirty-six feet with a total retail value $36,000. Each town within the ten districts received room to feature a product grown or produced in the area.[102]

By mid-February, however, the Executive Committee of the West Texas Chamber of Commerce began deliberations over the possibility of placing the exhibits at the Fort Worth celebration.[103] On February 22, D. A. Bandeen, the general manager of the chamber, announced the Executive Committee's intention to retool the displays of nearly 200 West Texas towns for exhibition at Fort Worth rather than Dallas. The chamber's Exhibit Committee received instructions to act as liaison between the Executive Committee and Fort Worth's centennial Board of Control. The chamber did not plan to abandon the Central Centennial Exposition altogether but intended to contribute a simple display emphasizing the region's agricultural significance similar to those of East and South Texas.[104] Contrary to the exhibits developed for Dallas, the chamber planned for the creation of permanent "all-resource" exhibits to be maintained in Fort Worth following the conclusion of the centennial year.[105] The placement of a permanent West Texas exhibit on the centennial grounds seemed particularly opportune as Camp Bowie Boulevard, the centennial ground's frontage road, converged with Highway 1, the main route into West Texas. Thus, Fort Worth would again become a symbolic gateway to West Texas.[106]

Officials in both Fort Worth and West Texas lauded the plans. Ray H. Nichols, chamber president, noted that 135 cities had already pledged support for the move. The prospect of developing a permanent exhibit in Fort Worth, he claimed, "offers West Texas the greatest opportunity in its history to tell the world about its progressiveness, its livestock and about its people." Of course, Executive Committee member Amon Carter and Fort Worth

Mayor Van Zandt Jarvis, who may have been behind shifting the West Texas exhibits to Fort Worth, promised support for the exhibit.[107] A few days later, the *Fort Worth Star-Telegram* pledged unqualified support for a permanent exhibit depicting the "partnership" as the culmination of a century of progress that "has linked Fort Worth more closely to the West Texas of which it was an early frontier point." The editorial concluded, "The Texas Frontier Centennial could have no greater impetus than the cooperation of 195 West Texas communities."[108] By March 3, 700 committeemen had been appointed by 135 West Texas towns to begin preparations for the Frontier Centennial exhibits. The West Texas Chamber of Commerce vowed to invest $66,000 in the development of the displays. As with the exhibits initially prepared for Dallas, display space would be divided between the ten districts represented by the West Texas Chamber of Commerce.[109]

The planning of the Texas Frontier Centennial in January and February 1936 ultimately illustrates the process by which elites used a commemorative celebration to shape collective memory, group identity, and civic image. Since the beginning of the twentieth century, city boosters and civic leaders worked to strengthen Fort Worth's ties with the American West and its progressive heritage. By the 1930s, the increasingly westernized Southwestern Exposition and Fat Stock Show and the city's livestock industry became the primary cultural links between Fort Worth and that western heritage. Given Fort Worth's central role in the Texas livestock industry, which played a singular role in shaping the state's history, centennial planners developed their plans around the Southwestern Exposition and Fat Stock Show and a corresponding commemoration of the Texas livestock industry.

The initiative to expand Fort Worth's centennial offerings resulted from not only the hopes held by civic leaders and boosters that such a move would attract more fairgoers from Dallas to Fort Worth, thereby generating additional revenue, but also their fears that having built modern livestock facilities in Dallas, Central Exposition officials intended to host a superior stock show. Trading on the prevailing popularity of the Texas cowboy in western literature and motion pictures, Fort Worth centennial planners announced their intention to commemorate the livestock industry and by extension the American West through the recreation of a "living, breathing" reproduction of the Old West as Americans experienced vicariously in the movies. A centennial commemoration of the Old West would, centennial planners believed, simultaneously generate more revenue than would a commercial exposition and fortify Fort Worth's identity and image as a western city. But the event would have to offer more than a few false store and saloon fronts; planners believed that only an "authentic" recreation of the Old West would be worth the price of admission.

Fort Worth's club women played a primary role in the process of refining the contours of the Frontier Centennial's commemorative message. Reflecting the city's rich tradition of club women participating in city boosterism and cultural offerings, the Centennial Commission's Women's Division marshaled the aid of thousands of club women. Although they led dozens of initiatives relating to centennial preparations, their contributions relating to the celebration's historic message are most distinctive. The Board of Control embraced a nebulous Texas frontier theme in time and space, allowing the Women's Division to explore the depths of the meaning of the Texas frontier heritage. In addition to gathering items from all the periods of Texas's history under the six flags, they also developed historical and cultural entertainment venues touching on the state's Spanish heritage and Fort Worth's history as a frontier outpost.

Particularly notable are suggestions to commemorate the history of the Old South and Texas's part in the Confederacy. Given the Frontier Centennial's dominant western theme, such suggestions seemed to reflect the duality of Fort Worth's heritage, a duality that was readily apparent to the city's club women. As the Board of Control accepted or rejected the suggestions of the Women's Division, the nebulous "frontier" theme narrowed. Suggestions considered beyond the desired scope of the centennial's message were either discarded completely or minimized. Other concepts such as the reconstruction of old Fort Worth and the renovation of the Van Zandt site included Fort Worth's history in its commemorative message. The cleansing of the Spanish, Mexican, southern, and African American influence from the Frontier Centennial's commemorative message according to perceived civic needs stood in sharp contrast to the Board of Control's stated desire for historic accuracy.

The significance of the participation of Fort Worth's club women in the initial planning of the Frontier Centennial increases when compared with the representation of women in the world's fairs. Many believed the inclusion of a Women's Building at Chicago's Columbian Exposition in 1893 brought a new era of significance for American women in spheres of social progress and culture. During the fair, the Board of Lady Managers, who managed the Women's Building, played an influential role in the way women would experience the exposition. The lack of offerings at subsequent world's fairs devoted to the aspirations of women seemed to counter the notion that the Columbian Exposition actually served as a harbinger of a new era for women. Scholars analyzing the century-of-progress expositions of the Depression Era, in particular, suggest that these fairs offered women little.[110] As noted by world's fair scholar Robert Rydell, these expositions "reconfirmed the status of women as consumable objects . . . to preserve dominant gender relations well into the future."[111]

The activities of club women under the direction of the Women's Division in the initial planning of the Frontier Centennial run counter to these depictions of women as sexual commodities at the century-of-progress expositions, including the Texas State Centennial in Dallas.[112] Club women headed dozens of planning initiatives for the celebration, including the development of the Frontier Centennial's commemorative offerings. These women also showcased the historic role of women in Texas through the development of the celebration's museum offerings. Preferring to support a modern image of Fort Worth women, the Women's Division refused to nominate an official women's costume for the celebration despite the urging of officials.

Planning a centennial celebration commemorating the Old West turned the Board of Control to Fort Worth's hinterland. As Fort Worth embraced its western heritage during the early decades of the twentieth century, a burgeoning common historical identity only strengthened longstanding economic ties that bound Fort Worth and West Texas. Historically, Fort Worth turned to West Texas as a source of cattle, agricultural products, and oil. Now centennial planners turned to the region as the ultimate source of its western heritage. Indeed, in the early stages of planning, the elusive search for authenticity made the Frontier Centennial as much a commemoration of West Texas as of Fort Worth or the Texas cattle industry. Seeing an opportunity to increase Frontier Centennial revenue, planners sought to encourage West Texans to support and attend the event. By alienating West Texas, state centennial officials inadvertently assisted these efforts, which culminated with plans to construct a permanent exhibit at the Frontier Centennial presenting the region's agricultural and commercial progress.

Despite the singular contributions of women and the desire to commemorate the Texas frontier with authentic attractions, in the coming months the direction of the celebration took a radically different course as Frontier Centennial planners searched for a vehicle to attract larger crowds. In the process, the role of women in the centennial changed, the objective of historical accuracy diminished, the scope of the centennial's western appeal broadened, and the relationship of Fort Worth's celebration to Dallas was defined.

PART 2

SELLING NATIONAL MYTH

CHAPTER 4

THE DEVIL'S BARGAIN

AMON CARTER, BUFFALO BILL, AND THE ARRIVAL OF BILLY ROSE

As plans for the Texas Frontier Centennial rolled forward in early March 1936, the Fort Worth dailies reported unexpected news. They announced that famed Broadway producer and showman Billy Rose had signed on to direct Fort Worth's centennial celebration. Accompanied by photographs showing Rose as a smartly dressed young man with slicked-back jet-black hair, the *Fort Worth Star-Telegram* clamored to introduce its readers to the new director of the Frontier Centennial, describing him as the "nationally recognized 'man of the hour' among showmen because of his 'Jumbo' now running at the Hippodrome in New York" and "Broadway's No. 1 producer," who inherited the mantles of famed showmen and creators of spectacle P. T. Barnum and Florenz Ziegfeld.[1] With William Monnig, the president of the centennial's Board of Control, and John B. Davis, the show's general manager, looking on, Rose signed the contract on March 9.[2] The contract obligated Rose to provide centennial amusement, develop publicity, and contract the show's concessions. Even with the opening day delayed to July 1, Rose had less than four months to make good on the spectacle he promised Fort Worth's city fathers and centennial planners.[3]

During the preceding weeks, centennial planners apparently concluded that hosting a successful celebration necessitated hiring a "nationally recognized showman" who could take advantage of the unique opportunity they believed the state centennial represented.[4] Precious few documents remain describing the path that led Fort Worth centennial planners to seek out a showman of national fame. To be sure, Amon G. Carter often spoke of the centennial in terms of stealing the spotlight from the exposition hosted by Dallas. And Rose would often describe his part in Fort Worth's celebration in competitive terms. Although rivalry makes for a better story and ad copy, economic and political necessity drove centennial planners to seek out and hire Rose rather than some longstanding vendetta held by Carter or Fort Worth against Dallas.

When Fort Worth's centennial planners announced the selection of a western theme, they reasoned that the "color, romance and action" of the Old West reflected a useful premise upon which sufficiently alluring attractions could be created. The earliest concepts for entertainment revolved around attractions depicting the cowboy and pioneer life of early Texas history with the reproduction of a frontier town representing the central attraction.[5] As plans for its construction materialized, entertainment accompanying the village emerged. Some of the larger attractions included a museum containing pioneer relics, a "dance hall-café," a gambling hall, and an "opery" house presenting period melodramas from the late nineteenth century. The main streets of the pioneer and Mexican villages would also contain "attractions of a pioneer days theme" including a penny arcade and shooting gallery.[6]

More nebulous were references to historical pageants and shows. Designs for the pioneer village included a stockade, later labeled an amphitheater for the production of "wild west attractions."[7] The Planning Committee proposed hiring a tribe of Native Americans and US cavalrymen to stage a nineteenth-century Plains war reenactment. By mid-February, planners began exploring the possibility of stationing the 2nd Cavalry of the United States Army on the centennial grounds.[8] Other possible plans included reenactments of an Indian attack or robbery of a stagecoach.[9] Finally, the Planning Committee considered the possibility of hosting athletic events and garden and pet shows, which had little to do with the state's frontier heritage.[10]

During January and February, plans moved forward with many aspects of the centennial. The architects drafted plans for the frontier city including the amphitheater and living space for US cavalrymen and Native Americans. The Women's Division's Museum and Fine Arts subcommittees gathered materials for exhibit at the Frontier Centennial. Despite the earmarking of centennial funds for "rodeo performers, livestock owners, dance bands and crooners," the Planning Committee had yet to solidify plans regarding the shows and pageants to be staged in the amphitheater or hire a troupe for melodramatic performances in the "opery" house in the pioneer village.[11] Moreover, several of the Frontier Centennial's major attractions, including the horse show and rodeo, could not begin until the completion of the new stock show facilities in October.

As the Dallas exposition's June 6 opening rapidly approached, Fort Worth civic leaders and city boosters became painfully aware of their promises in selling the show to the citizens of Fort Worth.[12] Frontier Centennial planners reasoned that the romance and color of an Old West theme placed Fort Worth on the best footing for developing a profitable celebration. However, they also continually warned that the entertainment must be worth the price of admission. In a typical statement, the *Fort Worth Star-Telegram* warned "an exaggerated carnival effect will not fill the order" and "There must be exhibits and entertainment worth the ticket price."[13] Without worthwhile attractions, centennial planners reasoned, Fort Worth would fail to entice sufficient numbers of central centennial-goers to travel the thirty-five miles west to the Frontier Centennial.

By the end of February, after more than two months of planning, Fort Worth had figuratively moved close to a point of no return. In addition to considerable time devoted to the creation of a "frontier centennial," several developments made the plausibility of calling off or scaling back Fort Worth's celebration nearly impossible. After the announcement of the centennial's proposed theme, city fathers and centennial planners launched a campaign to convince Fort Worth's citizenry of the economic expediency and viability of producing a western-themed celebration. Planners ultimately achieved victory at the polls on January 28 when through their vote the city's citizens essentially consented to the centennial plans by approving $250,000 in additional bonds to finance the celebration.[14]

Perhaps more important, Fort Worth officials boasted of their city's intention to stage a spectacular western-themed celebration. Fort Worth's centennial plans had already received acclaim by a host of state officials.[15] The state had also published and distributed centennial promotional pamphlets announcing Fort Worth's Texas Frontier Centennial as "a highlight of the Centennial year."[16] No longer a matter of boosting the city's economy or preventing the removal of the center of Texas cattle industry from Fort Worth to Dallas, according to William Monnig, the head of the Board of Control, "The city's reputation is at stake in this matter."[17] If the centennial planners abandoned their campaign for a frontier-themed centennial or produced a flop, city fathers believed, the municipality would have been better off never to have entered the centennial game.

The stakes increased in the last days of February when Fort Worth's Frontier Centennial made national news through its association with a controversy in Dallas over the placement of a statue of William F. Cody, the venerable plainsman and purveyor of western-themed entertainment.[18] The conflict began on February 22, when officials announced that a bronze replica of "The Scout," a statue of Buffalo Bill, would grace the entrance of the new Hall of Fine Arts on the centennial grounds in Dallas.[19] American artist Gertrude Vanderbilt Whitney sculpted the memorial for placement in Cody, Wyoming, on July 4, 1924.[20] The life-size statue depicted a mounted Cody with rifle in hand in the motion of pulling the reins tight as he inspects the ground for Indian tracks.[21] The selection proved anathema to a Confederate memorial group that stepped forward to issue complaints regarding the selection of the Buffalo Bill statue. Although some voiced objections on the grounds that Cody had little or no connection with Texas, many found his service as a scout for Union forces during the Civil War simply damnable. Frontier Centennial planners could not have devised an opportunity more suitable for publicizing its celebration—a sectional conflict engulfing the Central Exposition in Dallas capturing the attention of the national media over an iconic western plainsman of unparalleled symbolic importance to the meaning of the frontier and a creator of "West" in his own right. As Amon Carter observed the contest over the statue and the clamoring of the media to cover new developments, he perceived an opportunity to publicize Fort Worth's burgeoning centennial offering and simultaneously bolster Fort Worth's image as a progressive and modern city with roots deeply planted in western sod.

On February 26, Carter sent a telegram to Walter Holbrook, a member of the Publicity Department for the Texas Central Centennial, feigning to extend an amiable hand of support to Dallas. With the appearance of affability, he wrote, "I am surprised to note that Dallas, where everything usually proceeds so harmoniously, is involved in some sort of controversy over the proposal to erect a replica of Mrs. Whitney's famous statue of W. F. Cody." He conceded, "While I have not been given credit in the past for lying awake nights trying to help Dallas, at the same time the Centennial is an all-state endeavor and one so big and beneficial that like every other Texan I am interested in its success and willing to contribute everything possible to that end." Carter then proffered a solution making headlines across the nation: "If Dallas doesn't want a statue of Buffalo Bill Fort Worth certainly does."[22]

Prompted to "volunteer this suggestion" in the interest of aiding in the success of the state centennial, Carter claimed Fort

Worth did not desire to become embroiled in the controversy surrounding the Cody statue. His actions following the authorship of the telegram, however, suggest the contrary.[23] To guarantee that his commentary on the statue made headlines, Carter shamelessly called upon a network of associations and friendships he established during years of business in Fort Worth. He sent a copy of his telegram to Holbrook to nearly 250 individuals throughout the nation. The roll of recipients reads like a 1930s Who's Who directory of businessmen, politicians, and media moguls. A host of executives in the oil, automobile, airline, railroad, and finance industries received the telegram, in addition to numerous state and federal politicians including the secretaries of President Franklin D. Roosevelt, Vice President John N. Garner, a number of New Deal administrators, and congressmen. However, to ensure widespread media coverage, Carter also sent the telegram to dozens of newspaper executives, editors, and columnists throughout the nation including several managers with radio and motion picture companies.[24]

More important than Carter's proposal, the contents of the widely distributed telegram illustrate his intent to publicize the Old West theme of the Texas Frontier Centennial. Here Buffalo Bill proved extremely handy. "It occurs to me that the Frontier Centennial site would be far more appropriate," Carter wrote, "for while Buffalo Bill played no part in either the history or development of Texas he was a famous Indian scout, picturesque plainsman, typifies the spirit of the old West as no other figure does, and a statue to him on the Frontier Centennial grounds would be . . . wholly in keeping with our purposes."[25]

For Americans, Buffalo Bill embodied the frontier experience. Cody spent much of his life on the plains as a hunting guide and scout and took an active part in the Indian Wars on the Great Plains. Subsequently, Cody harnessed these experiences into his exhibition known as Buffalo Bill's Wild West. Given Cody's firsthand experience on the frontier, his presence imbued his shows with credibility. Indeed, Cody employed only genuine Pony Express riders and Native Americans who fought in the Plains

Indian Wars. In perhaps the ultimate example of blending reality and fiction, Cody reenacted his fight with the Native American warrior Yellow Hand using Yellow Hand's actual scalp as a prop during the performance.[26] As a result, the audience could not often distinguish the historical from the fictional. Thus, for many Americans, Cody's depictions circumscribed their understanding of the meaning and experience of the frontier.

The potency of Cody's frontier narrative also resided in his ability to draw upon prevailing symbols and myths widely accepted among Americans regarding the frontier. Using props such as the rifle and the stagecoach, Cody exploited a frontier mythology that cast westward expansion as a process in which the untamed and uncivilized West was subdued and civilized.[27] Cody's characterization of westward expansion intentionally promoted an image of American progress. The frontier, his show suggested, advanced a sequence of national and material growth.[28] As a result, Buffalo Bill became the icon of the frontier, the West, and nationalism and progress.

Although Fort Worth's centennial planners looked to Hollywood for conceptualizing the Frontier Centennial, Buffalo Bill, although unnamed, represented a fundamental influence. The characterization of possible entertainment and shows, including the reproduction of Indian raids on the Plains and stagecoaches, smacked of regular features presented in Buffalo Bill's Wild West. More than drawing upon Buffalo Bill's Wild West as a model for Fort Worth's centennial entertainment, Carter used the statue controversy as another means by which to attach Fort Worth to the larger narratives of progress and nationalism associated with the development of the greater American frontier described by Buffalo Bill. For Carter, Dallas's seeming rejection of the statue highlighted the fundamental difference between Fort Worth and Dallas. In his telegram to Holbrook, Carter noted, "I fear a hardy old plainsman such as [Cody] might not feel at home in the city atmosphere of Dallas and that if he could have a voice in the location of a statue he would select a place where he would feel at home and want an atmosphere in keeping with the period in which he lived and in which he played such a heroic part."[29] Because of what Cody represented, Carter's intermediation was more than a mere offer to take the statue, but rather a statement that Fort Worth was West and therefore progressive and Dallas was not.

The response likely exceeded Carter's expectations. On February 27, the day after he sent out the telegram, reports of Carter's commentary on the statue appeared in more than a dozen newspapers throughout the state, with more the following day. Given that Fort Worth still lacked any tangible western-themed "entertainment," Carter's telegram reflected a calculated gamble. On one hand, the telegram provided national exposure for the city and its centennial celebration. On the other hand, with such wide and sweeping publicity, now any failure to produce a celebration equal to Carter's boastings would certainly reflect poorly on the city and its leadership—a proposition all the more unacceptable given that Dallas appeared poised to host a successful and profitable exposition. Moreover, the centennial's June 6 opening date was only a little more than three months away. The high stakes culminating with Carter's involvement in the Buffalo Bill statue controversy help explain the frantic actions of Carter and the Board of Control in their search for a showman to produce the centennial's western entertainment. They also explain Carter's apparent desire to take a more hands-on approach in the planning of the centennial. During the first two months of planning, Carter operated mostly behind the scenes.

Within days of Carter sending out his telegram, a search began for a producer with the ability to create a successful show, in short order, worthy of Carter's big talk and with a reputation large enough to lend credibility to the production and draw crowds. Apparently, centennial officials extended an initial invitation to Major Gordon Lillie, who at the time operated "Pawnee Bill's Historic Wild West" in Oklahoma, to prepare a show for Fort Worth's exposition.[30] Since 1930, the aging showman had retired to a ranch outside Pawnee, Oklahoma, where he built an accurate replica of a pioneer settlement reminiscent of those established along the frontier in the nineteenth century. Operated by former members of Lillie's show and local Native Americans, Old Town, as it was called, featured a trading post, a museum displaying Indian relics, an Indian Village, and a herd of buffalo. Although constructed for the purpose of preserving "the atmosphere of the days of the pioneer," Lillie's Old Town proved wildly successful among tourists who flocked to the ranch.[31] With his fame and experience, Lillie possessed all the desired qualities sought by centennial planners. For reasons unknown, however, a contract never materialized. If anything, Lillie, though mentally alert at age 76, probably lacked the vigor he or Frontier Centennial planners believed necessary to produce in short order a successful celebration.

As centennial planners continued to scan the national landscape for a director, they focused their gaze on Hollywood. The studios in California, after all, produced the very films lionizing the Texas cowboy, a fact upon which celebration planners drew to sell the frontier theme to Fort Worth citizens. Moreover, from the very earliest conceptions, centennial planners hoped to recreate a functioning Old West similar to those represented on the silver screen. Carter initially brought the Frontier Centennial to the attention of a number of Hollywood moguls through his Buffalo Bill telegram including Harry Cohn, president of Columbia Pictures; Winfield Sheehan, an independent film producer and former vice president of Fox; and Irvin S. Cobb, an actor and screenplay author who hosted the 1935 Academy Awards.

Carter also sent the telegram to former Fort Worth resident Rufus LeMaire, the casting director for Metro-Goldwyn-Mayer.[32] For Carter, LeMaire represented a Hollywood insider with the connections to help locate a director with the right qualifications for the job. A few days following the telegram, Carter telephoned LeMaire hoping to enlist his services. As it turned out, Carter and the centennial planners erred in their calculations to contract a Hollywood director. The abilities needed to produce large-scale live entertainment were more likely found on Broadway. As a result, LeMaire found the task of locating an unengaged director with the necessary qualifications a difficult one. Fortuitously, one afternoon a few days after Carter's call, as LeMaire gazed out the window of his second-floor office onto a courtyard below, he spied an individual who had escaped his mind: the legendary Billy Rose crossing the way. LeMaire quickly beckoned him up to his office.

Recently arriving in Hollywood, Rose hoped to work out a movie deal with Hollywood executives for his latest Broadway production—*Jumbo*. Although Rose had authored dozens of popular tunes, run a number of successful nightclubs, and produced a moderately successful variety show, it was Rose's production of the acclaimed Broadway musical *Jumbo*, featuring dozens of circus acts and the participation of an elephant, that sparked LeMaire's interest. The show opened to critical and popular acclaim and played for five months in the historic Hippodrome in New York City.[33] More than the show's popularity, it was Rose's demonstrated abilities to stage successfully a gargantuan spectacle that led LeMaire to recommend him to Carter and the Frontier Centennial planners in Fort Worth.

Understanding the magnificence of the *Jumbo* production and its success begins with understanding Billy Rose (born William S. Rosenberg, 1899–1966), a lyricist, nightclub owner, and producer driven to establish a name for himself as one of the great producers of live entertainment. While his marriage to popular Ziegfeld comedienne Fanny Brice granted him entrance into the higher echelons of show business, it also came with a price. He became known as Mr. Fanny Brice—often the punch line in jokes contrasting Rose's short stature with the height of his wife.[34] Brice's fame, throughout Rose's marriage to the star, continually represented a yardstick by which he assessed his own celebrity. Rose believed producing his own Broadway show signified the surest way to establish an identity of his own and claim the recognition he desired.

In October 1930, Rose produced a show staged in Philadelphia starring his wife consisting of a string of unrelated acts unfortunately titled *Corned Beef and Roses*. Despite continued retooling, relocation to Broadway, and constant promotion, the show and its subsequent incarnations, *Sweet and Low* and *Crazy Quilt*, failed to turn a profit. After *Crazy Quilt*'s short two-month stint on Broadway, Rose met Ned Alvord, a press agent, who claimed *Crazy Quilt*, if properly promoted and revamped, would play to full houses across rural America. Rose, Alvord suggested, had to promote his production the way P. T. Barnum peddled his circus. In accordance with Alvord's recommendations, Rose "juice[d] up the show," hiring production director John Murray Anderson to direct, and toured the show throughout the East, South, and Midwest for a year.[35] Mentored by Alf T. Ringling, Alvord generated a scandalous ad campaign both shocking and tantalizing potential viewers.[36] Concomitant with its publicity, the show, with its blend of vaudeville acts and burlesque, generated controversy and was even banned in some cities, proved enormously successful.[37]

Rose found himself managing nightclubs again after a second attempt to produce a Broadway show ended in failure. His production of *The Great Magoo* in December 1932 closed after a week, with Rose's nearly $75,000 investment gone.[38] Following the closing of *The Great Magoo*, Rose accepted an offer from a group of New York mobsters to manage the Gallo Theater just west of Broadway. Although Rose's last experience partnering with mobsters ended badly, he found their willingness to grant him absolute autonomy, production rights, and a weekly salary of $1,000 irresistible. Rose's penchant for notoriety led him to prominently display his name in all promotional materials for his productions, making his productions and his name inseparable. When negotiating with the mobsters, Rose demanded his name be given prominence in all the theaters' promotional materials. Reimaging cabaret shows of earlier days, Rose planned to combine the successful elements of the theater and the nightclub in the production of a hedonistic extravaganza. The show would include a seemingly endless succession of quality carnivalesque sideshows, vaudeville acts, comedy, and music featuring well-known bands and showgirls. The Casino de Paree opened in December 1933 and became an instant success, receiving glowing reviews from the city's critics.[39] With the phenomenal success of the Casino de Paree, a second club patterned on the first titled the Billy Rose Music Hall opened in June 1934. Promotion for the club included a giant forty-foot-tall sign illuminating the name BILLY ROSE.[40]

Believing he had not yet "arrived," Rose began planning his next show. His interest in the capacity of carnival acts to entertain took him to Europe, where he attended several indoor circuses, among them the Cirque d'Hiver and the Cirque Medrano, and a circus in Budapest with a dramatic narrative.[41] His trip to Europe provided the inspiration for *Jumbo*. Rose returned to the US to find that the mobsters had run both of his clubs into the ground during his absence. Because of the intimate association of his name with both clubs, Rose found the situation intolerable and confronted the mob. With the aid of J. Edgar Hoover, Rose secured his safety after turning on the club owners. Walking away from both clubs, the unflappable Rose began work on his next production. "I felt I needed a big medium to channel all my energies," he later recalled. "The super-spectacle, the Big Show appealed to me. I knew the life stories of Barnum, of Thompson and Dundy, of the Ringling brothers. I knew that all who had functioned in the spectacle field were dead. If I was looking for a field devoid of competition . . . that required a certain kind of desperado cockeyed showmanship, . . . this was it."[42]

Since his days as a songwriter, Rose sought to surround himself with the most talented people in the business; now he drew upon those associations to present something grandiose and unprecedented. Rose pitched the idea for a musical about a circus to John Murray Anderson, who liked the concept and agreed to direct. Rose then called on former colleagues and writers Ben Hecht and Charles MacArthur to develop a script. Borrowing heavily from Shakespeare's *Romeo and Juliet*, the team fleshed out a story about feuding circuses.[43] MacArthur suggested naming the production after Barnum's famous elephant *Jumbo*, which likely appealed to Rose's megalomania.[44] Rose hired Albert Johnson to design the sets, including expanding the size of the stage and a massive renovation of the old and decaying Hippodrome Theatre, the only theater in New York judged large enough for the production.[45] Once financing was in place, Rose began hiring performers. To play the role of Claudius B. Bowers, Rose cast Jimmy Durante, famed comic actor and film and radio star. Rose also booked Paul Whiteman and his nationally renowned jazz orchestra.[46]

The show included all the complexities of a circus and a Broadway musical. Having hired the major actors, Rose began auditioning carnival acts. Ads went out for the show's specialty and sideshow acts, and Rose hired a host of attractions typical of circus fare including six-foot showgirls.[47] Rose also began collecting a variety of animals. The roster of animal performers included monkeys, tigers, lions, jaguars, wolves, bears, llamas, camels, horses, donkeys, reindeer, lambs, pigs, storks, and pigeons. The star of the show, a female elephant named Big Rosie, came from Coney Island's Luna Park.[48] Coordinating the various circus acts with Paul Whiteman's orchestra and the play's dialogue proved extremely difficult. The unpredictability of having live animals on stage only added to the complexity of the production.

Jumbo opened with fanfare equaling the menagerie of the production. The roping-off of seventeen blocks of Sixth Avenue to make way for the opening-night audience generated traffic delays and required pushing back the start time by one hour. Among the mob flooding the Hippodrome on the night of *Jumbo*'s premiere was a host of New York celebrities and showbiz luminaries including Gracie Allen, Tallulah Bankhead, Irving Berlin, Ben Bernie, Fanny Brice, George Burns, Marion Davies, Jack Dempsey, the Gershwins, Helen Hayes, Katharine Hepburn, the Marx Brothers, Ed Wynn, and Jimmy Walker, the mayor of New York City.[49] During its twenty-week run of 233 performances, it is estimated that more than a million people saw the show.[50] Despite glowing reviews and the longest run of a musical on Broadway in 1935, *Jumbo* failed to turn a profit.[51]

Still, with the production of *Jumbo*, Rose finally embodied the image press agents Richard Maney and Ned Alvord crafted for him: the Bantam Barnum. Drawing from the open-air traditions of P. T. Barnum and Buffalo Bill, Rose created a gargantuan exhibition that shattered the confines of traditional Broadway productions. The show's fantastic popularity only served to convince Rose that he would no longer be contented with producing the typical, no matter how successful. And Broadway did not possess a venue large enough for the spectacles he wanted to produce.[52] Even before *Jumbo* finished its run on Broadway, Rose began hinting at a greatly expanded venue for his next production, which he called "a world's fair on wheels."[53]

Certainly, LeMaire knew that Frontier Centennial planners would be hard-pressed to find someone with Rose's ability to imagine and produce a giant and elaborate spectacle that drew in more than a million viewers. And considering Rose's vocalized world's fair aspirations, LeMaire might have believed he would be an easy sell on the opportunity to produce Fort Worth's centennial exposition. Once Rose was in the casting director's office, LeMaire pitched the idea. Rose ironically told LeMaire, "It sounds like some sort of carnival proposition to me."[54] Despite the showman's initial misgivings, LeMaire apparently succeeded in convincing Rose to accompany him to Fort Worth to appraise the offer and discuss it with the Board of Control.[55] In the meantime, LeMaire informed Carter of his encounter with Rose. Having seen *Jumbo* while in New York, Carter, with the support of the Board of Control, completely supported LeMaire's nomination of Rose.[56]

After mulling over LeMaire's proposal, Rose cancelled his trip to Fort Worth, apparently believing that the city did not have the time to produce such a show nor the money to do it.[57] Learning of Rose's hesitation, Carter enlisted the aid of Rose's friend and financier Jock Whitney, hoping he might quiet Rose's fears and prod him "to drop over to Fort Worth and give the project the once over." Carter pitched the centennial to Whitney in terms Rose would find irresistible. Explaining the situation, Carter wrote, "The only thing lacking is an outstanding genius to develop and carry through the picturesque possibilities of cashing in on this great opportunity." Playing to his desire for recognition as the world's greatest showman, Carter wrote that Fort Worth's Frontier Centennial would provide Rose with "the possibilities and opportunities . . . to produce a great show even excelling Jumbo."[58]

Within a day of Carter's telegram to Whitney, Rose and LeMaire arrived in Fort Worth. No extant sources describe the negotiations between Billy Rose and the Board of Control.[59] However, stories about their interactions do appear in several secondary works. In these tales, Amon Carter and the other members of the Board of Control are often cast as cartoonish wildcatter Texas oilmen. As the story goes, the Board of Control, accompanied by Carter, greeted Rose and LeMaire on the morning of their arrival. While en route to the Van Zandt site, board members showed Rose pictures of the exposition grounds developing in Dallas and explained that Dallas already garnered all the relevant corporate and industrial exhibits, planning to invest $25 million in their celebration.[60] The presentation on the progress of the state centennial in Dallas likely signified the Board of Control's way of demonstrating the great opportunity the Frontier Centennial offered, with a ready-made centennial audience that only had to be attracted west. It seems extremely unlikely that the Board of Control, along with Amon Carter, believed or much less tried to convince Rose that Fort Worth could compete with the Dallas exposition, especially considering, as Carter explained to Rose, that Fort Worth, not counting the funding for the new stock show facilities, had garnered only $500,000 for its celebration.

The arrival of the entourage at the future Frontier Centennial grounds—which did not bear the marks of improvement of any kind—further reinforced the notion that the Fort Worth centennial could not have been about revenge or competition with Dallas. Once on location, the members of the Board of Control likely described their plans to build an "authentic" pioneer village including the Indian and Mexican villages, the replica of Fort Worth that would contain a museum with relics from the history of Fort Worth and West Texas, and a stockade for the presentation of pageants and western-type shows. As Rose scanned the landscape, he reportedly exclaimed, "This is a wilderness, not a site." Rose further explained to the board members what they already knew: "Do you boys realize what you've got to build here? It's not only a problem of putting up exposition buildings—but you've got to build a small city. You've got no lighting facilities here, no water supply, no sewage system. You've got to build all that."[61] The July 1 opening date made the Board of Control's proposal all the more daunting.

Following the visit to the site, Rose enjoyed a hearty repast of Texas favorites with Carter and the Board of Control at the Fort Worth Club. At the conclusion of the meal, Rose asked for some time to organize his thoughts. Once sequestered in a private room with a typewriter, Rose went to work putting his ideas to paper. Reportedly, after forty-five minutes he emerged with an outline that, with few departures, represented what would become the primary plan for the Frontier Centennial. Before he began to present his ideas, Rose allegedly paused and said, "I ought to say this. What I am laying out for your committee is pretty big and if . . ." Unable to complete his sentence, he was interrupted by Carter who exclaimed, "Nothing is too big for the state of Texas!" These words were purportedly supported by the members of the Board of Control by a series of whoops and hollers.[62] Not as radical as the above quote suggests, Rose's proposal in many ways worked within the bounds of what the Board of Control already planned. His agenda simply reoriented the purpose of the celebration and gave direction to the buildings already designed. Although he dropped the Native American and Mexican villages, he kept the idea for creating several blocks of buildings typical of the Old West. But the recreation of a pioneer town would house concessions and a saloon/cabaret and serve to connect major hubs of entertainment. Rose suggested a Wild West musical, a large open-air café, and the transplantation of the entire *Jumbo* production from New York headlined by nationally recognized talent. And because Fort Worth could not boast complete indoor air-conditioning of all exhibit buildings like Dallas, Rose recommended that Fort Worth's celebration operate only in the cooler evening hours.[63]

Rose's presentation thrilled those present. But, given the corner into which Carter and the Board of Control had backed themselves with the national publicity brought by the Buffalo Bill statue controversy and the sale of bonds, it seems likely they would have accepted just about anything Rose presented. The desperation of the situation also explains the group's response to Rose's financial requirements. Following the latter's presentation, William Monnig, president of the Board of Control, reportedly asked, "What will this here shindig of yours cost?"[64] Without mincing words, Rose projected between one and two million dollars. Likely drawing upon his experience with producing *Jumbo*, Rose educated the Board of Control regarding the improbability of generating a return on such a large investment in a few short months. He told the board members they should expect to lose at least half of their investment.

That the celebration could not be considered a financial windfall, as they had suspected, likely dashed the hopes of most of the men present. Perhaps sensing their dismay, Rose explained, "If you look at it as a venture in civic exploitation, it will pay big dividends in the long run. Some of the shows will show a profit on their dollars. . . . And if it's consolation to you . . . Dallas will be losing twenty million."[65] Monnig then asked what Rose expected for remuneration. Knowing the centennial planners were over a barrel, Rose asked for the now legendary sum of $1,000 a day for one hundred days of work. According to one source, LeMaire, who accompanied Rose out of the room while the Board of Control considered his offer, "berate[d] him for undue greed."[66] Rather than a demonstration of greed, it seems more plausible that Rose believed that, if accepted, the large fee would add to his reputation as a showman. Despite some apparent dissension regarding the large sums of money and the new direction of the celebration, Carter emerged with the support of the Board of Control and accepted Rose's terms. According to one version of the tale, offering his hand to Rose, Carter said, "Pardner, you got yourself a deal."[67]

In his autobiography, Rose later claimed that he earned his fee the next day when he pitched a slogan summarizing the concept he sold to the Board of Control: "Dallas for Education, Fort Worth for Entertainment."[68] Although the statement, which would eventually find its way onto nearly every piece of promotional literature printed for the Frontier Centennial, made a matter-of-fact distinction between the two celebrations, Rose clearly sought to juxtapose the banality of education with the excitement of entertainment. Rose's catchphrase represents the first in a series of promotions aimed at advertising the Fort Worth celebration at the expense of the Dallas-based exposition. Prior to Rose's involvement in the Frontier Centennial, a cooperative spirit had largely prevailed, as both cities worked together for the good of the state's celebration. Rex L. Lent, director of public relations for the Texas Centennial, told the Fort Worth Traffic Club, "We do not consider the Fort Worth celebration as a competing attraction; on the contrary, the two celebrations are complementary."[69] At a meeting of the Fort Worth Advertising Club, Charles Roster, the director of publicity for the Texas Centennial, praised the Frontier Centennial noting, "The average visitor will be looking for the type of frontier show" presented by the Frontier Centennial.[70] Urging unity for the betterment of all the state centennial celebration, George Dahl, technical director for the statewide celebration, told the Fort Worth Rotary Club, "All of us have a big job to get together and look through the same knothole. It is important that we see the picture together because that is the only way that we are going to put the Centennial over."[71]

Fort Worth officials also spoke of the Frontier Centennial in noncompetitive terms. Jack Hott, manager of the Fort Worth Chamber of Commerce, told the Fort Worth Traffic Club that "It will take both cities to take care of the crowds."[72] When James M. North Jr., a member of the Planning Committee and editor of the *Fort Worth Star-Telegram*, described the Texas Frontier Centennial to George H. Dern, the Secretary of War, he wrote, "It is not our idea to conduct the usual type of exposition or to compete in any manner with the central Centennial at Dallas."[73] Squashing the notion that civic rivalries would have an adverse impact on the state centennial, *The Texas Weekly*, which carefully reported on centennial developments, claimed, "Not only has [local rivalry] been completely averted, but there is already abundant evidence that the very diversity of the celebrations is promoting a spirit of all for one and one for all which is going to result in making both the Central Exposition and the other State celebrations greater successes than they would have been under a different plan."[74]

Rose's presence, however, brought an immediate and adversarial effect to the tentative spirit of cooperation that had existed between Fort Worth and Dallas. Following the slogan that pitted America's hunger for entertainment against its interest in learning, Rose began running ads in show business papers such as *Billboard* and *Variety* in mid-March calling for concessionaires interested in purchasing a concession with the Texas Frontier Centennial to contact Rose at the Sinclair Building in Fort Worth. The ad in *Variety* informed readers that Billy Rose, who had "wrapped the voluminous cloak of P. T. Barnum around his shoulders," signed on as managing director of the Frontier Centennial. "And with his cooperation," the ad noted, "Fort Worth will offer to America, not a pale carbon copy of the Chicago World's Fair, but a LIVING, BREATHING, HIGHLY EXCITING VERSION OF THE LAST FRONTIER." The ad in *Billboard* used Rose's catchphrase, "For education go to Dallas, for entertainment, come to Fort Worth."[75]

Rose's early digs at the Dallas exhibition resulted in a heated exchange between the planning organizations of the two centennials. In the days following the appearance of the ads in *Variety* and *Billboard*, Arthur L. Kramer, a member of the Management Committee of the Texas Centennial Central Exhibition, sent a letter to William Monnig, president of the Board of Control, regarding the content of the ads. Kramer took issue with both the implied characterization of the Dallas exposition as "a pale carbon copy of the Chicago World's Fair" and with the slogan "For education go to Dallas, for entertainment, come to Fort Worth." Believing that centennial leaders in Fort Worth would never "seek to hurt the Dallas exposition," Kramer assumed the content of the ads had simply escaped the Board of Control's attention.

Notwithstanding the presumed innocence of the error, he argued, "the Dallas exposition has the right to demand that no other city in Texas refer to it either directly or by implication in any advertisement or publicity relating to a competitive attraction."[76]

Apparently, Monnig shared Kramer's letter with the Board of Control. After discussing the contents of the letter, the Board of Control, Monnig wrote, believed, "you have become unduly disturbed." First, Monnig reiterated Fort Worth's continual support for the Central Exposition. "Our entire plans," he wrote, "are built around yours, in that ours largely are dependent upon the number of persons attracted to Dallas and the percentage of such we can attract to Fort Worth." Monnig also reminded Kramer of Fort Worth's good-faith effort to avoid duplicating any attractions planned for the Dallas celebration. As such, Monnig informed Kramer, the Board of Control was "somewhat surprised, after we had proceeded with the frontier theme, to have Dallas announce a rodeo, and again, after the employment of Mr. Rose, to read in the Dallas newspapers that the central exposition planned an enlargement of its entertainment features and duplication, to some extent at least, of what we had planned." Since Dallas drew first blood, Monnig and the Board of Control found Kramer's demands "somewhat impertinent." Although Monnig reserved the right for the Board of Control to publicize the Texas Frontier Centennial "in the manner best calculated, in our judgment, to achieve the desired ends," he claimed Fort Worth had "no thought of antagonizing Dallas."[77] This exchange over ads appearing in *Variety* and *Billboard* placed by Billy Rose in the days following his arrival marked the beginning of the centennial rivalry between Fort Worth and Dallas and would ultimately come to define the celebration in the national coverage of the state centennial.[78]

Like a devil's bargain, the hiring of Rose bought Frontier Centennial planners everything they desired in terms of creating and promoting a spectacle capable of attracting centennial-goers to Fort Worth. But the recruitment of Rose ultimately cost the centennial its soul. The ideology embraced in the catchphrase "Dallas for Education, Fort Worth for Entertainment" represented a fundamental shift in the conceptualization of the celebration. Early plans called for a commemoration of the Texas cattle industry through a celebration of the Texas frontier heritage. Planners believed that historic western-style attractions could serve the purpose of both commemorating and entertaining large crowds. Uninterested in commemoration or "authenticity," however, Rose emphasized the importance of entertainment. He simultaneously dropped the commemoration of Fort Worth's history as a priority and made the centennial function primarily as a promotional event to boost the City of Fort Worth. The Texas Frontier Centennial, after Rose's arrival, would become known as the Fort Worth Frontier Centennial.

Although Rose readily embraced the centennial's theme and favored creating entertainment with a "strong western flavor," what would attract and entertain visitors now represented the fundamental approach.[79] To achieve the desired effect, Rose would draw upon a larger western mythology in the frontier theming of Fort Worth's celebration rather local history. With the exception of making the centennial an exclusively promotional event, as director of the Fort Worth celebration, Rose, although invoking symbolic images of the Old West, would not trifle with larger ideological questions such as the meaning of the centennial's western message. Like all of Rose's previous productions, the Texas Frontier Centennial would become a production low on historical content and cultural value but high on spectacle. As an easterner and histrionic entertainer, Rose would take the Frontier Centennial in a markedly different path than initially intended by the centennial planners.

CHAPTER 5

"THE NEW WOMANLY BEAUTY"

MODERNITY, SEX APPEAL, AND THE ROLE OF WOMEN IN THE BATTLE FOR FORT WORTH'S SOUL

Even with a local live wire such as Amon Carter, Fort Worthians had likely never witnessed the level of unabashed egomania that poured from Billy Rose. Rose guaranteed the press a centennial spectacle without equal in history. He claimed the show would "make 'Jumbo' look like a peep show" and would be the "talk of the world."[1] He promised to bejewel the spectacle with Hollywood royalty such as Jack Benny, Shirley Temple, Mae West, Guy Lombardo, Dick Powell, and later Fred Astaire and Ginger Rogers.[2] The exposition, he claimed, "[would] be a sort of combination New York musical comedy, a circus, a rodeo and a country fair" featuring a three-ring circus, a livestock exposition, a replica of a frontier city, and a giant swimming pool containing "artificial waves." Besides importing the entire production of *Jumbo* to Fort Worth, Rose ballyhooed two additional entertainment venues to headline the Frontier Centennial. First, he promised to create a lavish musical titled the "Frontier Frolics." For this production he intended to build a large theater-restaurant presenting the nation's most notable entertainers weekly.[3] Second, he promised a Texas-themed "Musical Rodeo" showcasing America's top rodeo talent. Simultaneously illustrating his desire to capitalize on the Frontier Centennial's western theme and demonstrating his total ignorance of Texas history, Rose speculated he would call the show "'The Fall of the Alamo,' 'The Battle of San Jacinto' or some [other] Texas [name]" featuring "two thousand Indians and one thousand cowboys."[4]

Still, as large as Rose's ego was, he knew that Broadway-caliber productions and western-themed entertainment alone would not draw a substantial number of fairgoers from Dallas to Fort Worth. With the Central Exposition spending millions on new facilities and claiming sponsorship from industrial giants such as General Motors and Sinclair Oil Company, Rose, as a showman and nightclub owner, believed only one thing could give the Frontier Centennial an edge: unabashed sexuality. Rose jumped to this conclusion almost immediately upon seeing the desolate fields of the Van Zandt tract. Reportedly, Rose brazenly explained to show officials, "There's only one thing that can compete with twenty million bucks of machinery" (referring to the Dallas exposition) "and that is girls—pelvic machinery. . . . We have to give them girls and more girls."[5] Apparently, Frontier Centennial officials heartily approved of Rose's pitch for a highly sexualized celebration. When Rose brandished the theme "Fort Worth for Entertainment," there was little doubt as to the kind of entertainment he planned to present.

While Rose labored to produce "a super-bevy of 1000 show girls," the Women's Division continued to play a leading role in the preparations for the Frontier Centennial.[6] Most of their efforts focused on grassroots advertising, city beautification, and education of the centennial grounds.[7] The Women's Division's initiative to boost the show began in earnest with the creation of the West Texas All-States Centennial Club—a branch of the larger statewide organization. Covering the club's March 17 organizational meeting, the *Fort Worth Star-Telegram* explained, "The only obligation [of club members] is to pledge loyalty to the Texas Frontier Centennial and to spread news of it to their native States and home towns."[8] "Adopted Texans" responded enthusiastically to the club's call to enroll, and soon it boasted 450 members with groups representing all forty-eight states and nine countries.[9] All-States Club members also sent invitations to the governors of the states they represented and worked to establish special days for their states during the festivities.[10] By June 6, Mayor Jarvis's office in Fort Worth had received replies from at least eighteen governors.[11]

With the West Texas All-States Club up and running, on April 20 the Women's Division relinquished control of the club to focus on its other operations.[12] Still, the Women's Division continued to play an active role in promoting the Frontier Centennial. The All-States Committee became the Good-Will Committee, which sponsored a series of goodwill tours in May and June to boost the celebration in dozens of towns within a 100-mile radius of Fort Worth.[13] Traveling in a "rubberneck" sightseeing bus outfitted with a speaker system and a large sign reading "Women's Good Will Tour–Fort Worth Frontier Centennial," dozens of women dressed in pioneer garb representing all of the local women's clubs sang booster tunes, waved handkerchiefs, and hailed their destinations with song.[14]

The Women's Division's committee assigned to endorse an "official greeting" for the Frontier Centennial revealed tension in its presentation of Fort Worth as a city with strong western roots and as a modern metropolis. Initially, the committee endorsed the western-themed "Howdy, Stranger." Believing the folksy greeting inconsistent with the character of citizens living in contemporary Fort Worth, some argued it might perpetuate "Easterners' conception of Texans as uncouth people." The committee agreed and responded by endorsing the more sophisticated salutation: "How do you do?" Mayor Van Zandt Jarvis and a host of local women's clubs heartily approved of the new welcome and worked to promote its use throughout the city during the celebration.[15]

Women's Goodwill Bus Tour promoting the Frontier Centennial, Weatherford, Texas, May 1936. Courtesy, *Fort Worth Star-Telegram* Collection, Special Collections, The University of Texas at Arlington Libraries.

Although considered too unsophisticated for utterance by modern citizens of Fort Worth, planners apparently felt the western greeting fit nicely with the recreated Old West atmosphere of the Frontier Centennial grounds, where a large sign reading "Howdy Stranger" greeted those approaching the grounds via automobile.[16]

The committees of the Women's Division continued to carry out a host of other initiatives supporting the Frontier Centennial as well. To raise Frontier Centennial awareness, the committee on Centennial Work in Schools sponsored a scrapbooking contest among local elementary schools.[17] Other committees continued their efforts to improve the physical landscape of the city for the celebration.[18] The citywide clean-up dovetailed with the work of the Pilgrimage Committee, which developed a number of tours to acquaint centennial visitors with the various features of the city.[19]

Under the direction of the Women's Division, work also progressed on the restoration of the Van Zandt Cottage. They

Banner for the Frontier Centennial on opening day, Fort Worth, Texas, July 18, 1936. Courtesy, *Fort Worth Star-Telegram* Collection, Special Collections, The University of Texas at Arlington Libraries.

labored to make the structure to "look just as it did in 1871."[20] To match the original structure composed of rough-hewn logs and handmade bricks, the Women's Division's Research Committee, with the help of the local chapters of the DRT and the UDC (which would become its caretakers after the centennial) consulted members of the Van Zandt family and obtained furniture from the 1860s and '70s for the structure's interior.[21] The cottage officially opened on July 19, the day after the opening day of the Frontier Centennial. Reflecting the intent of the UDC to make the cottage a memorial to Fort Worth's southern heritage, those present christened the cottage by singing "How Firm a Foundation," reportedly Robert E. Lee's favorite hymn.[22]

The roles of women involved in the Frontier Centennial began to shift, with Rose limiting the influence of the Women's Division on matters relating to venues on the centennial grounds and strictly demarking their presence on the grounds. Rose appeared to have little use for the support or efforts of the city's club women.

A few weeks following his arrival, Rose attended a rally hosted by 200 representatives of thirty-six women's groups who pledged their organizations' support to Rose and the production of the Frontier Centennial. During the meeting, Rose requested that the Women's Division form a committee to act as liaison between his office and the five thousand women the division represented. He told the women present, "You can be of tremendous concrete help. But you can do it only by actually functioning. You have a magnificent spirit and I'd like to see you capitalize on it."[23] Rose's comment seems to suggest that the Women's Division had failed to contribute anything of value to the Frontier Centennial and that they could only do so under his direction. Considering the sizable role the Women's Division already played in the planning of the celebration, Rose's comments must have insulted those present.

Notwithstanding Rose's slighting remarks, evidence suggests that Fort Worth's club women initially embraced the showman. Rose appeared to agree with their design for the Centennial grounds that drew heavily upon historic architecture and that he valued their participation.[24] But what the Women's Division failed to understand is that Rose's vision for the Frontier Centennial included little room for commemoration, education, or culture—issues pursued by club women.

As Rose's plans for the Frontier Centennial began to unfold, the Women's Division discovered how little he valued their contribution to centennial planning. On April 7, the Planning Committee of the Women's Division met with Rose and the Board of Control to synchronize the plans developed by the Women's Division and those laid out by Rose. Rose and the Board of Control seemed to welcome the contributions of the Women's Division in areas such as grassroots advertising, education, and city beautification, activities they believed simply bolstered civic awareness and participation. But the centennial grounds, the primary moneymaker of the celebration, were another matter entirely. Viewing the centennial grounds as sacrosanct, the Board of Control believed decisions regarding the character of their construction and content should be left entirely to Billy Rose. And the endlessly self-important Rose did not relinquish control of his productions to others. In February, the Women's Division had convinced the Board of Control to include both a reproduction of Old Fort Worth and a Mexican Village in the designs for the centennial grounds. The addition of these structures represented important victories for the Women's Division, which worked to include both the frontier history of Fort Worth and the diversity of Texas cultures in the centennial's commemorative memory. During the April meeting, however, the Women's Division learned that Rose intended to cut both the reproduction of the original Fort Worth and the Mexican Village from the centennial grounds. Rose's apparent uninterest in things historical and the inability of the Planning Committee to preserve portions of the celebration perceived as significant to the event's commemorative message led chairman Margaret McLean to complain, "We've had a hard time holding on to our part of the show."[25]

As it turned out, the collection of western art and Texas relics for presentation on the centennial grounds was the only part of the "show" Rose allowed the Women's Division to hold onto. Moreover, from the beginning Rose made it clear that the Women's Division would only involve themselves in the collection of materials, not necessarily their presentation. "If you'll assemble it," he explained, "we'll serve it in a colorful, interesting form. . . . We will put the picture frame around it, but you must gather what goes in it."[26] To the relief of the Women's Division, Rose promised to provide ample exhibit space in the designs of the frontier city.

With their commemorative and cultural contribution on the centennial grounds limited to a historical and fine arts museum, the Museum and Fine Arts Committees began in earnest to collect materials for exposition. Initially, these groups planned for as many as sixteen exhibits educating patrons in the culture and way of life on the Texas frontier.[27] The displays featured pioneer furniture, relics from ranching life in Texas including a collection of cattle brands and guns, materials from Fort Worth and Civil War history including uniforms and weapons, a large collection of Native American artifacts from the Leyland Collection, thousands of pieces of frontier china, clothing from the various periods of Texas history, a collection of 700 dolls from the region, and materials from the state's Mexican heritage.[28] The Museum Committee also assembled more than 600 books and manuscripts on the subjects of West Texas pioneer history, the cattle industry, Texas Indians, and works of poetry and fiction.[29]

Complementing the Museum Committee's collection of artifacts and relics illustrating the state's frontier history, the Fine Arts Committee of the Fort Worth Art Association collected materials illustrating life on the frontier and in the American West for display at the Frontier Centennial. The committee amassed what must have been an unprecedented collection of western art including fifty-five paintings, seventeen sculptures, and eleven lithographs, among which were the works of West Texan Harold D. Bugbee and notable western artists such as George Catlin, Frederic Remington, and Charles M. Russell.[30]

When the time came to begin arranging the frontier relics and works of art for exhibition on the centennial grounds in mid-June, the Women's Division lost further control of their part in the "show." Once the Museum and Fine Arts Committees began working on the exhibit space on the centennial grounds, Rose began to show an interest in their work. Reportedly, Rose, who micromanaged every detail of the exposition, demanded the Women's Division secure his approval on all aspects of the displays down to the color of the walls, window treatments, and rugs. Not surprisingly, the members of the Women's Division who interacted with Rose apparently found his dictatorial style and lack of deference to historicity off-putting. But Rose's treatment of the club women could be downright reprehensible. On one occasion, in speaking of an exhibit Rose told the club women their museum looked like "hell and a bunch of Spinach" and proceeded to explain why museums were naturally dull.[31]

Billy Rose's plan for the Frontier Centennial provided little room for women to play a leading role as preservers and promoters of culture, history, or education. Notwithstanding the manifold contributions of the Women's Division to the planning of the celebration prior to his arrival, under Rose club women became increasingly associated solely with the exhibits of Texas frontier history and western art.[32] Ironically, with Rose's constant criticism and direction, even the museum no longer represented an expression of the Women's Division. Rose successfully pushed the Women's Division to the periphery of Frontier Centennial developments. For Rose, concepts such as commemoration and historical accuracy could not attract or wow centennial visitors and therefore belonged at the periphery along with the club women. Juxtaposed to club women who sought to preserve and promote Fort Worth's heritage and culture, Rose sought to place women in the contrasting role of sexual commodity. Rose conceived of attractions far more seductive than frontier china, dolls, uniforms, old photos and books, and furniture to place on the center stage of his show.

During the splash of Rose's arrival in Fort Worth, he made dozens of statements hinting at the extravaganza he planned to produce. Perhaps his most oft-repeated claim was that a feature he called the "Frontier Frolics" or "Frontier Follies" would showcase one thousand beautiful showgirls.[33] The logistics of making good on that claim, like most of Rose's early promises, appeared more easily said than done. Budgetary constraints made transporting one thousand showgirls from Broadway to Fort Worth cost prohibitive. As a result, Rose began his search for what he called "pelvic machinery" in Fort Worth. Rose's initial pleas through the media produced a lackluster response. On March 15, the first day of tryouts, only five young women appeared before Rose. Appalled, Mary Wynn, a columnist for the *Fort Worth Star-Telegram*, chided local young women for their apparent apathy about the opportunity and challenged them to do better. "You let the little man with the big ideas," she wrote, "sit practically undisturbed for an hour." If he didn't find "beauty" in Fort Worth, she warned, Rose would have to "import it from New York, Chicago, Los Angeles—or Dallas. Would your pride stand for that?"[34] The article must have struck a chord with Fort Worthians, as the following day Rose found 100 ladies lined up outside his office.[35]

After the first week of tryouts, Rose hatched an ingenious plan to exploit the showgirl audition process and its associated sex appeal to promote the Frontier Centennial. Rose announced he would hold the second audition prior to the final rodeo of the Southwestern Exposition and Fat Stock Show in the Stockyards Coliseum.[36] Contrary to Rose's early estimates that the first week of tryouts would result in hundreds of callbacks, they only produced sixty-eight candidates for a second audition. On the night of the second audition, all sixty-eight young women lined up on the pock-marked dirt floor of the Stockyards Coliseum in high-heeled shoes and swimsuits. On a makeshift platform, they sashayed and danced before Rose and the rodeo crowd. The showman's "talent" for picking out beauty was as much on display as were the young women. Passing swift and, at times, unforgiving judgment, Rose barked at the various participants, "Ask your mother to spend more money on your dancing lessons" or "I can't say much for your dance, dear, but that smile is worth a million bucks!"[37] By the end of the audition, Rose promised at least five contenders a part in the show.

The scene at the Stockyards Coliseum provided a poignant example of the role Rose intended women to occupy in the Frontier Centennial. Like livestock, the young women were reduced to commodities presented for audience consumption. Young women shuffling before a judge in the Stockyards Coliseum with the aroma of manure hanging in the humid air proved a little too reminiscent of the activities of the Fort Worth Livestock Exchange for Joe Cooper, a columnist at the *Fort Worth Star-Telegram*. He described the scene in the headline of his column: "Rose Qualifies as Show Judge; Splits Sheep from Goats."[38]

Ever the optimist, Rose explained to local newspapers that, in his experience, the discovery of five talented young women from a thousand represented a good crop. Rose quickly devised yet another plan to both attract talented and beautiful Texas young women to Fort Worth and simultaneously generate statewide interest in the city's celebration through the commodification of women. He announced that Fort Worth would host a beauty contest for the title of "Texas Sweetheart #1." He called on newspaper editors, radio stations, local chambers of commerce, and club women from every Texas town with a population greater than one thousand to promote the contest. Each city would host its own competition to select a representative to send to Fort Worth. Lending legitimacy to the enterprise, Rose promised that the legendary Clark Gable would be in attendance to judge the May 30 final competition. The winner would become something of a symbol for the Frontier Centennial, receiving a starring role in the Frontier Follies and a six-month movie contract with Universal Studios. Moreover, he claimed, the top thirty-six runners-ups would also receive parts in the Frontier Follies.

The scheme worked. Within weeks, cities from around the state, but especially West Texas, announced their own competitions to determine their city's most beautiful woman.[39] All told, eighty-eight towns planned to send representatives to Fort Worth. The *Fort Worth Star-Telegram* regularly covered, often on its front page, the local contests from around the state and announced the winners.[40]

In mid-April, Fort Worth began preparing for its own competition. Eventually, the Fort Worth competition garnered nearly fifty contenders. Helping to generate interest in the local contest, the *Fort Worth Press* and *Star-Telegram* began regularly publishing revealing photographs of the contestants.[41] On the evening of May 26, the contestants put on a seven-act floor show, with each contestant performing specialty numbers in the Lake Worth Casino. The principal judge was none other than John Murray Anderson, Rose's stage director, who named Alice McWhorter, a recent high school graduate who worked at a local department store, "Miss Fort Worth."[42]

In the days immediately preceding the statewide completion, eighty-two contestants and their families and friends descended upon the city. Free of charge, the hundreds of visitors and locals filled the auditorium at Paschal High School to witness the selection of the most beautiful girl in Texas. Unable to secure the participation of Clark Gable, Rose selected Anderson to again assume

Faye Cotton, winner of Texas Sweetheart #1, Fort Worth, Texas, May 1836. The statewide beauty contest was designed to promote the Frontier Centennial but also to discover young women to hire as showgirls for the celebration. Courtesy, *Fort Worth Star-Telegram* Collection, Special Collections, The University of Texas at Arlington Libraries.

the mantle of judge.[43] With Rose as master of ceremonies and Anderson as head judge, the competition appeared virtually indistinguishable from other auditions for the Frontier Centennial. Although the crowd, full of locals, favored the selection of Miss McWhorter, the panel of judges crowned nineteen-year-old Faye Cotton of Borger Texas Sweetheart #1.[44]

Despite Rose's intent to procure the bodies of Texas's young women to promote the celebration, the local media preferred to view the competition for Texas Sweetheart #1 as an expression of virtue and patriotism. Descended from alleged highbrow revues and burlesque shows produced by the likes of Florenz Ziegfeld, American beauty competitions became but one of the acceptable "theatrical forms" for displaying the female body among middle-class Americans. In 1935, the Miss America Pageant sought to counter the prevailing reputation of beauty competitions as "leg-and-more shows" by recasting itself as the antithesis of such performances, heralding its contestants as societal role models for young women. Strengthening the ties between the competition and civic promotion, participants now acquired sponsorships from cities, regions, and states rather than businesses. Deemphasizing the show's sex appeal, contestants also began to appear in costumes other than bathing suits.[45] Although the emphasis of the Texas Sweetheart #1 competition rested primarily upon appearance in a bathing suit, the local media preferred to cast the sweetheart competition, like the Miss America Pageant, as an expression of patriotism and wholesome beauty.

Columnists from both the *Fort Worth Star-Telegram* and the *Fort Worth Press* depicted Cotton as the archetypal Texas young woman exuding the qualities of all Texas women. Mary Crutcher of the *Fort Worth Press* asserted that Cotton embodied a new era for women in show business. Perhaps drawing a sharp contrast between the natural beauties of Texas and the well-packaged and streamlined glamour look made popular by scantily clad actresses in the 1930s, she quoted John Murray Anderson, who described Cotton as "typical of the new type of womanly beauty" he had discovered in Texas that needed no makeup or artificial enhancement.[46] This new era, Crutcher claimed, would draw agents to Texas seeking women endowed with natural beauty allegedly rare in New York or California.[47] Further associating Cotton with cherished Texas ideals, the *Fort Worth Press* covered Cotton's visit to Dr. Sam Jagoda's renowned gun collection. Featuring a photograph of Cotton aiming a 400-year-old blunderbuss, the headline read: "Faye Cotton, True Daughter of Texas, is Fond of Guns."[48] *Fort Worth Press* columnist Edith Alderman Guedry also praised Cotton's humility, integrity, and independence. Speaking of the young woman's sense of modesty, Guedry recounted Cotton's claim that she would never participate in any contest that required her to wear anything scantier than a bathing suit.[49]

Also quick to praise her humility, the *Fort Worth Star-Telegram* noted that Cotton "passed a mirror in the Hotel Texas lobby without even a side glance, ate a man-sized steak without bothering about her figure, let her nose get faintly shiny without hauling out a powder puff and talked with startling candor about the very ordinary pattern of her life up to now." Moreover, the paper explained, Cotton neither drank nor smoked and always had a full night's sleep.[50] By identifying Cotton and the rest of the participants as possessing the traits of natural beauty, civic pride, modesty, humility, and morality, the media defined a new standard of femininity in modern Texas. Conjoining these traits with the contestants also reinforced the acceptability of presentation of the female form and created a yardstick by which future female participants in the Frontier Centennial would be judged.[51]

It soon became apparent that Rose would not find enough local talent to support the production he planned. The impresario simply needed more pretty faces. More important, he required experienced dancers. He sent newly arrived Broadway dance director and protégé of John Murray Anderson, Robert Alton, back to New York in mid-May to recruit dancers and showgirls. Contracted female dancers, showgirls, and some male dancers began arriving the day before the scheduled June 8 rehearsals.[52] In all, Rose imported 150 showgirls and dancers from New York, more than three times his early estimates. The Board of Control again turned to the Women's Division to see to the housing needs of the group.

The Fort Worth dailies regularly published images of the newly arrived showgirls and dancers as well as rehearsals for the show.[53] And as with the coverage of Faye Cotton and the competition for Texas Sweetheart #1, the *Fort Worth Press* and *Star-Telegram* depicted the visiting chorines as virtuous, hardworking, Texas-loving beauties. An article in the *Star-Telegram* reported that Mrs. Phillips of the Women's Division held reservations about the incoming dancers and showgirls but changed her mind after discovering they were the "'the best behaved and hardest working' young women she had ever seen."[54] Another piece described a troupe of seventeen women known as the Foster Girls performing in *Jumbo*. According to the story, the group "live[s] by rules almost as strict as those of a convent." The girls were not permitted to date, smoke, or drink; they ate regularly; and they always traveled in a group to and from the hotel.[55] Apparently, show planners also took some precautions to preserve an image of modesty for the dancers while in public. A sign placed in Monnig's Warehouse, the location of dance rehearsals, exclaimed, "Dress Decent."[56]

Rose's initial description of the content of Frontier Centennial entertainment seemed to reinforce the depiction of female participants as beautiful and virtuous models of modern Texas womanhood. Within days of his arrival, Rose quickly eschewed any intimations that he would produce anything amoral or indecent. He assured Jack Gordon of the *Fort Worth Press* that although he planned to include hundreds of beautiful showgirls in the entertainment venues, there would be neither nudity nor "smut." "Nine persons out of 10," he explained, "are revolted by smut. It has no place in show business."[57] Initially, his actions appeared as good as his words. During the auditions at the Stockyards Coliseum, a young lady took off her jacket and, according to Jack Gordon of the *Fort Worth Press*, did "a snake-hips that would make the boys up on the midway blush." To the performance, Rose exclaimed, "It's not gonna be that kind of show."[58] As late as March 31, Rose, alluding to traditional world's fair midway entertainment, claimed the Frontier Centennial would "have lots of pretty girls. [But] No fan dancers or nudist camps. Everything would be clean."[59] Given his reputation as the "Barnum of Sex," it seems likely that Rose's early comments concerning Frontier Centennial nudity reflected an attempt to preserve an image of propriety.[60]

Prior to his work on *Jumbo* and the Frontier Centennial, Rose helped pioneer a unique style of nightclub fusing dining and cabaret entertainment. A believer in the "big night out" concept, Rose provided, in the midst of a time of poverty and want in the Great Depression, inexpensive and abundant culinary offerings and liquor coupled with novelty acts, comedians, and musical numbers that New Yorkers found irresistible. Sex appeal also played an important role in the success of the Casino de Paree and later Billy Rose's Music Box. Rose featured numerous showgirls prominently and reportedly selected only tall women because they kicked higher and gave the appearance of more skin.[61] Moreover, scantily clad waitresses wandered the club tending to the needs of patrons. A giant fishbowl containing an unclothed woman attracted patrons to the bar at the Casino de Paree. Likewise, the Gay Nineties bar in Billy Rose's Music Hall featured a wishing well offering those who peered inside reflected glimpses of a naked woman residing inside the well.[62] Rose's claim to the local press in Fort Worth that his venues did not contain nudity or smut constituted bald fabrication.

With midways at the recent world's fairs becoming expressions of pure hedonism, it seemed a foregone conclusion that Rose would have eventually become a purveyor of entertainment at such expositions. Rose knew well that world's fairs had become showcases for the exotic—offering scenes that fairgoers could not see in their hometowns.[63] In many instances this meant nudity. Both the growing popularity of nudity in nightclubs such as Rose's and in burlesque shows and the burgeoning sexual freedoms experienced by young women in the 1930s played important roles in shaping the character of midway attractions available at Depression Era world's fairs.[64] In fact, the revenue garnered from the Streets of Paris exhibit at the Century of Progress prompted officials, who favored a healthy bottom line over unflinching morality, to look the other way.[65] In so doing, Century of Progress officials helped increase the "commoditization of women's sexuality at the world's fair."[66] Planners, however, never wanted such entertainment to define the exposition.[67] Prior to a public outcry of indecency and the elimination of offensive entertainment, the nude dancers at Zorro's Gardens and a stripper named Gold Gulch Gertie were among the more popular attractions at the 1935–'36 San Diego World's Fair.[68]

Even the annual Southwestern Exposition and Fat Stock Show offered entertainment reminiscent of the offerings at world's fairs. In the automobile building, the Rainbeau Garden, boasting a "French Village Atmosphere" and "Sixteen Glorious Continental Beauties," offered matinee and evening dance and floor shows.

The headlining event, the *Folies de Paree*, featured bubble dancer Reggie Roth and Muff Dancer Tyna Ravel. Ads in the stock show's program and the *Fort Worth Star-Telegram* featured young women in various stages of undress.[69]

Despite the prevailing atmosphere of sexualized spectacle Americans had become accustomed to seeing at world's fairs, the celebration in Dallas initially appeared devoid of the exotic entertainment featured at the midways of these expositions. Extant evidence suggests the increase of sex appeal at the Central Exposition in Dallas appeared after Billy Rose's arrival in Fort Worth. In August 1935, Nat D. Rogers, concessions director for the Central Exposition, speaking of one of the more popular offerings at San Diego's World's Fair, "ridiculed the idea of a nudist colony as crude and vulgar" but understood its appeal.[70] The only publicized hint of sexual allure came in December 1935 when the official Texas centennial publication, *Centennial News*, announced the organization of the Texas Rangerette Company. Dressed in boots, spurs, and ten-gallon hats, this group of twenty-five "of the most beautiful girls in Texas" assumed the role of official centennial hostesses.[71] Rose's reputation as a showman, creator of spectacle, and purveyor of sex appeal likely gave Dallas officials pause. Within weeks of his arrival, Dallas planners began augmenting the centennial exposition with additional sexualized entertainment venues, some of which would duplicate planned features of the Frontier Centennial.[72]

The Texas Centennial Exhibition, however, lacked the primary attraction that made the Streets of Paris a smashing success in Chicago: the notorious Sally Rand. Rand, an actress turned fan dancer, emerged not only as the most memorable feature of the Century of Progress but also its financial savior.[73] Initially, Chicago planners disdained the notion that they would allow the debauched entertainment exhibited at the Columbian Exposition to tarnish the reputation of their own exposition. A major reason for hosting an exposition was to counter the city's notoriety for vice and poverty through demonstrations of progress. Despite such claims, the Century of Progress did host numerous exhibits featuring displays of the female body in beauty contests and dancing and modeling shows. Eventually, Chicago planners would count on the revenue produced by tawdry late-night entertainment ranging from nude posing and stripping to taxi dancing at venues such as the Streets of Paris.

As at Chicago's Century of Progress, Sally Rand would become an important figure in the Frontier Centennial and the ensuing battle regarding the role of women as commodified sexual objects and the identity and image of Fort Worth as a modern city of the American West. Although Rose never mentioned his intention to bring Rand to the Frontier Centennial, it seems likely she was on his list of candidates. Rand represented the gold standard for exotic entertainment on the midway of Depression Era world's fairs. While it is unknown whether Rose extended an invitation to meet with her, Rand stopped for a layover in Fort Worth during the first week of April.[74] Offering advice about the content of the Frontier Centennial she told reporters, "Your show's got to have sex appeal." She quipped, referring to Dallas, "People don't go to expositions to get educated. They go to see things they don't see at home." When reporters pressed Rose as to whether he was interested in Rand's offer, he said coyly, "I'm considering everybody."[75] Rose evidently offered Rand a spot in the Frontier Centennial, which she accepted.[76] And almost immediately Rose changed his tune regarding fan dances and the propriety of nudity in the Frontier Centennial. A few weeks after his meeting with Rand he told the press, "I am supposed to keep it clean, but [it] will probably be a little on the nude side."[77] Rose's comments about the possibility of nudity aside, Fort Worthians initially appeared indifferent to the contracting of the infamous dancer.

Still, the hiring of Rand and the sexualized promotion of the celebration that shortly followed denoted a significant shift in the role women would play at the Frontier Centennial. Promotional material for the centennial until mid-April consisted of small and innocuous blurbs noting Fort Worth's celebration as one of many events hosted by Texas cities during its centennial year. On April 14, Ned Alvord, Rose's longtime press agent, arrived to help Rose sell the fledgling celebration to Americans.[78] Alvord played an important role in several of Rose's previous productions and relished the opportunity to promote the Frontier Centennial.[79] The western theme, the musical rodeo, Frontier Follies, *Jumbo*, and of course the girls, according to Alvord, provided "more chance for exploitation" than any of the previous venues he had promoted. He told the press he planned to saturate the region from Albuquerque on the west to Mississippi on the east and Hutchinson, Kansas, on the north to the Gulf on the south with posters, billboards, handbills, and newspaper ads promoting the show.[80] In all, centennial planners estimated the promotional materials would reach twelve million people.[81]

Although Rose made no secret that showgirls would occupy center stage in the Frontier Centennial, many Fort Worth citizens were ill prepared for the content of the promotional campaign Rose and Alvord intended to mount on behalf of the exposition. Millions received their first impression of the Frontier Centennial and Fort Worth from a young woman mounted atop a bucking steed covered only by a bandana cinched at the waist. The image, created by a local woman, borrowed heavily from promotional photographs of rodeo queens appearing atop a rearing horse to appear in the early 1930s.[82] Signaling a fundamental shift in the attitudes of Americans towards the place of women in a sport traditionally dominated by men, the image emerged as part of a growing acceptance of the athleticism exhibited by women participating in rodeo concomitant with the glamorization of the cowgirl both in movies and dime novels. Movie stars and entertainers regularly posed for these "cheesecake shots," and by the second half of the 1930s glamorized images of cowgirls saturated the media.[83] By 1936, the Southwestern Exposition and Fat Stock Show hosted the third largest rodeo in the nation, likely making the image a familiar one among Fort Worthians.[84] Although not responsible for the image itself, Fort Worth is certainly responsible for its overt sexualization as a result of the Frontier Centennial.

The further sexualization of an image, which formed part of a trend legitimizing the display of the female body, signaled another important step in the commodification of women for sexual

The *Wild & Whoo-Pee!* pamphlet promoted the Frontier Centennial's entertainment venues based on western mythology using sexualized imagery. Courtesy, Amon G. Carter Papers, Special Collections, Mary Couts Burnett Library, Texas Christian University.

appeal during Fort Worth's celebration. "Miss Fort Worth," as the image came to be known, became the primary symbol of the centennial. The "official hostess" of the celebration graced nearly all promotional signage and literature including stickers, posters, leaflets, and billboards.[85] Eventually, nine versions of the Miss Fort Worth image, each one posing in various degrees of undress, appeared on promotional literature and show programs for the celebration.[86]

A new slogan also accompanied the debut of Miss Fort Worth. Here again Rose and Alvord drew upon well-known western terminology and altered it to hint at a naughtier side of the exposition's entertainment. They conjoined the terms Wild West, borrowed from William F. Cody's frontier show, and whoopee, an expression for wild revelry but also a double entendre for sex, to create the slogan "Wild and Whoo-Pee!"[87] Pairing the image of

Miss Fort Worth and the new motto made a sexual interpretation implicit.

The ad campaign made use of other advertising venues as well. Sporting signs with the phrases "Wild and Whoo-Pee" and "Where the Fun Begins" and a poster of Miss Fort Worth, a ten-passenger Stinson plane traveling to destinations throughout the nation would advertise the exposition.[88] Local radio stations also trumpeted the centennial. Amon Carter's radio station, WBAP, broadcast a show providing progress reports for the centennial grounds, novelty acts, and music from the Frontier Centennial programs performed by the Frontier Troubadours.[89] In a blatant attempt to draw centennial-goers west to spend their dollars in Fort Worth, Frontier Centennial officials constructed a large sign advertising the show outside the main gate of the Dallas exposition. Weighing in at two tons, the 40 x 130-foot sign claimed to be the second largest in the world and could reportedly be viewed from anywhere on the grounds of the Texas State Centennial.[90] In giant neon letters, the sign beckoned to visitors: "WILD & Whoo-Pee, 45 minutes west," accompanied by an animated bucking bronco moving across the sign.[91]

The rivalry between Fort Worth and Dallas helped spur commodified sexual roles played by women at both celebrations. Believing healthy competition would benefit both expositions, officials in Fort Worth, and to a lesser extent those in Dallas, embraced the rivalry. At the annual West Texas Chamber of Commerce meeting in May, representatives of Fort Worth and West Texas pledged with R. L. Thornton, chairman of the Managing Board of the Central Centennial Exposition, to "outrival" each other, believing the entire state of Texas would benefit from a "finish fight" between the two metropolises.[92] The rivalry also proved invaluable to Fort Worth for promotional purposes. At Rose's urging, the Board of Control hired Richard Maney, one of Rose's former press agents, to represent the show in New York.[93] Maney worked to arrange media coverage in the major national media outlets, and the rivalry made a convenient angle to pitch to reporters and columnists.[94] Although occasionally mentioning

Fort Worth Frontier Centennial sign placed outside the entrance to the Texas State Centennial, Dallas, Texas, 1936. Courtesy, W. D. Smith Commercial Photography, Inc. Collection, Special Collections, The University of Texas at Arlington Libraries.

showgirls or the frontier theme, the press found the rivalry irresistible. Publications such as *Collier's*, *Vogue*, *The Literary Digest*, *Business Week*, *Time*, *Variety*, and *Architectural Forum* all couched their coverage of Fort Worth's participation in the centennial in terms of the rivalry.[95] In the process, the national media elevated Fort Worth alongside Dallas and provided the Frontier Centennial with free publicity.

Most coverage, however, focused on the central exposition in Dallas and in some cases dismissed Fort Worth's centennial offering as a petty and vindictive sideshow produced in an attempt to harm Dallas. Unprepared for such an interpretive tack, an irate Carter fired off a letter to *Collier's* magazine complaining about Owen P. White's article that described Fort Worth as "resurrect[ing] its ancient animosity on the strength of which it is planning to put on a special show."[96] White's "treatment of the Fort Worth Frontier Centennial," wrote Carter, "is both niggardly and unfair." Although he objected to the limited coverage of the Frontier Centennial compared with that of the central exposition, Carter found the article's assertion that Fort Worth staged its own celebration purely out of hatred for Dallas disconcerting. "There is no animosity between Fort Worth and Dallas," Carter quickly explained. "There has been a friendly rivalry for generations, and, in my opinion, the rivalry has done both good, for it has been a competitive rivalry that has kept both on their civic toes."[97]

Carter's complaints regarding the *Collier*'s article and his rebuttal illustrate his primary desire that Fort Worth be depicted on equal footing with Dallas in the rivalry. Although a subsequent article appearing in *Vogue* also gave the Frontier Centennial short shrift, Carter loved the piece because it noted, "The two cities always have hated each other," and also perhaps because it claimed that "Fort Worth, despite its occasional pretensions to culture, remains somewhat proud that it is distinctly a western town, while its sister to the East is as stuck-up as anything."[98] Notwithstanding the discrepancy between space devoted to the central exposition and that of the Frontier Centennial, Carter and Rose reveled in the cheap publicity provided by the national media coverage.[99]

In mid-May, Rose achieved a major promotional coup that would have implications for the depiction of women as objects at the Frontier Centennial. On May 15, he arranged with a representative of the monthly motion picture newsreel *The March of Time* to shoot a full-length episode covering the Frontier Centennial. The wildly popular news series debuted in 1935 and introduced audiences to "a new kind of pictorial journalism." Surpassing existing newsreels, *The March of Time* offered twenty to thirty minutes of interpretive analysis and dramatic coverage of a single news story. Despite its high journalistic aims and production values, *The March of Time*'s sharp interpretive slant bordered on rhetoric rather than journalism and in several instances embroiled the newsreel in controversy. Still, by 1936, episodes of *The March of Time* regularly screened in more than five thousand theaters in 3,200 cities nationally and internationally.[100] Coverage of the

Frontier Centennial in an episode of *The March of Time* extended the promotional campaign far beyond the media blitz in the Southwest and the coverage in the national print media.

By mid-June, *The March of Time* episode billed as "The Battle of a Centennial" began showing in theaters nationwide.[101] True to form, the reel presented a deeply biased and inaccurate picture of the centennial developments in the state. Placing the Fort Worth-Dallas feud at the heart of the story, the reel claimed the centennial rivalry between the two cities represented the most recent fight in a long heritage of fighters in Texas. Noting the honor accorded to Dallas after defeating Fort Worth in the contest to host the official exposition, the story cuts to a reenactment featuring Amon G. Carter rallying a group of boosters to put on a rival celebration. "You'd think Dallas invented Texas," Carter shouted from a pulpit, "just because they bid higher for the centennial than any other city. But we're going to put on a show of our own and teach those dudes, over there, where the West really begins." The reel moves onto the hiring of Billy Rose including a reenactment of Rose proposing the legendary fee of $1,000 a day for one hundred days from his office in New York. Cutting back to Fort Worth, Rose tells a group of boosters from atop a horse, "The battle between Fort Worth and Dallas is right up my alley. And if you people string along with me, I'll make Texas the biggest state of the Union."

Amid scenes of the *Jumbo* circus-theater and the Casa Mañana theater (the building intended to house Rose's Frontier Follies, rising on the Frontier Centennial grounds), the narrator delineates the subject of the most recent competition. He explains that the buildings rising on the centennial grounds are "to be filled to bursting with . . . eye bedeviling coryphées [dancers], mostly nude." With shots of Jonny McMahon, the reel explains that "Dallas resolves to liven up its own midway" by adding sex lectures and the Streets of Paris concession. Along with shots of showgirls rehearsing, Sally Rand packing her ostrich feathers, the Rangerettes, and a shot of Lady Godiva from the Streets of Paris, the balance of the reel provides shots of Fort Worth and Dallas each attempting to top the other with more girls and more nudity. The narrator concludes, "The keynote of the Texas centennial becomes sex appeal." The final scene features Colonel Andrew Jackson Houston, the only surviving son of Sam Houston, shaking his head in disbelief at the content of the centennial celebration.[102]

Fort Worth received a lion's share of the nearly seven-minute spot. Moreover, the newsreel merged the two themes that Frontier Centennial officials cultivated in the promotion of the exposition: sex appeal and the rivalry with Dallas. The reel's focus on the risqué and the rivalry, however, came at the expense of the celebration's western theme. Not only did the reel fail to mention the name of Fort Worth's centennial offering—with the exception of Frontier Centennial signage in the background, several shots of Miss Fort Worth posters, Rose and Carter in cowboy garb, and Carter's rant about showing Dallas where the West really begins—it made no mention of the frontier or the Old West. Rather than providing glimpses of the reproduced frontier buildings or the sets and stage of the *Last Frontier*, Rose's musical rodeo/Wild West show, *The March of Time* episode only provided scenes of the Casa Mañana theater and the *Jumbo* circus-theater. Notwithstanding the omissions, the content of the newsreel no doubt elated Rose and the Frontier Centennial planners.[103]

The March of Time's characterization of the Frontier Centennial as "a monster leg show" with "eye bedeviling coryphées, mostly nude" played right into the promotional tactics devised by Alvord. As a bill poster for Ringling Brothers, Barnum & Bailey circus, Alvord learned his promotional techniques from Alf T. Ringling. Alvord specialized in whipping up controversy around the shows he promoted through chicanery. One of his favorite schemes included conning the moral authorities in rural communities in which his shows toured to denounce the show as filth. After tricking the local newspaper to print ads featuring a spread of nearly nude women, Alvord, dressed as a clergyman, met with local pastors prior to the arrival of the show and convinced them to condemn the production. The ads promising a show featuring forbidden delights and the accompanying religious denunciation made the shows irresistible, especially to a rural population. Such tactics not only packed local theaters but also earned Alvord a nickname: "The Dirty Deacon."[104] The ultimate irony of Alvord's promotional schemes was that the show never actually delivered naughtiness on the scale implied by the ads and the denunciations.

Without the prompting of a collar-clad Alvord, the Fort Worth clergy fell into his trap. Although the hiring of Sally Rand and her rumored "Nude Ranch" became potent symbols of the immoral direction of the Frontier Centennial, ultimately Alvord's promotion pushed local religious organizations to act. While the nearly nude Frontier Centennial symbol Miss Fort Worth and the accompanying slogan "Wild and Whoo-Pee" likely gave the resident pastors pause, they found the promotional pamphlet highlighting the various features of the celebration intolerable.[105] The offending leaflet featured teasers for each of the major centennial shows claiming "The Old West, Out Where the Fun Begins" had been "Recreated in the flesh" and contained a blurb for the "Frontier Follies," now called *Casa Mañana*, which labeled the show the "BIGGEST GIRL SHOW EVER PRODUCED."

The ad also included an ink sketch featuring nearly a dozen totally nude bathers in the Casa Mañana theater's stage-side pool and a number of dancers posed on stage in various stages of undress before a crowd of diners. The illustration in the brochure provided the first glimpse of the entertainment Rose planned to present at Fort Worth's centennial. In connection with Rand and the "Nude Ranch," the message unequivocally stated the celebration would feature full nudity. Moreover, as per Rose's original suggestion to the Board of Control to make the celebration an exercise of civic boosterism, the pamphlet gave a new title to the centennial celebration strengthening its ties with Fort Worth. No longer referring to the "Texas Frontier Centennial," the pamphlet promoted the "Fort Worth Frontier Centennial"—explicitly linking Fort Worth with Wild and Whoo-Pee.[106]

The offending brochure precipitated a heated exchange, most of it appearing on the front page of the *Fort Worth Press*, between local religious organizations and Rose and the Board of Control, which likely sent Alvord into a state of euphoria.[107] Taking aim at the Frontier Centennial during a May 22 district conference, the Methodist Episcopal Church drafted and unanimously adopted a resolution denouncing the publicity campaign and the forms of entertainment it represented as an insult to the city's heritage. Designed to appeal to "the hoodlum element," the statement argued, the publicity campaign is "in so low and vulgar character as to be wholly unworthy" of our city and its history. "We wish to denounce," the statement continued, "the drinking of intoxicating liquors, legalized or other forms of gambling, lewd and nude dancing as morally degenerating and as subversive to the noble ideas of those pioneers whose lives and achievements we celebrate this Centennial year."[108]

William Monnig, Chairman of the Board of Control, immediately responded to the allegations of the Methodist Episcopal Conference. Monnig explained to the press that the Frontier Centennial would be "a decent show." However, he quickly added, "but it won't be a Sunday school." He dismissed the criticisms of the Methodists, noting that after its debut those protesting the show would be proven wrong. On the matter of Sally Rand's "Dude Ranch," he claimed reports had been exaggerated and denied allegations that Rand would host a "Nude Ranch" at the centennial.[109]

Within days, the Tarrant County Baptist Pastors Conference also discussed the possibility of issuing a statement in opposition to the Frontier Centennial. At the meeting, a call for a resolution condemning the show based upon the rumors concerning Sally Rand's "Nude Ranch" and the promotion of the Frontier Centennial failed to pass. Some at the meeting apparently objected to the resolution, claiming they could not vote to condemn the Frontier Centennial without concrete evidence of the actual centennial plans. The conference appointed a four-person committee to investigate the show.[110] Upon learning of the committee, Rose invited the group to meet with him, claiming he would "be glad to go over the complete plans of the show with any legitimate committee." Rose then appended, "But any pastor jumping on the show's to get his name in the papers will get a cold reception."[111]

On June 1, the committee, chaired by Reverend C. E. Matthews, met in a closed meeting with Billy Rose and the Board of Control.[112] Following the factfinding mission, the conference again met to deliberate the findings of the committee. Based upon the plans presented to the committee, their inspection of the show's costuming, and the assurances of the Board of Control, Matthews reported that the centennial plans called for no nudity in any of the celebration's venues. In a frenzied state of incredulity, a Reverend Fred Swank shouted from the crowd, "I don't believe it!" Notwithstanding the lack of nudity, Matthews remained unconvinced of the inherent moral and civic value to the celebration under the direction of Billy Rose. "The show is mercenary in spirit throughout," he explained. "It is not concerned with promoting the welfare of Fort Worth." However, because the committee found no evidence that the show itself would include outright nudity, the conference drafted a strongly worded resolution taking issue with the advertising only.[113] For the Baptists, like the Methodists, whether or not the Frontier Centennial included nudity made little difference; the celebration under the management of Rose and the commodification of women for publicity, they believed, had become a detriment to both Fort Worth's honorable pioneer heritage and its future growth as a modern American city.

Dismayed by the direction of the Frontier Centennial, Fort Worth's club women attempted to resolve their concerns directly with celebration officials. Shortly after the debut of the official Frontier Centennial icon, Miss Fort Worth, the leadership of the Women's Division presented a resolution to the Board of Control requesting more dignified promotional literature for the Women's Division's use in promoting the show to friends, relatives, and convention groups throughout the nation. More specifically, they urged the incorporation of historical facts relating to Fort Worth and the region.[114] The Women's Division also requested the modification of Miss Fort Worth's costume into something "more typically western." Although the Women's Division provided no specifics of what they considered "more western," they clearly preferred an alternative to her current attire, "which seems to be kept in place only by an act of Providence."[115] According to John Murray Anderson, representatives of the Fort Worth Woman's Club also approached Ned Alvord to request changes to the provocative images of the ad campaign, particularly the images of the nude women playing in the stage-side pool at the Casa Mañana theater. In response to their objections, Alvord exclaimed, "Who did you expect me to put in the pool—John the Baptist? Wouldn't draw a nickel at the box-office!"[116] Apparently, club women chose to endure the sexualization of the centennial in muted anguish rather than chance bringing the city and celebration to financial ruin by launching a heated protest or boycotting the celebration they worked so hard to help produce.

Local papers appeared amenable to the sexualization of the celebration. Although the *Fort Worth Star-Telegram* and the *Fort Worth Press* cast participants in the Texas Sweetheart #1 competition and showgirls as models of a modern generation of civic-minded and virtuous beauties, they nevertheless depicted the commodification of women as innocent fun. Making great copy, headlines regularly employed clever wordplay to describe centennial developments. For example, accompanying the pictures of four young women in bathing suits participating in a public showgirl audition at the Southwestern Exposition and Fat Stock Show, the caption, thumbing its nose at the education exhibits at the Dallas exposition, read: "Part of 'Educational' Exhibit at Coliseum Tonight."[117] The heading above a picture of Billy Rose and Sally Rand supplementing an article addressing their discussions of the Frontier Centennial asked: "Recognize Her with Her Clothes On?"[118] In addition, "Picking Dancers No Job for Man with High Blood Pressure" headlined several images of the local showgirl auditions.[119]

Finally, the *Fort Worth Star-Telegram*'s coverage of several peeping toms trying to catch a glimpse of showgirl rehearsals represents perhaps the greatest example of the paper's complicity in the sexualization and commodification of women for the centennial celebration. Under the front-page headline, "No Fair Peeping!

2 Youths Nabbed as Follies Cavort," the paper jovially rehashed the details of two voyeurs who were caught watching the "scantily clad young women going through their dance routine."[120] The simultaneous depiction of young women as role models of virtue and beauty and as items existing to fulfill the visual pleasures of men suggests fluidity between the two roles in the minds of Texans in particular and Americans in general.

The *Fort Worth Press* also supported Rose and the sexual orientation of the Frontier Centennial. After receiving "letters from several citizens who are afraid Fort Worth's Frontier Centennial will represent smutty entertainment to our visitors this summer," the paper in an editorial defended Rose and the Board of Control's choice to hire him. "This city would be foolish indeed to import Rose, John Murray Anderson, famous stage designer, and their corps of professional theater experts from New York at such great cost," the paper explained, "merely to put on a bawdy peep show. Any cheap burlesque director can do that."[121] *Fort Worth Press* columnist Edith Alderman Guedry also discounted rumors of nudity at the Frontier Centennial. She told the story of a Miss Marion and the 200 seamstresses charged with the task of creating the costumes for the centennial shows. Considering the fifty thousand yards of material going into the costuming, Guedry wrote, they "get a good laugh every time they see the word nudity connected with the . . . Frontier Centennial." According to the columnist, the seamstresses seemed more concerned with "how the show girls will be able to stand so many coverings in the Texas heat."[122] The press's apparent kowtowing to the wishes of Rose and the Board of Control only served to enrage the religious opposition. In several letters to the *Fort Worth Press*, Reverend C. V. Dunn of Stephenville chastised the paper for trivializing centennial nudity. "I have seen no word from the editor," Dunn wrote, "condemning the infernal thing."[123]

Despite the complicity of the press in the sexualization of the Frontier Centennial, like the officials at the San Diego World's Fair—who, after a year's run, eliminated all the sexually explicit entertainment from their exposition because it "threatened the moral economy of the Southland's conservative and evangelical Protestant residents"—Rose and Alvord made a tactical error in the strategy for publicizing the Frontier Centennial.[124] They failed to realize that Fort Worthians viewed the Frontier Centennial and its promotion as a reflection of their city's image and heritage. As a result, Fort Worth citizens were much more inclined to concern themselves with the contents and implications of the promotional campaign than were other cities in which previous Rose productions played. Moreover, because the previous "girl shows" Alvord promoted remained in a town for only a short time, generating a controversy around the show proved safe because the show left town as quickly as it arrived. The short engagement of a show prevented a major opposition movement from taking root. Four months of construction and rehearsals and the four-month run of the Frontier Centennial meant that the development of a powerful opposition movement pushing a boycott could have a crippling impact on attendance at the centennial.

Fearing that his reputation might turn into a liability for the celebration, Rose headed off allegations of centennial filth raised by the Methodists, Baptists, and other religious organizations at an open public forum in which concerned citizens could ask questions about the show.[125] Rose told those present, "The Fort Worth show will be in excellent taste. I don't go in for smut. I don't abstain for any religious reason. I simply have found through years in the show business that dirt doesn't pay." But, he added, "Sure, we'll have girls, lots of girls." As evidence of his virtuous approach to entertainment, Rose mentioned that in the preceding year the Catholic Church in New York placed *Jumbo* at the top of its "white list."[126] On another occasion, Rose again backpedaled from his former veiled references to centennial nudity, when asked by the press if the frontier show would "shock" anyone. Rose responded, "There'll be nothing any more shocking about our show than you will find in the movies being shown every day in Fort Worth's family theaters. We'll have no more nudity—and no less."[127]

More direct measures were required to avoid the possibility of additional negative publicity coming from religious firebrand J. Frank Norris. The head pastor of First Baptist Church in Fort Worth, Norris played a significant role in bringing Christian fundamentalism to the American South. Unafraid to denounce insufficient enforcement of vice laws, in 1912 he had launched a series of tent meetings preaching against the city's failure to implement prostitution and liquor laws in the notorious red-light district "Hell's Half Acre."[128] Amon Carter astutely believed Norris would find the ad campaign, Sally Rand, and a "nude ranch" repugnant. Fearing Norris would issue scathing criticisms from his pulpit and mobilize religious sentiment against the centennial, Carter allegedly contacted Norris personally. As the story goes, after Carter explained that the Frontier Centennial planned to show nude girls and sell liquor, Norris offered to begin his planned national summer tour of revivals early to avoid a moral conflict with the show and the city.[129] Although the story might be apocryphal, it nevertheless illustrates that Carter recognized the danger in alienating one segment of the population.

Centennial planners also took decisive action to curtail the most offensive features of promotional materials. On all posters and billboards featuring the scene of nude maidens bathing in the pool at the Casa Mañana, the offending women were retouched with a painted-on bathing suit.[130] Prior to the public protest issued by the Baptists, Carter's paper the *Fort Worth Star-Telegram* brazenly published the same advertisement of the Frontier Centennial featured in many other papers in the Southwest. In addition to the Casa Mañana pool scene and Miss Fort Worth, the ad included a large picture of Sally Rand posing with her famed bubble. Although taken from the side with her arms and legs arranged to give only a view of her silhouette, the picture presented a clearly nude Rand.[131] The ad never again appeared in the paper. Subsequent ads for the centennial featured no images and did not hint at anything "wild or whoo-pee."[132] The Frontier Centennial handbills continued to include the infamous pool scene at the Casa Mañana; however, the scene now obscured the immodesty of the bathing maidens.[133]

Although Miss Fort Worth remained the symbol of the Frontier Centennial, the Women's Division successfully lobbied for promotional materials emphasizing Fort Worth's western heritage and prominence in the Texas livestock industry and its advantages as a modern metropolis. Acquiescing to the request of the Women's Division, the board issued a pamphlet under the title *Fort Worth Frontier Centennial in the Capital of the Cattle Kings*. In contrast to earlier promotional materials, the pamphlet omitted the use of overt sex appeal to boost the Frontier Centennial. Omitting references to "Wild & Whoo-pee," it featured a significantly modified Miss Fort Worth. Still sitting astride a bucking bronco, she now wore a pair of shorts and a riding vest. The pamphlet did mention Sally Rand, but it referred to her ranch as the "D'Nude Ranch." With images of Native Americans, cowboys and cowgirls, bison, and rodeo scenes, the tract also brought the emphasis of celebration back to the cattle industry and the frontier.

Because the Women's Division planned to send it to attract convention business to Fort Worth during the centennial year, the pamphlet also boosted Fort Worth, emphasizing its western heritage and image as a modern city. In addition to the western imagery of the Frontier Centennial, it further connected Fort Worth to a western heritage by including photographs of a prize-winning Hereford presumably from the Southwestern Exposition and Fat Stock Show and the color guard of the 2nd Cavalry of the United States Army that initially occupied the old Fort Worth army outpost in 1849. Perhaps most interesting is the juxtaposition of Fort Worth's western past with its modern growth and prosperity, connecting past and present. In a large layout, occupying a quarter of its space, the pamphlet included side-by-side drawings of the "Pioneer Village" with architectural renderings of the new Art Deco livestock facilities. The brochure also placed side by side an aerial photograph of downtown Fort Worth including the new Moderne Texas and Pacific Station and Post Office Building with detail sketches of the recreated first railroad station in Fort Worth

The *Fort Worth Frontier Centennial in the Capital of the Cattle Kings* pamphlet toned down the sexuality exhibited in earlier Frontier Centennial promotional materials while highlighting Fort Worth's ties to the cattle industry and contrasting its historic past with its modern present. Courtesy, Amon G. Carter Papers, Special Collections, Mary Couts Burnett Library, Texas Christian University.

and the false-façade buildings of "Frontier Village Street" including a post office to appear on the Frontier Centennial grounds.[134] The intentional combination of old and new served to foster Fort Worth's image as a modern American city sharing in the heritage of progressive nation-building on the frontier west.

Initially, Rose and centennial planners viewed the booking of Sally Rand as a major promotional coup; however, with an opposition movement brewing in Fort Worth, she became another potential liability to the centennial. To help curb public outcries of immorality relating to Rand's participation, show officials ceased providing the press with any information on the content of the Rand's "Nude Ranch" and deemphasized that attraction in promotional literature.[135] Claiming the fan and bubble dances were "dated," Rose also told the press that Rand would not perform either during her stay at Fort Worth.[136] Aided by city officials and the media, upon her arrival in early July, centennial planners began a campaign to tame Rand's persona for Fort Worth citizens. Contrary to the inclinations of Alvord, who believed "[n]obody must shoot Miss Rand till they can see the white of her thighs," the centennial planners orchestrated speaking and photo opportunities for Rand at a number of civic events, often accompanied by city officials.[137]

In a tribute to pioneer womanhood, Rand's first appearance before the public was in a "split-bonnet and old-fashioned gingham frock" aboard a prairie schooner with members of the Board of Control and heads of the Women's Division.[138] Members of the Women's Division apparently only appeared to welcome Rand at the airport after the "fervent behest" of the Board of Control.[139] Disarmed by Rand's charm, Anna Shelton, president of the Fort Worth Woman's Club, claimed, "I was amazed. She's a cute little thing." Mrs. J. B. Hamilton, former president of the Junior League, noted, "I was agreeably surprised. She was bright, witty."[140] She tossed the first pitch and encouraged women's participation in sports at the dedication ceremony of the new softball field in Forest Park.[141] On several occasions, Rand used the podium to soft-pedal Frontier Centennial nudity and distance herself from the "Nude Ranch." During her first dinner in Fort Worth, she told the press, "My work in the theater is confined to the creation of a beautiful illusion. I won't dance in the Nude Ranch."[142] Answering questions about the Frontier Centennial, she told the Kiwanis Club, "It's true there won't be anything cheap or tawdry in the entertainment."[143]

While stopping short of describing Rand as a role model for Fort Worth young women, as they had with Faye Cotton and the showgirls, the local newspapers endowed Rand with the more acceptable traits of domesticity, civic-mindedness, talent, and intelligence. Highlighting Rand's domestic side, in a blurb accompanying a picture of Rand in an apron preparing dinner in her kitchen, the *Fort Worth Press* claimed she "was 'whooping up' a meal."[144] The *Fort Worth Star-Telegram* reported on Rand's interest in Texas history as she traveled to "the Alamo and other historical spots."[145] Poking fun at those protesting and "beat[ing]

Sally Rand, in pioneer dress, accompanied by members of the Women's Division upon her official arrival in Fort Worth, Fort Worth, Texas, 1936. Courtesy, *Fort Worth Star-Telegram* Collection, Special Collections, The University of Texas at Arlington Libraries.

their tom-toms" about the hiring of Sally Rand, Jack Gordon wrote, "A half hour's conversation with Sally Rand, will convince any fan-devouring brother or sister that here is no Jezebel or Terpsichore, but a witty, charming and astonishingly well-informed young woman."[146] In a description of her first encounter with Rand, Edith Alderman Guedry wrote, "I was oft sold on Sally Rand's personality. She has personal charm, intellect, and believe it or not is demure in manner."[147] In the end, the public appearances and positive press coverage successfully co-opted Rand's persona as exotic purveyor of the immodest and conjoined it with those traits exhibited by Cotton to create an image tolerable to Fort Worth citizens.

That the vocalized opposition to centennial immorality subsided suggests that the campaign to roll back overt Frontier Centennial sexuality succeeded. Still, when the Central

Exposition's midway opened on June 6 with plenty of tawdry entertainment, some Fort Worth centennial planners wondered if Dallas stole "the edge" from the offering of the Frontier Centennial.[148] Carter and others had no intention of losing the sex appeal game to Dallas. As opening day neared, information regarding Sally Rand's "Nude Ranch" began to reappear in the *Fort Worth Star-Telegram*. Centennial planners, however, remained tight-lipped concerning the contents of the venue. The building itself remained one of the last structures to take shape on the centennial grounds. Just ten days before the opening, Rand began auditions for positions in the Ranch's "Sun Garden," which would present the Frontier Centennial's most explicit forms of commodified sex. Apparently attempting to preserve the image of virtue among Fort Worth young women, locals were prohibited from trying out for one of the eighteen positions at the ranch.

Exactly what the women would do at the Nude Ranch remained a secret to outsiders, but Rand promised the *Press* it would be "artistic."[149] Three days before the beginning of the exposition, the *Fort Worth Star-Telegram* reported on the costuming of the women to perform at the ranch. The ensemble represented another step in sexualization of the cowgirl image. Reflecting the attire of Miss Fort Worth, the outfit included boots, a 10-gallon hat, and gun holsters.[150] Rand's sexualization of the cowgirl at the Nude Ranch brought about one of her most enduring legacies. The performer's conjoining of the cowgirl imagery and the fan dance represented the primary source for the cowgirl striptease, which "would become one of the most widely imitated [strip] numbers during the Cold War."[151]

Lack of evidence makes evaluating the reaction of the general population to Rose's approach to the celebration, its promotional literature, and the arrival of Sally Rand difficult. Although the *Fort Worth Press* referred to incoming letters from readers concerned with "smutty entertainment," the paper only published a few, and the *Fort Worth Star-Telegram* never published a single letter commenting on the content of the publicity or the sexualization of the Frontier Centennial in general. The letters published by the *Fort Worth Press* suggest a mixed response. Perhaps most intriguing is that those commenting on the sexualized role of women at the Frontier Centennial appear to make their evaluations from a perspective of progress and modernity. For example, 72-year-old M. Jordan told readers he deplored the trend toward increased public nudity. He wrote, "I have learned that young beauties flaunting their half-nude selves, either on paper or in public, are not conducive to pure desires or thoughts." Jordan suggested that the decline in morality resulted from demands for instant gratification spurred by wealth resulting from greater education in modern society.[152]

Columnist Edith Guedry also argued that the "emphasis on the risqué" was decidedly unprogressive. "It gives one a certain feeling of shame," she wrote, "to know that during this, a year set aside to observe a Century of Progress in Texas we should have to give risqué shows to spotlight so." What would "our pioneer ancestors, whom we are honoring, think of us . . . and our so-call[ed] progress?" she asked. For Guedry, the need for explicit sexuality at the Frontier Centennial for greater appeal indicated a nation bereft of its morality. Ultimately, she concluded that Americans had progressed in science and materiality, but not spiritually. Like the Greek and Roman civilizations that collapsed at the height of their golden eras, modern America stood on the precipice of a spiritual if not physical pitfall.[153]

A Tarleton woman also wondered if the city's embrace of Sally Rand signaled a shift in the standards expected of modern young women. "In our midst," she wrote, "is a woman who pulls her [shirt] off with such a rip that the whole U.S. has learned to use her name as synonymous with birthday suits, and the home town takes her to its bosom and appears to be proud of her for doing it." She added, "One wouldn't be surprised at her being taken to the male bosom, privately speaking, while being given the keys to the city and other places, but the female bosom is another matter." She chastised "city fathers and mothers" for teaching young women that it was no longer enough for women to be "clever, pretty, smart, demure, [and] naïve"; young women must take their clothes off too. The writer concluded, "Hasn't the experience of the 'Rose' taught us some important things about womanhood?"[154]

Notwithstanding the conviction among some of an erosion of women's position in society, others believed the sexualization of the Frontier Centennial represented an important step in the city's path toward modernity. More specifically, they argued that the sexualization of the Frontier Centennial was an indication of Fort Worth's arrival as a city of the modern American West. An editorial in the *Fort Worth Press* challenging the Women's Division's request that Miss Fort Worth don clothing more "typically western" asked, "[H]ave the ladies visited a bathing pool lately?" The piece posited that if "Fort Worth is Where the West Begins . . . they might conclude that the poster girl's costume is typical of the modern West, at least."[155]

Embracing the traits of the modern woman emerging from the Frontier Centennial, the Tarrant County Medical Society linked the image of Miss Fort Worth with women's education when it hired Pauline Belew, one of the original creators of the Miss Fort Worth image, to design the cover of the June 1936 issue of the organization's publication, the *Bulletin*. The cover featured two women sitting on the top of an outline of the State of Texas—one atop the North Texas-Oklahoma border, the other with her back to the Panhandle. On the right sits Miss Fort Worth, legs crossed and extending a flirtatious invitation. On the left in a near mirror image, a woman dressed in cap and gown, holding a stack of books, likewise extends an invitation with an arm outstretched.[156]

The picture captured perfectly the prevailing conflict inherent in the bifurcated roles occupied by women in the 1930s as Rose assumed direction of the Frontier Centennial. Assuming a more traditional role of modest preservers of culture and promoters of female education, Fort Worth's club women, under the direction of the centennial's Women's Division, worked to develop Frontier Centennial attractions meant to create a greater sense of the city's frontier heritage, to educate, and to enlighten. Under Rose's direction, the influence of the Women's Division, particularly as it related to attractions and their involvement on the centennial grounds, shrank. The move toward creating a new role for women at the Frontier Centennial began with the competition for Texas Sweetheart #1. Commodified presentations of young women such as beauty pageants represented the verge of acceptable displays of the female body. Helping to define a tolerable role for these young women in the celebration, the media depicted them as virtuous, civic-minded, natural beauties. Similarly, when showgirls began arriving from New York, the media cast these young women as modest, hardworking, and talented.

The overtly sexualized promotional materials and the hiring of Sally Rand transcended the bounds of the acceptable role women played in mainstream society. World's fairs, particularly during the Depression Era, became important avenues for expanding the role of women in America to that of sexual commodity. "By suffusing the world of tomorrow with highly charged male sexual fantasies," Robert Rydell, world's fair scholar has argued, "the century-of-progress expositions not only reconfirmed the status of women as objects of desire, but represented their bodies as showcases that perfectly complemented displays of futuristic consumer durables everywhere on exhibit at the fairs."[157] Although the centennial grounds included no industrial exhibits presenting advances in American material culture, the significance of progress to Fort Worth's identity as a city and the repeated linkages of the Frontier Centennial to a prosperous future made the association of commodified sex at the celebration and modernity implicit.

Billy Rose himself perhaps viewed his participation in the Frontier Centennial and the entertainment he produced as contributing to the city's cultural modernity. Originally, Rose liked the title *Casa Diablo* for the premier entertainment venue at the Frontier Centennial but, believing his show to be on the cutting edge of Broadway entertainment, he found *Casa Mañana*—or House of Tomorrow—more fitting.[158] The city's religious groups and club women, however, contested the increasingly sexualized role of women, viewing it as at odds with the city's heritage and image as a modern city. They considered the commodification of women to be undignified for Fort Worth's honored pioneer heritage and modern and progressive aspirations. Appropriately, it was the Women's Division that pushed for new promotional materials that simultaneously returned the advertising of Frontier Centennial to its western theme and preserved the city's modern image.

CHAPTER 6

"IS IT TEXAS? IS IT FRONTIER? IS IT WESTERN?"

BILLY ROSE AND THEMING THE MYTHIC WEST

When Billy Rose stood before the Board of Control to pitch his concepts for the Frontier Centennial, his only original contribution was bringing in hordes of showgirls and presenting Broadway-caliber entertainment. He pitched two shows, the vaguely titled "Frontier Frolics" (which became known as *Casa Mañana*) and a musicalized Wild West show/rodeo he later titled *The Last Frontier*. He also suggested vacating his production of *Jumbo* from the Hippodrome Theatre in New York and moving it to Fort Worth for the celebration. Rose liked the idea of a "frontier" or "western" centennial but had no previous experience in producing western entertainment. Still, as a showman, Rose exhibited an astute sense for what would attract audiences. He knew that in the business of drawing crowds, creating overtly historical pageants or museums would not pay rich dividends. As for many Americans, the fountainhead for Rose's understanding of the American West came from mythic portrayals in western novels and films. Rose immediately seized upon the symbols of the mythic West and used them as a framework for presenting his entertainment creations.

From the very beginning, the Board of Control viewed the Frontier Centennial grounds as a means to promote not only Fort Worth's western identity but also its image as a modern metropolis. Recent world's fairs in Chicago and San Diego provided important models for the creation of themed space. World's fairs had become showcases of both modern and historic architecture. Rose kept the concept developed by the Board of Control to reproduce a frontier settlement of the Old West. However, rather than referring to historical records and photographs, Rose turned to western mythology to resurrect the Old West. In addition, the showman used the "six flags" of Texas as a framework upon which to structure his centennial amusements. The conflating of time and space created a unique environment some believed looked more like a "fairyland" than a frontier settlement of the Old West.[1] Such inconsistency created problems as, prior to Rose's arrival, the Board of Control worked to create an experience true to history for commemorating the past. Unencumbered by historical inconsistencies or architectural accuracy, in the recreation of the frontier settlement Rose produced an experience meant to evoke a sense of historicity and nostalgia without referencing any facts of the past. In this sense, the Frontier Centennial is best understood as a themed space.

Rose saw in the centennial planners' concept to recreate the Old West of literature and film an innovative source for entertainment. As a producer, Rose imagined the West as a grand stage from which he could create an unprecedented spectacle. With *Jumbo*, he produced a phenomenon, splicing the excitement and thrill of the circus with the drama and music of Broadway. The Frontier Centennial provided Rose an opportunity to replace the big top with a rustic frontier town, the circus performer with the heroic cowboy, and the clown with the "savage" Native American. He also understood that more than the circus, the frontier of the American West tapped narratives of a time and place for which Americans still longed. This must have been particularly appealing to Rose. As a producer, Rose exhibited a knack for playing on the nostalgia his audiences felt for days gone by. It became a trademark of his works. In his 1924 production of *The Fatal Wedding*, Rose presented audiences with a wistful look at the 1890s. The success of the production convinced Rose that audiences found entertainment mixing nostalgia, satire, and comedy universally appealing. Rose's successful implementation of this formula, which he repeatedly turned to over the years—including in his production of *Jumbo*—played an important role in his success as producer.[2] Mixing the excitement of the Old West with the near overwhelming nostalgia Americans felt for the frontier made perfect sense to Rose and likely contributed to his decision to assume direction of the Frontier Centennial.

Rose easily slipped into the role of cowboy showman once occupied by Buffalo Bill. Like many easterners, Rose, as a youth, imbibed the nostalgic depictions of the mythic West in pulp novels and Western films. He later recalled in his autobiography, "As a kid, I had read Zane Grey with a flashlight under the blankets after my old man had chased me off to bed. In the nickelodeons I had whooped 'Look out!' when the bad guy snuck up behind William S. Hart."[3] Upon Rose's arrival in Fort Worth, Amon Carter immediately baptized Rose a Texan and dropped a "twenty-gallon Stetson" on his head.[4] Later, the Fort Worth sheriff's office strapped a .45 caliber "shooting iron" to his waist, pinned a "gold five pointed badge" to his chest, and deputized him a special sheriff.[5] To publicize the centennial, Rose regularly appeared duded up in cowboy boots, hat, and chaps, with six-guns, twirling a lasso on or near a horse.[6] Rose's affinity for his new cowboy image led him to brag to the New York press, "I am now a Texan."[7] Emphasizing his transformation from New Yorker to Texan, Rose's publicity agent, Richard Maney, told the New York press that Rose had become "Billy Rose of the Rancho." In the course

Billy Rose, in cowboy attire, poses for publicity photographs after being contracted to direct the Frontier Centennial, Fort Worth, Texas, April 1936. Courtesy, *Fort Worth Star-Telegram* Collection, Special Collections, The University of Texas at Arlington Libraries.

of the celebration, the local and national press provided Rose a number of clever monikers reflecting his new cowboy image. For example, *Architectural Forum* labeled the showman "Billy 'wow puncher' Rose."[8] In their regular feature "America's Interesting People," *The American Magazine* dubbed Rose a "Frontiersman."[9]

Although Rose donned the cowboy imagery primarily for publicity, it might have lent some credibility to his ability to produce a western-themed exposition. Some questioned the "little Jew boy's" knowledge of the West. In an interview, Ernie Pyle, a Scripps Howard columnist, asked, "Do you think people may not like the idea of a Broadway hot shot putting on a Wild West show?" Rose responded, "I told them they'd just have to have confidence in me. I know the Southwest well enough."[10] Those who questioned Rose's missing western pedigree did not realize that the fundamental nature of the celebration had changed. The day after

Rose signed the contract, William Monnig told the press, "[W]e wanted to make it [the Frontier Centennial] the greatest amusement attraction of the State during the Centennial year and we got the greatest show man we could find."[11] Describing the aims of Frontier Centennial planners in a letter to Franklin Delano Roosevelt, Amon G. Carter wrote that the Fort Worth event would be "the most colorful, thrilling and interesting show ever produced in Texas."[12] Suggesting that planners no longer thought of their celebration as an opportunity to commemorate the city's or state's frontier heritage or the Texas livestock industry, they increasingly referred to the Frontier Centennial as a "show." As such, the only credential that mattered to planners was that Rose knew how to stage a spectacle that attracted large audiences.

Only Rose's continued bluster for Frontier Centennial pulchritude overshadowed his denunciation of all things historical. At least part of Rose's disregard for history resulted from the historical tone struck by the Central Centennial Exhibition in Dallas. On more than one occasion Rose labeled the exposition in Dallas, with its scientific, industrial, and historical exhibits, a "carbon copy" of Chicago's Century of Progress.[13] Naturally, Fort Worth stood to profit from offering something original. Moreover, Rose also believed historical exhibits and museums were boring and antithetical to entertainment. Rose shared his antipathy for the historical when he told the *Fort Worth Press*, "Dallas has all the historical stuff so we don't have to worry about that. We can just show the folks a good time."[14] Desiring to separate permanently history from the Frontier Centennial in the mind of prospective centennial-goers, Rose even sought to eliminate the word "centennial" from the title of the show. Ned Alvord, the show's promoter, placed an ad in the *Fort Worth Press* seeking ideas for a new title. In the ad, Alvord stated, "Centennial sounds too much like history. And there'll be dam' little history in the show when Billy Rose gets through."[15] Although some Fort Worth citizens responded to Alvord's plea with suggestions such as "Frontier Fiesta" and "Frontier-Frolic," Rose apparently failed to convince city fathers and centennial planners to change the title of the celebration.[16]

For all of Rose's anti-history rhetoric, he astutely recognized that producing a successful western show did require some references to western history. As with Western films, the show could not succeed without some elements anchoring it to the past. Moreover, Rose understood that such references to the past must be clearly and immediately recognizable to the intended audience. He explained this in his initial meeting with the Board of Control. He told those present that the Frontier Centennial needed "[e]ntertainment on a grand scale, with a strong western *flavor*" (emphasis added).[17] Like Buffalo Bill, pulp novelists, and movie producers, Rose hoped to situate the Frontier Centennial within the parameters of the mythic West by using western or Texas-sounding names and western symbols such as the epic struggle between cowboys and Indians and deemphasizing the influence of women, African Americans, Mexicans and Native Americans.[18]

Beyond western novels and films, Rose turned to several additional sources to help generate ideas for creating an Old West atmosphere and developing a layout for the grounds of the Frontier Centennial. A few days after Rose agreed to direct the celebration, the Southwestern Exposition and Fat Stock Show began. By the 1930s, the Old West had become the overriding theme of the annual stock show—and 1936 would prove a hallmark year in the history of the stock show. Although Galveston, Houston, San Antonio, and Huntsville all hosted centennial-related events prior to the commencement of the Southwestern Exposition and Fat Stock Show, civic and stock show officials regularly referred to the exposition as the opening act not only of the Frontier Centennial but of Texas's centennial year.[19] Officials also believed that attendance and participation in the stock show provided a significant indicator of the Frontier Centennial's future success. For months, Fort Worth businessmen promoted the stock show in cities around the Southwest through a series of goodwill tours.

Amon Carter, through the *Fort Worth Star-Telegram,* also continually charged local readers with the duty of supporting the stock show. "Fort Worthians," an editorial argued, "owe a record attendance to that institution . . . being no less than the 'curtain raiser' for the [Texas Centennial]."[20] As a "curtain raiser" for the state's centennial year—and more important, as a forerunner of the Frontier Centennial—the stock show continued its western theme. Anticipating the pomp of the opening scenes of the festivities, the *Fort Worth Star-Telegram* boasted, "The Spirit of the Old West will live again in Fort Worth this afternoon as a picturesque procession swings through city streets to herald the opening of the fortieth annual Southwestern Exposition and Fat Stock Show."[21] The *Fort Worth Press*, describing the sights of the stockyards, noted, "Cowboys from all over the West are to be seen, with their sombreros, highly colored bandanas and flashy shirts, slacks and high-heeled boots. There are bronc and wild Brahma bull riders, bull-doggers, trick riders and trick ropers."[22] On Billy Rose's first night in Fort Worth, Amon Carter whisked the former to the stock show where he no doubt drank deeply of the show's western atmosphere.[23]

Rose also traveled to several locations to help generate ideas for the Frontier Centennial. First, he arranged to visit Pawnee Bill's Ranch in Oklahoma. Major Gordon W. Lillie, former partner with Buffalo Bill and retired Wild West showman, owned a 3,000-acre ranch in Pawnee County, Oklahoma. Featuring replicas of an Indian trading post and an Indian Village called "Old Town" from the 1880s, Pawnee Bill's Ranch became a center of tourism in the state. During his visit to Pawnee Bill's Ranch, Rose hoped to "garner ideas for Western atmosphere at the show here."[24] Rose also traveled west to San Diego to visit the California Pacific International Exposition, which opened in spring 1935. Although little is known of his trip to San Diego, Rose explained to the press that he wanted to assess the fair's "general layout."[25] Rose must have found "Gold Gulch," one of the fair's most popular attractions, useful. A recreation of a street from an old mining town of the 49ers, Gold Gulch featured a row of seemingly dilapidated wooden structures housing honky-tonks and a burlesque show featuring Gold Gulch Gertie.[26] The design of the Frontier Centennial would ultimately include characteristics from both Pawnee Bill's ranch and San Diego's World's Fair.

Rose's production of *The Last Frontier* included authentic Native Americans and a herd of bison. On the other hand, Rose used a layout structured around a midway to organize the recreated structures of the frontier village and the venue for Sally Rand.

In the broader conceptualization of the Frontier Centennial as a historical themed environment, world's fairs played perhaps the most important role. Although planners sought to capture the Old West as it appeared in Western films and novels, since the construction of the Crystal Palace at the Great Exhibition of Works of Industry of All Nations held in London in 1851, world's fair expositions represented prominent examples of themed architecture and environments. The 1893 World's Columbian Exposition held in Chicago featured "ethnological" attractions along its midway including German, Irish, Chinese, and Japanese villages, as well as villages for Dakota Sioux, Navajos, and Apaches. The midway also housed exhibits to the "Mohammedan world" and West and East Asia.[27] Other Victorian era fairs such as the Atlanta Cotton States and International Exposition in 1895 featured the usual ethnological villages but also a reconstructed old plantation house.[28] These exhibits, like those at the Columbian Exposition, were meant to reinforce the colonial status and hegemonic control of a pluralistic society.[29] The Painted Desert exhibit at the 1915 Panama-Pacific International Exposition in San Diego featured a large pseudo-pueblo building to display the culture of the Pueblo Indians of the Southwest. The exhibit appealed to fairgoers' "fascination with Indian primitivism and tourist yearnings to escape from the industrial age in the rustic lifestyle of the Southwest."[30]

The century-of-progress expositions of the 1930s also used themed architecture to reinforce their messages. During the economic turmoil of the Great Depression, the world's fairs of the 1930s, according to Robert Rydell, "stressed America's historical progress towards becoming a promised land of abundance."[31] Planners hoped to connect a progressive past with a modern and prosperous future in the minds of fairgoers through the juxtaposition of themed landscapes of the past and the modern architecture structures housing the industrial and manufacturing exhibits. At the Century of Progress Exposition in Chicago, planners intentionally situated the Native American village and an exact replica of a Mayan Temple next to General Motors' automobile manufacturing exhibit. A publicity release for the exposition noted, "The General Motors tower rises, a bright orange tribute to Modernism, over the wigwams and tepees and hogans of the oldest Americans, over the dances and feathers and beads in the Indian stadium . . . . 'What a distance we have come,' is the theme of the World's Fair, but nowhere does it come home so sharply to the visitor as when he attends the Indian ceremonials."[32] Like the Century of Progress, the California Pacific International Exposition juxtaposed Gold Gulch with exhibits such as "Modeltown and Modernization Magic," which offered fairgoers a futuristic look at suburbia.[33] By the time of the Frontier Centennial, world's fairs had generally become buffets of themed environments, of both modernity and the past.

Similarly, Fort Worth civic leaders and centennial planners sought to write messages of progress and modernity into the physical landscape of the Frontier Centennial grounds. Hoping to bring the local livestock industry into harmony with the city's projected image of a modern metropolis, civic leaders and city boosters fought for the purchase of the Van Zandt site to build the modern livestock facilities for the stock show. By placing the stock show facilities adjacent to downtown, civic leaders worked to link Fort Worth's livestock industry and larger western heritage with the growth and progress manifest in its modern skyscrapers.

In addition to its location, the design of the new stock show facilities was meant to make them prominent members in the cast of buildings that composed modern Fort Worth. During the campaign to acquire New Deal funds for the stock show facilities in September 1935, Amon Carter described the new livestock buildings as part of a larger process of modernizing Fort Worth. In a letter to Harry L. Hopkins, Carter wrote that the planned PWA building projects in Fort Worth, of which the stock show facilities were foremost, "will . . . give us [a] thoroughly modern city in every respect."[34] During campaigning for the bond issue to provide funding for the stock show buildings, editorials in the *Fort Worth Star-Telegram* also described the modern livestock buildings as the "the greatest of all opportunities to improve the city" which would also "make the Stock Show one of the foremost livestock shows of the country."[35] The construction of modern livestock facilities would not only repackage Fort Worth's livestock industry to conform to its modern identity but also secure a place for the Southwestern Exposition and Fat Stock Show in the upper echelon of the nation's premier stock shows.

Civic leaders intended the stock show buildings, in both layout and design, to represent the most advanced livestock facilities in the United States. As such, the plans for the new facilities submitted by Wyatt C. Hedrick and Herman P. Koeppe to the PWA blended classical composition with the austere Moderne or Art Deco style emerging from Europe in the 1920s and 30s.[36] From its inception, the plans called for a coliseum and auditorium anchored by a memorial tower. The final plans included a 208-foot tower flanked by a 6,161-seat coliseum on the left and a 2,994-seat auditorium on the right with auxiliary buildings situated behind the main buildings. As "the city's most conspicuous Art Deco landmark," the signature tower with stair-stepped ziggurat pinnacle topped by a beacon light immediately tied the new livestock facilities to the city's image of modernity.[37] Moreover, the coliseum boasted a revolutionary domed ceiling. Designed by Herbert M. Hinckley Sr., the self-supporting dome spanned the 250 x 125-foot arena and required no support beams to obstruct the views of spectators.[38]

More than a symbol of modernization, the new facilities also memorialized the state's western heritage. Named the Pioneer Tower, the focal point of the complex honored the early pioneers who settled Texas. City councilman and head of the Department of History at TCU, W. J. Hammond, selected quotations from the writings of Britain Rice Webb, Mirabeau Lamar, and Lawrence S. Ross, and portions of the Texas State Constitution for display on four plaques in the Pioneer Tower's rotunda.[39] The lobby of the coliseum houses several Monel plaques inspired by

Coliseum and auditorium architectural drawings submitted by Wyatt C. Hedrick and Herman P. Koeppe, Fort Worth, Texas, 1936. Courtesy, *Fort Worth Star-Telegram* Collection, Special Collections, The University of Texas at Arlington Libraries.

the western theme of the stock show. Of particular interest is an image of a rancher with his livestock. Art Deco historian Judith Singer Cohen suggests, "The rugged cattleman is an obvious tribute to the resourceful settlers of the Southwest who were responsible for developing the region's cattle industry."[40] On its east-side façade, the coliseum also featured a sculpture of a bucking horse and rider, a familiar symbol for the stock show's rodeo.

Perhaps the most striking tribute the state's western heritage are two 10 x 200-foot tile friezes situated atop six stone piers on the main entrances of the coliseum and auditorium. W. J. Hammond selected the content for the mosaics, meant to present "the various historical development of the state," while Kenneth Gale of the Zanesville Tile Company created the panels.[41] Although both friezes run chronologically, the pair presents different themes from Texas history and together do not convey a linear narrative. For example, the first of the six scenes in the frieze over the coliseum, to the left of Pioneer Tower, includes a depiction of several

Native Americans presenting a gift to two frontiersmen with the Alamo in the background alluding to the Texas Revolution. (It should be noted that the frieze depicts the Alamo as it looked in 1936, not 1836.) The first of the six scenes in the frieze over the auditorium, to the right of the Pioneer Tower, includes several Spanish conquistadors, a Catholic priest, and a Mexican woman and two men with a Spanish mission in the distance connoting the presence of the Spanish and Mexican settlers in pre-independence Texas history.

Presenting Texas history within a broader narrative of frontier progress and settlement, the mosaic over the coliseum included images of the Alamo, Native American Plains culture, frontiersmen, pioneers, peace settlements with the Native Americans, the arrival of the railroad, and cowboys at play. In contrast, the frieze over the auditorium presents a more diverse portrait of Texas history, one that emphasizes the state's progress toward modernity and prosperity. The first two scenes include tributes to Texas's Spanish and Mexican roots, frontiersmen, and a pair of Confederate soldiers wearing blue hats, and Union soldiers wearing gray hats, moving a cannon together, signifying the reunion of North and South. The final four scenes highlight the significance of the livestock industry; agricultural development; oil extraction and refining; and construction, manufacturing, and shipping. Although the content of the friezes was meant to depict Texas's history, the panels clearly present a skewed perspective of history promoted by Fort Worth's civic leadership during the first decades of the twentieth century. Of particular interest is the innocuous glancing reference to Texas's part in the Confederacy and, with the exception of an agricultural scene depicting several African Americans picking cotton, the lack of portrayals of the Old South. Moreover, while it acknowledged Texas's cultural and racial diversity in including the historic presence of Native Americans, Spaniards, and Mexicans, the mosaic emphasized the state's white heritage.

Even before construction on the complex began, the project added to an image of prosperity and progress by removing an unsightly shantytown from the site. At least fifteen families living in tents, shacks, and huts were evicted from the site when preparations for construction began. Victims of the depressed economy, some of the relief-roll families had resided on the property for as long as three years. Attempting to put a good spin on the face of progress, Delbert Willis, reporting the story for the *Fort Worth Press*, claimed the families felt it their civic duty to vacate for the new centennial grounds. "Shanty towners are willing to give it up," he wrote, "all for Billy Rose and the Centennial."[42]

A groundbreaking ceremony held on March 10 marked the beginning of construction. To the tune of "The Eyes of Texas" played by the TCU Reserve Officers' Training Corps (ROTC) band, William Monnig, Mayor Van Zandt Jarvis, Uel Stevens (chief engineer-examiner for the state PWA), and Amon Carter plunged gilded shovels into the ground. Reflecting the symbolic nature of the new facilities, the comments made by those officiating pointed to the importance of the building in memorializing Fort Worth's western heritage and image as a modern metropolis. Commenting on the significance of the structure, Lionel Bevan, president of the Fort Worth Chamber of Commerce, exclaimed, "We are again making history for Fort Worth and all of Texas, especially West Texas." He added, "We want this to be a monument and memory of the West for the thousands and millions of visitors who will come here." Not omitting the significance of West Texas to Fort Worth's western identity, he noted, "'This is particularly West Texas' interpretation of Texas history." Following Bevan, Carter reminded those present of the importance of the new facilities to Fort Worth's future. He declared, "We not only are celebrating 100 years of progress, but we are laying the groundwork and foundation for another 100 years." Mayor Van Zandt Jarvis also addressed the significance of the modern livestock facilities to the city's future economic opportunities. He "envisioned Fort Worth as the leading convention city in the South because of facilities to be made available by the construction of the new buildings."[43]

Amon G. Carter, Mayor Van Zandt Jarvis, Uel Stevens, and William Monnig breaking ground for the Frontier Centennial memorial buildings, Fort Worth, Texas, March 10, 1936. Courtesy, *Fort Worth Star-Telegram* Collection, Special Collections, The University of Texas at Arlington Libraries.

The ceremony signaled the beginning of the foundation work for the three prominent features of the new facilities: the coliseum, the auditorium, and the memorial tower. The actual work of excavation began the following day as engineers and surveyors defined the layout of the buildings and carpenters began constructing temporary offices and work sheds on the site.[44] In the coming weeks, work also began on the remaining auxiliary exhibit structures. These included the Rodeo Horses and Stock Building and the Horse Show Horses Building.[45] In total, the new stock show facilities would cost the City of Fort Worth $1,550,739.[46] At the official dedication of the coliseum on September 21, 1936, Amon Carter announced the plans to call the edifice the Will Rogers Memorial Coliseum after Carter's friend, the popular cowboy-humorist.[47] The auditorium was dedicated a few months later on

December 23, 1936, marking the completion of the three main structures in the complex.[48]

Just as centennial planners hoped the placement of modern stock show facilities near downtown would link Fort Worth's western heritage with its contemporary urban growth and prosperity, they also hoped the reconstruction of a frontier village next to the modern stock show buildings would evoke a powerful message of progress. In an editorial, the *Fort Worth Star-Telegram* suggested this interpretation when it stated that the Frontier Centennial grounds "must be a thing of prideful reminder in the history of Fort Worth's civic progress"[49] The notion to build an "authentic reproduction" of a frontier town as a counterpoint to the new stock show facilities represented a central component of the earliest centennial plans.[50]

Not long after his trips to Pawnee Bill's Ranch and the San Diego World's Fair, Rose began to make more specific comments on the direction he would take in the development of the grounds. Describing his conceptualization, he said, "I want to recreate a typical city of the days of '49." He added, "I want to have the atmosphere of a Texas town 100 years ago—a city of soldiers, surrounded by herds of wild buffalo, Indians, cowboys, gambling halls, etc."[51] Interestingly, his description of the grounds differed little, if at all, from comments made earlier by centennial planners and city boosters.[52] Although such comments seem to suggest a narrow definition of the historical environment Rose intended to create, over time his conceptions of the "west" appeared far broader. Likely after learning that Rose brought in Albert Johnson, renowned Broadway stage designer from New York, to design the lands, the Women's Division expressed their concerns that "native architecture" would no longer be used in the design of the fairgrounds. At a Women's Division rally, Rose assured them that in the construction of the grounds his test questions would be: "Is it Texas? Is it frontier? Is it Western? If it is, it is right. If it's Forty-Second Street, if it's New York, if it's Broadway, it's wrong." Comments made by his publicist also suggest Rose's conceptualization for the Frontier Centennial grounds were no longer anchored in the Texas of 100 years before. Richard Maney explained the frontier town "will combine the best features of Deadwood, Virginia City and San Francisco of '49."[53] As did dime and pulp novels and Western films, Rose moved toward a generic conception of the mythic West that extended from the Great Plains to the Pacific Ocean and from the 1830s to the 1870s or 1880s.

Late in March 1936, Johnson began working with architect Joseph R. Pelich to develop a general layout for the Frontier Centennial. Within days, Johnson drafted a layout radically altering Pelich's original organization of the Pioneer Village.[54] Meant to give "a surprise at every turn," the new "frontier city" featured a W-shaped midway half a mile long consuming nearly twenty-three acres.[55] Later, *Architectural Forum* praised the layout as "a simple but effective plan which led traffic along short avenues with a major interesting building at the end of each vista."[56] Like modern shopping malls, each of the four points along the midway featured an entertainment "anchor." In addition to layout, Johnson also scrapped Pelich's original architectural designs based upon historic West Texas ghost towns. Johnson and Rose developed an ingenious way to depict Rose's broad notions of Texas and the American West. Each of the major entertainment venues and the midway itself featured an architectural representation of one of the six nations to fly flags over Texas.[57] Johnson's design represented a conflation of all the eras of Texas's past into one uniform park. Because Rose had yet to flesh out the content of his major attractions (with the exception of the importation of *Jumbo*), the designs only hinted at the attractions the sketched buildings would eventually house.[58] With a July 1 opening day, construction on the major "temporary" Frontier Centennial buildings commenced soon after the work on the new stock show facilities began.[59]

Rose's themed vision of Texas history and the Old West began to take shape on the Frontier Centennial grounds directly to the east of the new stock show facilities. Work first began on the buildings housing the major entertainment venues. Although he

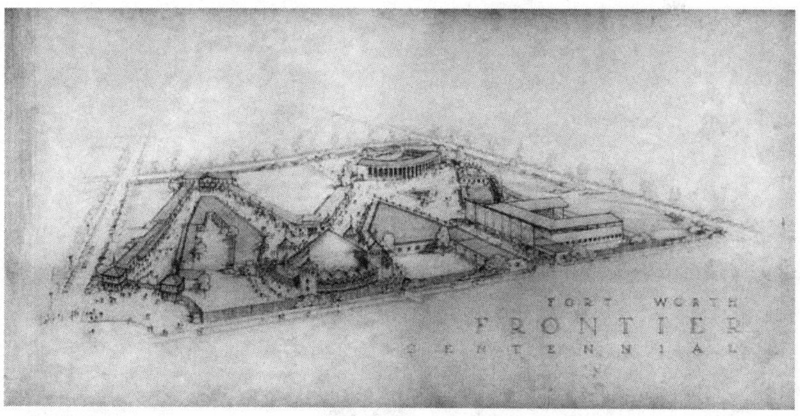

Frontier Centennial grounds sketch by Joseph Pelich, Fort Worth, Texas, 1936. Courtesy, *Fort Worth Star-Telegram* Collection, Special Collections, The University of Texas at Arlington Libraries.

claimed each building would, in its architectural styling, represent an era of Texas history, Johnson's designs maintained no allusions to historical accuracy. Detailed plans for what would become the iconic and most expensive "temporary" building debuted on the first of April.[60] For the presentation of what Rose called the "Frontier Follies," Johnson conceived of a giant horseshoe-shaped open-air café-theater with a seating capacity of four thousand. Intended to reflect the architecture of the "Spanish flag," the plans called for 600 arches accompanied by Spanish lanterns and a copper-and-white color scheme. In addition to claiming the distinction of being the largest café-theater on earth, the designs included several engineering features intended not only to enhance the stage productions but also to impress and attract audiences. The 130-foot revolving stage, also billed as the world's largest, rested above a pool of water. The hidden mechanisms that turned the great stage also allowed for forward and reverse lateral motion. When moved in reverse, the stage drew away from the front rows to reveal a pool featuring a set of fountains. Moreover, during the show, gondolas and other boats could move freely between the audience and the stage. From the stage, rows of tables and chairs fanned outward in

The Casa Mañana theater headlined as Billy Rose's main entertainment venue during the Frontier Centennial, Fort Worth, Texas, 1936. Its design was intended to represent Texas under the Spanish flag. Courtesy, *Fort Worth Star-Telegram* Collection, Special Collections, The University of Texas at Arlington Libraries.

escalating tiers to meet first- and second-floor box seats at the sides and rear of the interior.[61] To serve dining guests, the centennial officials employed 200 African American waiters—the only part African Americans played during the Frontier Centennial.[62]

Within a week of the unveiling of the plans, work began on the massive café-theater with an exterior façade stretching 280 feet.[63] The contractor employed 150 workmen on that structure alone. In early May, as the theater began to take shape, Rose christened the building. Because of its futuristic features, which Rose claimed far surpassed those of existing theaters, he named the building Casa Mañana or House of Tomorrow.[64]

Soon after the debut of the plans for the café-theater, Johnson introduced designs for the other three major entertainment buildings. For Rose's masterwork *Jumbo*, he envisioned a

The *Jumbo* Theatre housed Billy Rose's relocated New York production of *Jumbo*. Its design was intended to represent Texas under the French flag. Courtesy, *Fort Worth Star-Telegram* Collection, Special Collections, The University of Texas at Arlington Libraries.

2,500-seat circular auditorium reminiscent of the "famous old circus building in New Orleans in the [18]70s, the Hippotheatron in New York in the [18]60s and older structures in Europe." Like the Casa Mañana, Johnson meant the Circus Building to represent one of the six flags to fly over Texas. With the addition of details "typical of French structures," such as French scrollwork, the Circus Building represented the French period in Texas history.[65] The intricacy of the light gray scrollwork against the building's scarlet exterior and white coned roof made for a striking and unique edifice. The interior consisted of a large bowl surrounding the circular stage or circus ring, which reached forty feet in diameter. Plans also called for two fan-shaped menageries flanking the structure for holding and viewing the animals between performances.[66]

Far less striking than the Casa Mañana or the Circus Building, Johnson's Rodeo Building would house Rose's much-touted

The Last Frontier Arena contained Billy Rose's frontier-themed musical rodeo / wild west show, Fort Worth, Texas, 1936. Courtesy, *Fort Worth Star-Telegram* Collection, Special Collections, The University of Texas at Arlington Libraries.

"musicalized Wild West Show." The simple, although large, concrete-and-wood structure consisted of a U-shaped 3,000-seat grandstand covered by a canvas awning. Characterized as "a sideshow structure," the exterior featured a series of rectangular panels colored in the earth tones of brown, green, and orange. Each panel featured alternating images of a large bearskin and an "Indian Shield" with crossed tomahawks.[67] Unlike the designs of the Casa Mañana and the Circus Building, which exhibited some architectural preferences of the nations they intended to represent, neither the façade nor the interior of the Rodeo Building reflected the design motifs of the Mexican flag—the nation centennial planners claimed it represented. In fact, the tent-like canvas awning and grandstand seating around the arena seemed more reminiscent of Buffalo Bill's Wild West shows than as an homage to Mexico. Early plans called for two sets of train tracks to meet on the dirt floor of a 120-foot arena for reenacting the 1869 joining of

The Pioneer Palace featured a massive dance floor and bar, Fort Worth, Texas, 1937. Courtesy, *Fort Worth Star-Telegram* Collection, Special Collections, The University of Texas at Arlington Libraries.

the transcontinental railroad. Later, centennial planners instead opted to build an artificial mountain functioning as both stage and backdrop to Rose's musical rodeo.[68]

Construction on what would be the fourth and final major entertainment structure began nearly a month after the previous three.[69] When Rose first announced the structure, he described it as "[a] real, old-time honky-tonk." He promised to fill the bar with pretty girls, a Mexican orchestra, singing waiters, and dance hostesses. Initially titled the "Gay Nineties Casino," the building was eventually dubbed the Pioneer Palace.[70] Essentially a massive dance hall and bar, the Pioneer Palace included a large dance floor 300 feet long and 175 feet wide at the center, with a forty-foot bar with an elevated stage behind running its entire length. The exterior of the one-story wedge-shaped ultramarine building featured deep-set windows with white shutters and scalloped points on the roof.[71] Neither Rose nor Johnson ever revealed which of the six flags the design of the Pioneer Palace reflected.

Johnson's plans, keeping with the six flags theme, originally called for six large entertainment structures. In the process of construction, however, several features of his "Frontier City" ultimately fell by the wayside. Borrowed from earlier plans for the centennial grounds, Johnson's plans included space for a 400-seat "old-time gas-lighted 'opery house'" to present melodramas. Rose later argued that, because of the proliferation of melodramas in recent years, the concept lacked the requisite novelty for a major attraction at the Frontier Centennial and was therefore dropped from the plans. Other sources suggest that Frontier Centennial planners simply ran out money.[72] Interestingly, this venue represented Texas under the Confederate flag.[73] By the end of April, Rose began considering the placement of carnival-type rides and attractions on the plot on which the Opery House would have stood.

On April 29, Rose hosted the designer of the Century of Progress's "Sky-Ride" who developed plans for a 250-foot tower that would spin and lift a number of "Stratoships" simulating the experience of flight. However, Rose ultimately contracted Bill Hames, who annually provided midway entertainment for the Southwestern Exposition and Fat Stock Show.[74] Although the "Stratoships" tower never materialized, Rose did construct an artificial mountain surrounded by a moat and wire netting to display 200 monkeys.[75] Rose also dropped plans for a "Trading Post Exhibits" building that Johnson had situated across from the Circus Building. With the omission of the Opery House representing the Confederacy and the Trading Post, perhaps representing the Republic of Texas, by the time work began on the Pioneer Palace, centennial planners mentioned nothing of its possible representation of the American Flag. Even though it never fully materialized, the six flags theme at the Frontier Centennial represented the first use of such theming for entertainment purposes, subsequently embraced by the Six Flags Over Texas theme park in 1961.[76]

Centennial planners eventually added a fifth building, incongruent with the six flags theme, at the behest of the West Texas Chamber of Commerce. Officials in Dallas originally offered West Texas 6,000 square feet of space to exhibit the region's resources. After officials cut the region's exhibit space down to 1,300 square feet, the West Texas Chamber of Commerce turned to Fort Worth and the Frontier Centennial as an alternative for presenting the region's resources to centennial visitors. From the beginning, Fort Worth boosters, civic leaders, and Frontier Centennial planners sought the participation of West Texans in the development of Fort Worth's centennial celebration. Naturally, centennial planners, many of whom actively participated in the West Texas Chamber of Commerce, happily acquiesced to the placement of a West Texas display at the Frontier Centennial.[77] On March 4, chamber president Ray H. Nichols and general manager D. A. Bandeen issued a letter announcing a two-pronged plan for presenting the region's resources to centennial visitors. First, an "All-Resources and All-Community exhibit" originally planned for the central centennial in Dallas would be exhibited at the Frontier Centennial. Second, the West Texas Chamber of Commerce would "cooperate fully" with the creation of a "general agricultural exhibit" on par with those presented by East and South Texas. However, "Responsibility for gathering the West Texas exhibit will rest upon the Central Exposition."[78]

Bandeen met with both Frontier Centennial architect Joseph R. Pelich and Billy Rose to discuss the needs of the West Texas Chamber of Commerce.[79] Although "educational" exhibits did not fit with Rose's conception of the Frontier Centennial, planners developed a novel space for the West Texas Chamber of Commerce. Contributing to Rose's western-themed space, Pelich designed a rectangular building resembling the old Texas and Pacific Station at Fort Worth. Painted in red-and-black stripes with a flat-top tar-covered roof, the replica included "verandah, spittoons, and 1876 time tables."[80] The inclusion of a replica of the city's first railroad station represented the only building on the grounds to architecturally tie the Frontier Centennial to Fort Worth's history.

To add to the station's authenticity, the City Council passed an ordinance permitting the St. Louis, San Francisco and Texas Railway to build a 1,900-foot spur to the West Texas Chamber of Commerce building. The St. Louis, San Francisco and Texas Railway also rebuilt and refurbished old railroad equipment for presentation at the centennial.[81] The interior of the building provided the West Texas Chamber of Commerce with space to display a number of dioramas and panels depicting the various raw materials and goods produced in the region, a collection of West Texas branding irons, a color motion picture boosting the region, and a replica of the office of the recently deceased Will Rogers containing many of his personal belongings.[82]

Tying together the conflated eras of Texas history, Johnson's design called for structures typical of the "Old West" to line the entire length of the midway. Unlike Pelich's design, which implemented features of Fort Worth's frontier heritage and the state's Mexican and southern past, Johnson presented a series of buildings representing the conventional props in formula Westerns of the era.[83] These props became so important to portrayals of the mythic West by the 1930s that without them the Old West would not be recognized by audiences. As such, an editorial in the *Fort Worth Star-Telegram* affirmed, Frontier Centennial planners carefully followed the canon of western mythology. "The reconstructed Frontier Village," the editorial explained, "the Block house, the Indian Camp, the Second Dragoons—they are all parts of a ritual."[84]

After entering the turnstiles, Frontier Centennial-goers walked through a row of old and weather-beaten buildings scattered haphazardly along the midway, complete with hitching posts, that Rose dubbed the "Sunset Trail." To add an "authentic" weatherworn appearance, each board went through a carefully measured process of charring.[85] Those allowed to view the Sunset Trail prior to opening day praised the designers and marveled at the details giving the buildings an aged appearance, including the appearance of leaning, worm holes in the wood, grass growing in the cracks, and desiccated lumber.[86] Buildings included a pair of frontier

Features such as this well lined the "Sunset Trail," the frontier-themed midway of the Frontier Centennial, Fort Worth, Texas, 1936. Courtesy, *Fort Worth Star-Telegram* Collection, Special Collections, The University of Texas at Arlington Libraries.

stockades, a general store, a two-story town hall, a saloon and dance hall, and two hotels known as the Astor House and Palmer House.

These buildings of false-front design contained a string of 20 x 20-foot rooms containing the Women's Division's museum of pioneer relics and western art.[87] Continuing to occupy the role of civilizers, volunteers from the Women's Division in frontier attire

A pair of wooden block houses marked the entrance to the Frontier Centennial's pioneer village. Courtesy, *Fort Worth Star-Telegram* Collection, Special Collections, The University of Texas at Arlington Libraries.

saw to the hospitality needs of centennial visitors in a replica of a village church complete with an old organ.[88] Commenting on the location of the Women's Division's museum on the first leg of the W-shaped midway, columnist Ernie Pyle claimed the organization was intentional "so that the public can get through them first and have it over with, and then be free to have fun with a clear historical conscience."[89]

Other frontier buildings included the blacksmith shop, the Wells Fargo building, *The Weekly Star* printing house distributing a mock frontier paper, and the livery stable that featured old buggies and coaches. An adobe house containing Mexican arts and crafts provided the Frontier Centennial's only hint to the state's Mexican heritage. Celebrities attending the show were often brought by blue-coated soldiers before the court of Judge Roy Bean's "Law West of the Pecos." Along the midway, Frontier Centennial-goers could also find other western-themed

The barber shop was among the old and weather-beaten false-front buildings that ran along the Frontier Centennial's midway, Fort Worth, Texas, 1936. Courtesy, *Fort Worth Star-Telegram* Collection, Special Collections, The University of Texas at Arlington Libraries.

amusements such as a "tintype" photo studio, wax museum, old-time leather shop, tonsorial parlor, and shooting galleries.[90] For meals, centennial visitors ate at The Chuck Wagon, an eatery designed to look like a row of prairie schooners.[91]

Although the Frontier Centennial grounds conflated numerous times and places and architectural styles in the history of Texas and the American West, its allusion to "authenticity" was intended to produce a sense of nostalgia for the mythic West—a West that most Americans knew well and of which Fort Worth claimed to be a part. Still, little remained in the physical layout of the centennial grounds to connect Fort Worth and the mythic West. Ironically, the distancing of the physical layout from Fort Worth by omitting structures such as a reproduction of the military outpost of the city's namesake coincided with a greater connection of Fort Worth to the Frontier Centennial. For example, as early as April 1936 the letterhead for centennial correspondence as

Aerial view of the Frontier Centennial Grounds, Fort Worth, Texas, 1936. The W-shaped midway was designed to pull visitors to each of the main entertainment venues. Courtesy, Fort Worth Frontier Centennial, Special Collections, The University of Texas at Arlington Libraries.

well as subsequent promotional material now carried the title "Fort Worth Frontier Centennial"[92] The change in title reflects the culmination of a process that altered the purpose of Fort Worth's celebration of the state centennial from commemorating the state's livestock industry to an exercise in civic boostering. When President Franklin Delano Roosevelt visited Dallas to inaugurate the state's centennial celebration, Fort Worth civic leaders found an opportunity to validate their own centennial offering.[93] On June 12, civic leaders arranged for the president to make a stop in Fort Worth. To ensure that the president would receive a "patriotic and loyal welcome," Mayor Van Zandt Jarvis declared June 12 a holiday beginning at 1 pm and dubbed it "Fort Worth and West Texas President's Day."[94]

After arriving at the Texas and Pacific Station, Roosevelt's entourage headed north through the city lined with flag-waving Fort Worthians to Marine Park, where the president gave a speech.

Following Roosevelt's remarks, the presidential motorcade moved south to the centennial grounds touted as "Fort Worth's No. 1 pride."[95] During the five-minute stop, the president and Mrs. Roosevelt met the architect of the new stock show facilities Joe Pelich and his wife. Afterward, Amon Carter approached the president's limousine and stood next to the seated Roosevelt, pointing out the four major temporary centennial buildings still under construction. Reportedly, Roosevelt responded to Carter's boostering with an enthusiastic "wonderful."[96] Like pioneer societies that sought legalization through the attendance of celebrities at their annual meetings, Fort Worth civic leaders likely viewed Roosevelt's visit as a means to validate Fort Worth's western identity through the affirmation of the Frontier Centennial grounds by the President of the United States.[97]

Together, the ramshackle buildings of the Sunset Trail, the unique Circus Building, the exotic Casa Mañana with its round stage and moat, and the modern design of the new stock show buildings must have constituted a compelling spectacle for Frontier Centennial-goers. Although the group of structures seemed otherworldly, their form and organization were precisely planned to convey meaning in the present. City fathers intentionally juxtaposed the structures of the past with those of the present to convey the city's progressive and modern image. Moving beyond the itemized themed spaces of world's fairs, Rose sought to create in totality the mythic West. Rose tapped deeply meaningful symbolism to create, with a sense of nostalgia, a historic Texas and Old West, without any overt reference to the past. By conflating diversely different times and places, Rose sought to sell an easily recognizable and consumable mythic West and, in the process, placed Fort Worth within the nation's epic frontier past in the minds of centennial-goers.

EPILOGUE

The turnstiles counted nearly one million visitors to the Frontier Centennial grounds during the summer and fall of 1936. Attracting guests from around the nation, the celebration played host to dozens of dignitaries and celebrities. Notable political attendees included Vice President John Nance Garner and his wife; director of the FBI J. Edgar Hoover; Texas governor James Allred; Texas senator Tom Connally; and Florida governor Dave Sholtz. Other celebrities to attend included Ernest Hemingway, former heavyweight boxing champ Max Baer, and Broadway producers Earl Carroll and George White.[1] MGM studios also took an interest in the Frontier Centennial and sent a film crew to Fort Worth to film *Casa Mañana*.[2] In addition, audiences around the nation experienced the Frontier Centennial vicariously through a number of coast-to-coast broadcasts of *Casa Mañana* and *The Last Frontier*.[3]

During its four-month run, the Frontier Centennial operated with only a few major setbacks. Behind the scenes, centennial planners struggled against a chronic lack of capital. Perhaps more disconcerting, the design of the Circus Building, one of Johnson's architectural wonders, reduced *Jumbo*, one of the three major entertainment attractions, to a financial failure. The building suffered from a lack of air conditioning or even proper ventilation. Although *Jumbo* played mostly evening performances, the sweltering summer heat concentrated under the conical ceiling of the Circus Building made viewing the show unbearable for audiences.

Hoping to solve the problem, planners pared down the length of the show by half and installed water-cooled fans, all to no avail. To boost ailing profit margins, Frontier Centennial planners even abated their Jim Crow policies and began admitting African Americans to *Jumbo.*[4]

As anticipated, even during the height of the religious protest over the sexual content of Frontier Centennial promotional materials, visitors to the celebration found presentations of the female form in Rose's productions, including Rand's performance of the bubble dance at the Casa Mañana and her Nude Ranch, innocuous. Frontier Centennial planners prepared for the worst when J. Frank Norris appeared on the centennial grounds unannounced, after returning from his summertime evangelist travels. Rose used several methods of chicanery, hoping to divert the preacher's attention from Rand's performance. Norris surprised the press after his visit when he announced, "My hat is off to Amon Carter and his associates. They've done a real job."[5] Although the Tarrant County Baptist Association and other religious leaders continued to object to Frontier Centennial nudity, these complaints—unlike the earlier religious protests against the celebration's promotional materials—went unheeded.[6]

Similar to the world's fairs of the era, in terms of revenue and attendance, the Frontier Centennial failed to meet the high expectations of civic leaders and city boosters. The celebration lost $97,000 and brought in less than one-fourth the number expected to attend.[7] Despite the dismal figures, centennial planners and civic boosters judged it an unmitigated success. As a vehicle for civic promotion, the celebration achieved its aims. As William Monnig explained to the unpaid bond holders following the celebration, "the Fort Worth Frontier Centennial was worth all it cost to Fort Worth, in the advertising it gave the city, the favorable impression made upon visitors, and the business activity for which it was responsible, estimated at approximately $5,000,000."[8]

Amon Carter shared Monnig's assessment of the success of the exposition in promoting Fort Worth and gave much of the recognition to Billy Rose. In a farewell telegram to Rose, Carter wrote, "You did a magnificent job in the creation of our Frontier Centennial. I appreciate it and I feel that everyone intimately connected with the enterprise feels the same way. It has been an outstanding success. I think in advertising value alone it has been worth to Fort Worth all its cost. . . . I regard it as the biggest and best thing Fort Worth ever has done and no little of the credit goes to you, for without you and the magnificent shows you created none of this value could have been obtained." Monnig's and Carter's comments reflect the extent to which the Texas Frontier Centennial had become Fort Worth's Frontier Centennial after the arrival of Billy Rose.[9]

For those associated with the West Texas Chamber of Commerce, the decision to promote West Texas at the Frontier Centennial rather than the central exposition in Dallas with the "All Resource, All Community" exhibit represented a shrewd decision. The West Texas Chamber of Commerce estimated that more than 700,000 fairgoers visited the exhibit during the celebration, exceeding the number who visited the West Texas agricultural exhibit in Dallas by a factor of ten. Based upon the exposure the region received at the Frontier Centennial, officials with the West Texas Chamber of Commerce considered making the exhibit a permanent part of the Southwestern Exposition and Fat Stock Show, a move that would further strengthen the economic and cultural ties between Fort Worth and West Texas.[10]

Rose returned to Fort Worth for an encore in 1937. Billed as the Fort Worth Frontier Fiesta, the second run of the Frontier Centennial promised visitors new and more exciting entertainment offerings. Retrofitting expositions for a second year to help make up for first-year losses had become standard practice among world's fair host cities. Dallas also announced it would host the Greater Texas and Pan American Exposition in 1937. Continuing to promote the Dallas/Fort Worth rivalry, Rose told the press, "We'll be all-American, not Pan-American."[11] Rose's persistent hostility toward Dallas did not reflect the tone struck by the new management of the Frontier Fiesta. In April 1937, James F. Pollock, who replaced John B. Davis as general manager, began a dialogue with the officials of the Pan American Exposition, suggesting the two cities work together in promoting special days, promising "that Fort Worth, officially and generally, will enter wholeheartedly into this new relationship, which cannot but result advantageously to both cities." Officials of the Pan American Exposition responded favorably and sought an opportunity for officials of the two expositions to meet.[12]

For the most part, the Frontier Fiesta lacked the western focus and grandeur of Texas patriotism inherent in the centennial celebration of the previous year. Rose brought back many of the same personnel who shaped the Frontier Centennial such as John Murray Anderson, Albert Johnson, and costume designer Raoul Pène du Bois. Personalities such as Everett Marshall and Paul Whiteman also returned.[13] Although advertising materials continued to promote the Sunset Trail, claiming "it's a hairy-chested he-man's town of the Texas frontier" which looked "more like the Old West than the pioneers knew," Rose did away with his musical Wild West show *The Last Frontier*.[14] The Rodeo Building now housed a circus-type attraction called "Flirting with Death." On the grounds where Sally Rand's Nude Ranch once stood, seventy-two hackberry trees ornamented with ten thousand twinkling lights provided a stage for "Firefly Garden" featuring performances from the Salici Marionettes.[15]

Although Sally Rand and her Nude Ranch no longer graced the grounds, the issue of sex appeal and nudity at the Frontier Fiesta remained pertinent for city officials. Prior to the 1936 celebration, image- and heritage-conscious religious leaders and club women convinced Rose and civic leaders to curtail overt depictions of nudity in promotional materials. During the celebration itself, civic leaders turned a blind eye to centennial nudity. However, Frontier Fiesta nudity now came under scrutiny. To boost ailing revenue at the Pioneer Palace, Billy Rose hired Hinda Wassau, who performed a number titled "The Evolution of the Strip-Tease." Initially, the City Council passed a resolution condemning the act and later threatened to stop the number entirely. Defying the City Council's censure, Wassau continued to perform her dance unaltered. Eventually, however, she bowed to the council's wishes performing a more modest version of the dance.[16]

As with the Frontier Centennial, *Casa Mañana* remained the premier attraction of the Frontier Fiesta. For the new *Casa Mañana*, Rose drew upon scenes from four popular literary works. These included *Gone with the Wind*, *Wake Up and Live*, *Lost Horizon*, and *It Can't Happen Here*. Without Sally Rand to draw crowds, Rose counted on more elaborate costuming and stage designs to attract audiences. For example, the scenes from *Gone with the Wind* were performed before a façade of an antebellum mansion 200 feet across and three stories tall. As the stage rotated to the next scene, the mansion burst into flames.[17] Given the lengths to which the Board of Control went to omit any references to the South or the Confederacy at the Frontier Centennial, Rose's selection of *Gone with the Wind*, a novel romanticizing the Old South, is interesting and perhaps suggests that the City Council, who approved Rose's selections, did not consider the Frontier Fiesta as important a vehicle for civic identity as the Frontier Centennial.

Primarily through the participation of Billy Rose, the Frontier Centennial would play a role in shaping the entertainment content of several Depression Era world's fairs. In fall 1936, the Great Lakes Exposition held in Cleveland was finishing its first year, and both attendance and income fell well below expectation. Looking to boost revenue during the fair's second year, the general manager, Lincoln Dickey, traveled to Fort Worth to attend the Frontier Centennial hoping to generate ideas for revamping the fair's entertainment offerings. After seeing *Casa Mañana*, Dickey believed Rose to be the person to boost the exposition's appeal.[18] During a visit to Cleveland, Rose pitched an idea for an outdoor aquatic spectacle featuring divers, swimmers, and a chorus he would call *Aquacade*. Officials agreed to pay Rose $100,000 to produce the show for the exposition's 1937 season. To create *Aquacade*, Rose called on John Murray Anderson, Albert Johnson, and Ned Alvord to promote the show.[19]

Rose borrowed heavily from staging concepts and musical numbers he developed for both the 1936 and 1937 seasons of *Casa*

Mañana and spent much of 1937 traveling between his shows in Fort Worth and Cleveland. Similar to the Casa Mañana stage, the stage for *Aquacade* revolved and could slide both forward and backward to reveal a pool of water between the stage and guests. Rose also included tables for dining customers. Unlike that of the Casa Mañana, *Aquacade*'s stage rested on two floating barges anchored to the shore of Lake Erie. *Aquacade* often played to sold-out crowds, and thanks to good weather it contributed significantly to aiding the Great Lakes Exposition end its second season in the black.[20]

Following the conclusion of his engagements with *Aquacade* and *Casa Mañana*, Rose set his sights on the New York World's Fair planned for 1939. In summer 1936, the planners of the exposition sent a fourteen-person delegation to Fort Worth to inspect the Frontier Centennial.[21] However, when Rose approached New York planners, they initially rejected his proposals for a show at the world's fair, believing his brand of entertainment too undignified for what was perceived to be a cultural event. Undaunted, Rose appealed to the vanity of fair president Grover Whalen by producing a show for the new Casa Mañana in New York City titled *Let's Play Fair*. The revue told the story of Whalen's search for talent to exhibit at the world's fair. After Whalen viewed the production, he contracted Rose to produce a show in the New York State Amphitheater.[22]

In Fort Worth, the Frontier Centennial and the accompanying Stock Show facilities initially brought few changes to the Southwestern Exposition and Fat Stock Show. For the following year's show, the stock show Executive Committee voted to continue holding the exposition at the old stockyard facilities. After learning of the decision, Amon Carter sent a scathing letter to the president of the stock show and Fort Worth mayor Van Zandt Jarvis. Carter bitterly protested the decision. Providing a detailed recitation of the events that led to the construction of the new facilities, including the arguments he and Van Zandt Jarvis both made to convince Fort Worth citizens to vote for stock show bonds, Carter asked, "How do you suppose the public regards our pleas that the Show could not long survive in the old quarters; that unless given larger ones it would gradually die? Or, what of our claims that unless we did something worthwhile our friends across the river would absorb our Stock Show. . . . To say the position in which the committee has placed all of us is awkward and embarrassing is to use terms that do not adequately depict the situation as I see it."[23]

Notwithstanding Carter's pleas, the stock show remained on the North Side for another six years. As the result of a flash flood down Marine Creek damaging the stockyards facilities and the overwhelming demand for livestock to support American military action in World War II, stock show officials canceled the 1943 show.[24] The following year, lingering damage to the stockyards forced officials the hold all stock show events at the new facilities. For several years, the stock show was held there, and the success of these shows demonstrated to the Stock Show Association that the proximity of rail lines to the facilities was no longer essential for livestock transportation to the show. In 1948, some twelve years after the Frontier Centennial, the Fort Worth City Council named the centennial exposition grounds as the permanent home of the Southwestern Exposition and Fat Stock Show.[25]

More than simply altering the location of the stock show, for Fort Worthians the Frontier Centennial has become a golden era in the history of the city. Recording her memory shortly after the celebration, Ella Daggett—sister of Mary Daggett Lake and amateur Fort Worth historian and head of the Women's Division's Historical Research Committee—preferred to remember the Frontier Centennial as "the Cinderella of Centennial plans" or a bride to whom Billy Rose whispered, "Be different, my dear, and be gay. . . . Different and Gay!" As a bride, Daggett explained, the celebration needed "Something Old, Something New, Something Borrowed, Something Blue."[26] Escorting readers through a nostalgic tour of the centennial grounds, Daggett described the Sunset Trail, the Circus Building, the Will Rogers display in the West Texas Chamber of Commerce Building, and the Casa Mañana as meeting the marital requirements. Sharing Daggett's longing for the summer of '36, *Fort Worth-Star Telegram* reporter E. Clyde Whitlock noted on the celebration's tenth anniversary that "To this day those who lived here then talk about it with wistful nostalgia and a far-away look in their eyes."[27]

By the time Fort Worth celebrated Fiesta-Cade, its own centennial celebration, in 1949, the Frontier Centennial had become memorialized as a defining feature in Fort Worth's history. A promotional pamphlet placed Fiesta-Cade's commemoration of the Frontier Centennial alongside its celebration of the founding of Fort Worth, the coming of the railroad, the cattle drives, and Fort Worth's participation in World War I and announced, "The memory of Fort Worth's thrilling Casa Mañana show of 1936 conceived by Billy Rose will be revived by a re-enactment of Fort Worth's theme song, 'The Night Is Young and You're So Beautiful.'"[28]

Others did not share the view that the Frontier Centennial should occupy a center space in the glories of Texas or Fort Worth history. As deliberations began for the celebration of Fort Worth's centennial, some preferred to forget the Frontier Centennial and the blatant use of sex for its promotion and shows. Dr. Kathryn Garrett of the Fort Worth and Tarrant County Historical Society exclaimed, "Fort Worth doesn't want to be disgraced as Texas was in 1936. That year we had posters out all over the State of a modern cowgirl with very few clothes on. . . . We had those, instead of the romantic figures of conquistadores with flowing capes to advertise the one hundredth birthday of Texas."[29] Writing a history of the Women's Club, a year before the Fiesta-Cade, Elizabeth Miller shared Garrett's assessment of the Frontier Centennial. Miller described Fort Worth's centennial year as "The Year of Great Foolishness," pointing out that "It is interesting to recall the lively discussions as to what style of cotton dresses would be most suitable for the Women's Division to wear when one realizes that nobody noticed the women who wore dresses."[30]

Although the Fiesta-Cade remained commemorative in nature and proceeded without sex appeal, throughout the remainder of the twentieth and into the twenty-first century Fort

Worthians remembered the Frontier Centennial primarily as the year Billy Rose brought showgirls and Sally Rand to Fort Worth and made the city the entertainment capital of the Southwest. Capturing this sentiment, *Fort Worth Star-Telegram* columnist Jack Gordon quoted John Murray Anderson on the show's forty-fifth anniversary as saying, "Not since the days of Nero has such a show been put together."[31] Two factors helped fortify this memory in the public's consciousness. Because of the temporary construction of the Frontier Centennial grounds, by the celebration's twentieth anniversary the only physical reminders of the Frontier Centennial included the dilapidated ruins of the Pioneer Palace and the skeletal machinery of the Casa Mañana's revolving stage.[32] In 1958, the City Council sponsored the construction of a theater-in-the-round on the old Frontier Centennial grounds. Becoming a living monument to the pomp and splendor of Billy Rose's revue featuring hundreds of showgirls and Sally Rand, the theater was dubbed Casa Mañana.[33] A photograph published in the *Fort Worth Star-Telegram* on the twenty-fifth anniversary of the Frontier Centennial, two years after the opening of the new Casa Mañana, illustrates how the new venue fortified civic memories of the old centennial revue. Over the caption "In 1936, an Office Was Here," the paper published a photograph of James F. Pollock, former board member of the Frontier Centennial and general manager of the Frontier Fiesta, pretending to dictate a letter to Carly de Onis, a showgirl at the new Casa Mañana, with the new theater in the distance. According to the caption under the photo, the image was meant "To link the past with the present."[34]

The holding of showgirl reunions and published showgirl accounts also strongly linked the memory of the Frontier Centennial with showgirls and sex appeal. Although Fort Worth dailies reminded readers of the anniversary of the Frontier Centennial, they also reported on reunions held for women who worked as showgirls in *Casa Mañana* in 1936. For example, in 1981, on the forty-fifth anniversary of the Frontier Centennial, the Fort Worth Hyatt Regency Hotel hosted a cocktail party for showgirls and dancers from *Casa Mañana*.[35] Former showgirl Mrs. Jack T.

Homes also hosted a reunion for former dancers at her home.[36] As recently as 2001, the *Fort Worth Star-Telegram* published stories on the lives of several local women who worked as showgirls in the 1936 revue.[37] Reinforcing the public memory of the Frontier Centennial, popular histories of the celebration have also emphasized the importance of Billy Rose, *Casa Mañana*, and showgirls.

Perhaps more significant than showgirls and sex appeal are the ways in which the Frontier Centennial helped mold and cement its host city's identity as an urban center in the modern American West. In the early twentieth century, civic leaders and city boosters began shifting the civic memory of Fort Worth from a city of the Old South to an urban center born out of America's western frontier. Civic leaders found in the western narrative of national progress and development a more usable history upon which to build Fort Worth's economy. The city's annual livestock show provided city leaders a valuable vehicle to reinforce their interpretation of the past. At a time in which Americans consumed western-themed films and literature in great quantities, the western theming of the stock show also ensured the event's financial success. As the power of the city's meatpacking interests waned, stock show officials found a willing partner in the show's host city—a move further validating the city's western heritage and culture. Concomitant with Fort Worth's growing western identity, civic leaders and boosters also began developing an image of modernity. Together, Fort Worth's embrace of a western heritage and projected image as a modern metropolis provided a unique identity to distinguish itself from Dallas.

The celebration of the state's centennial year provided Fort Worth an opportunity to further establish itself as a western and modern place. Although the stock show offered Fort Worth a link to ranching in the West, the stockyards appeared increasingly out of step with Fort Worth's pursuit of modernity. Cramped, out-of-date facilities limiting the show's ability to grow prompted civic leaders and city boosters to seek both state centennial funds and New Deal funds to host the state's celebration of the livestock industry including the construction of modern livestock facilities for the city's stock show. In the push for new livestock facilities, some members of the City Council and city boosters believed removing the show to more appealing grounds to be essential to the repackaging of Fort Worth's livestock industry and western identity—a move hotly contested by North Side residents. Thus, the struggle to move the stock show facilities to a new location had important ramifications for Fort Worth identity and image. That the stock show through its new location and facilities became a member of Fort Worth's modern landscape remains an important legacy of Fort Worth's centennial celebration.

After claiming the funds for constructing new stock show facilities on the west side of Fort Worth, centennial planners announced the celebration's frontier theme. Hosting a western-themed celebration achieved two ends. First, it reinforced Fort Worth western memory and identity. Second, centennial planners believed a western-themed celebration sufficiently enticing to attract tourists from around the state and nation, ensuring the financial success of the celebration. Thus, the celebration would become a boon for the city's depressed economy. Initially, centennial plans revolved around celebrating the frontier through the recreation of an "authentic" and "living" frontier town akin to what Americans experienced only in the movies. To further validate Fort Worth's connection to the American West, centennial planners reached out to West Texas, its economic hinterland, as the subject of commemoration. For the construction of the celebration's primary attraction, the recreation of an authentic frontier settlement, civic leaders stipulated that the designs be based on historic photographs of early West Texas settlements. The decision to commemorate West Texas's frontier heritage reveals the extent to which Fort Worth was as beholden to its hinterland for its economic prosperity as it was for its western culture and identity.

Frontier Centennial planners would ultimately find the standards of historical authenticity nettlesome. As the Women's Division worked to develop historical attractions based upon the varieties of Texas heritage, centennial planners found themselves in a position to accept or reject ideas based upon their conceptions of the state's frontier history. As a result of the city's rejection of its Southern heritage, centennial planners omitted attractions intended to commemorate the Old South, the Confederacy, or African Americans. Centennial planners also chose to deemphasize the place of non-white historical participants in commemorating the state's past. In this way they embraced their own versions of a mythic Texas West. At the same time, they embraced the Women's Division's suggestion to include a recreation of the original Fort Worth military outpost. The inclusion of the old Fort Worth represented the first step toward making the centennial festivities a celebration boosting Fort Worth and West Texas only.

Fearing historical exhibits alone would fail to attract a sufficient number of visitors, centennial planners sought a western showman capable of producing a spectacle. What they found was an eastern showman who offered them a devil's bargain. Billy Rose cared little for history, authenticity, or commemoration, the primary impetus for the celebration, but promised to make a spectacle that in the process would elevate Fort Worth's profile in the nation. While Amon Carter and others salivated over Rose's penchant for boosterism, Rose's direction cost the celebration its commemorative soul. It also forced Fort Worthians to consider the role women would play in modern Fort Worth. In the planning of the Frontier Centennial, the Women's Division played an essential role, working to preserve Fort Worth's history and culture, promote education, and boost and beautify the city through grassroots advertising and city cleanup efforts. Rose viewed women in terms of their ability to attract audiences and placed a premium on beauty and skin. While Fort Worthians embraced public showgirl auditions and beauty competitions, both acceptable presentations of the female form, some found the subsequent use of overt sexuality in the promotion of the celebration and the announcement of Sally Rand's Nude Ranch disconcerting. Those who protested believed the sexualized depictions of women an insult to Fort Worth's western heritage and threat to its progressive and modern identity. To prevent a boycott, Rose and Frontier Centennial planners brought the depiction of women, including Sally Rand, into acceptable bounds of American society.

Unrestrained by authenticity or historical accuracy, Rose freely drew upon prevailing concepts of the mythic West in the preparation of the centennial grounds. Sampling from standardized plots that had become ritualized on film and in literature, Rose created a western vision centennial-goers immediately recognized and that appealed to their nostalgia. In his creation of the Frontier Centennial grounds, Rose drew upon principles used in modern theme parks. As long as fairgoers are presented with the illusion of the historic or authentic, they accept themed spaces that conflate historic times and places. Taken as a whole, the Frontier Centennial grounds also reinforced both the city's western identity and its image of modernity. By placing the recreated frontier village next to the newly constructed modern livestock facilities, centennial planners physically linked the city's western heritage with its modern development, suggesting to visitors an image of progress.

The tandem themes of the West and modernity so carefully articulated during the Frontier Centennial remain central to Fort Worth's urban identity and image. One reason Amon Carter and others hailed the celebration as the "biggest and best thing Fort Worth ever has done" is because it successfully expressed these themes in the minds of those who attended. Since the centennial year, Fort Worth civic leaders and boosters have continued to maintain a balance between its small-town western heritage and modernity and growth. Fort Worth's continued effort to pursue an image of modernity while retaining a western heritage during the twentieth and twenty-first centuries is reflected in its historiography. For his study of Fort Worth's urban growth through the 1950s, Robert H. Talbert titled his work *Cowtown-Metropolis.*[38] Later, Caleb Pritle's study *Fort Worth: The Civilized West* juxtaposed a photograph of Fort Worth's 1980 skyline with an image of a string of false-front buildings connoting the Old West on its front cover.[39] In perhaps the most recent example, Ty Cashion labeled his survey of the city's history *The New Frontier: A Contemporary History of Fort Worth & Tarrant County.*[40]

Following the Frontier Centennial, the Fort Worth Chamber of Commerce and Fort Worth companies continued, for the next twenty years, to commission artwork placing pioneers and prairie schooners in the midst of modern skyscrapers and oil refineries with planes, trains, and automobiles in the distance.[41] Believing "Cowtown" to be passé, civic leaders worked to bolster a "Nowtown" image during the mid-1950s. They sought to revitalize the city's downtown area and its modern identity by hiring Victor Gruen, famed designer of retail space turned city planner, to apply his ultramodern concepts to downtown Fort Worth. In his plan "A Greater Fort Worth Tomorrow," Gruen suggested an automobile-free, pedestrian space where citizens worked, shopped, and lived with large pedestrian thoroughfares instead of streets. Unable to obtain sufficient civic support, the plan fell by the wayside.[42]

By the late 1970s, Fort Worth, with the aid of Sid Richardson Bass, began to develop its modern and western image through the revitalization of downtown Fort Worth. The revitalization of the city began around reconstructing two square blocks that would become known as Sundance Square, named after The Sundance Kid, the infamous outlaw who reputedly lived in the area. Subsequently, a number of high-end western-themed boutiques, art galleries, and restaurants lined Sundance Square.[43] Simultaneously, the restoration and redevelopment of the stockyards as a tourist destination in the mid-1970s bolstered the city's western heritage.[44] The purchase of the Van Zandt site in 1936 paved the way for the creation of Fort Worth's cultural district, which speaks to Fort Worth's western heritage with museums such as the Amon Carter Museum, the Cowgirl Hall of Fame, and the Cattle Raisers Museum, but also its modern identity with the Modern Art Museum of Fort Worth, affectionately known as The Modern.[45] Bridging the gap between Fort Worth's western and modern identities, the Amon Carter Museum, which originally housed Carter's collection of western art, recently broadened its name to the Amon Carter Museum of American Art. The press release that offered a justification for the name change quoted from the museum's first director, Mitchell A. Wilder, who stated that he "believed the history of American art could be interpreted as the history of artists working on successive frontiers, both geographic and artistic."[46] Today, western icons and modern images freely comingle in museums and on cab tops, police cars, and billboards in contemporary Fort Worth, declaring a western urban identity refined and reflected in the modern landscape—a legacy of the Frontier Centennial.

NOTES

Introduction

1. "Route Impulse Will Travel to Open Frontier Show," *Fort Worth Star-Telegram*, July 17, 1936, 1. Unless otherwise noted, all references to the *Fort Worth Star-Telegram* come from the morning edition. Opening day brought twenty-five thousand visitors to the Frontier Centennial, see Jan Jones, *Billy Rose Presents . . . Casa Mañana* (Fort Worth: Texas Christian University Press, 1999), 76, 77.
2. For example, see Laura Hernández-Ehrisman, *Inventing the Fiesta City: Heritage and Carnival in San Antonio* (Albuquerque: University of New Mexico Press, 2008).
3. See Terry G. Jordan, *Trails to Texas: Southern Roots of Western Cattle Ranching* (Lincoln: University of Nebraska Press, 1981).
4. Oliver Knight, *Fort Worth: Outpost on the Trinity* (Norman: University of Oklahoma Press, 1953), 46–58. Michael Q. Hooks estimated that 75 percent of Fort Worth's early boosters came from the South. See Hooks, "The Role of Promoters in Urban Rivalry: The Dallas-Fort Worth Experience, 1870–1910," *Red River Valley Historical Review* 7, no. 2 (Spring 1982): 5.
5. Because of the changes in topography, vegetation, and climate, Walter Prescott Webb suggested, the 98th parallel represented the dividing line between the eastern and western United States. See Webb, *The Great Plains* (1931; repr., New York: Ginn and Company, 1959).
6. Glen Sample Ely, *Where the West Begins: Debating Texas Identity* (Lubbock: Texas Tech University Press, 2011), 9, 11–12.
7. For a review of Texas historiography see Ely, *Where the West Begins*, 5–7; Walter L. Buenger and Robert A. Calvert, "The Shelf Life of Truth in Texas," in *Texas Through Time: Evolving Interpretations*, ed. Walter L. Buenger and Robert A. Calvert (College Station: Texas A&M University Press, 1991), ix–xxxv. Buenger claimed that Texas was "a southern place—with a Texas twist." Walter L. Buenger, "Texas and

the South," *Southwestern Historical Quarterly* 103, no. 3 (January 2000): 309.

8. See Noa Gedi and Yigal Elam, "Collective Memory—What Is It?" *History & Memory* 8, no. 1 (Spring/Summer 1996): 30–50; Wulf Kansteiner, "Finding Meaning in Memory: A Methodological Critique of Collective Memory Studies," *History and Theory* 41, no. 2 (May 2002): 179–97; and Alon Confino, "Collective Memory and Cultural History: Problems of Method," *The American Historical Review* 102, no. 5 (December 1997): 1386–1403.
9. Gregg Cantrell, "The Bones of Stephen F. Austin: History and Memory in Progressive-Era Texas," *Southwestern Historical Quarterly* 108, no. 2 (October 2004): 148.
10. Ibid., 177.
11. Walter L. Buenger, *The Path to a Modern South: Northeast Texas between Reconstruction and the Great Depression* (Austin: University of Texas Press, 2001), 258. See also Jacob W. Olmstead, "'Un-southern': Buffalo Bill, the Texas State Centennial, and Texas's Western Turn," *Southwestern Historical Quarterly* 122, no. 4 (April 2019): 371–94.
12. See Robert H. Talbert, *Cowtown-Metropolis: Case Study of a City's Growth and Structure* (Fort Worth: Leo Potishman Foundation, Texas Christian University, 1956), 2–7.
13. Carl Abbott, *Boosters and Businessmen: Popular Economic Thought and Urban Growth in the Antebellum Middle West* (Westport, CT: Greenwood Press, 1981), 4; Buenger, *The Path to a Modern South*, 258.
14. Patricia Nelson Limerick, *The Legacy of Conquest: The Unbroken Past of the American West* (New York: W.W. Norton, 1987), 88–89.
15. Diamond Jubilee Committee, *Diamond Jubilee*, (Fort Worth: Claud Gross Co., 1923), and Diamond Jubilee Dinner [Program], 1923, Box 89, Folder "Fort Worth Diamond Jubilee Celebration, Amon G. Carter Papers, Special Collections, Mary Couts Burnett Library, Texas Christian University, Fort Worth, Texas. (TCU/SC).
16. W. Fitzhugh Brundage, "No Deed but Memory," in *Where These Memories Grow: History, Memory, and Southern Identity*, ed. W. Fitzhugh Brundage, 1–28 (Chapel Hill: University of North Carolina Press, 2000), 9.
17. Frank E. Manning, "Cosmos and Chaos: Celebration in the Modern World," in *The Celebration of Society: Perspectives on Contemporary Cultural Performance*, ed. Frank E. Manning (Bowling Green, OH: Bowling Green University Popular Press, 1983), 4, 7, 11 (quotation).
18. For recent discussions of the construction of public image in the West, see Bonnie Christensen, *Red Lodge and the Mythic West: Coal Miners to Cowboys* (Lawrence: University Press of Kansas, 2002), xiv–xv; and Alicia Barber, *Reno's Big Gamble: Image and Reputation in the Biggest*

Little City (Lawrence: University Press of Kansas, 2008), 5–6.

19. Hernández-Ehrisman, *Inventing the Fiesta City*, 12–13. Chris Wilson, *The Myth of Santa Fe: Creating a Modern Regional Tradition* (Albuquerque: University of New Mexico Press, 1997), 7–8 (quotation).
20. Phoebe S. Kropp, *California Vieja: Culture and Memory in a Modern American Place* (Berkeley: University of California Press, 2006), 1.
21. Christensen, *Red Lodge and the Mythic West*, xii–xiii.
22. Fort Worth Chamber of Commerce, "Fort Worth, 1929," (no publication data); Fort Worth Chamber of Commerce Papers, Box 21, Folder 45, TCU/SC.
23. See Judith Singer Cohen, *Cowtown Moderne: Art Deco Architecture of Fort Worth, Texas* (College Station: Texas A&M University Press, 1988).
24. Ely, *Where the West Begins*, 3; Michael L. Johnson, *Hunger for the Wild: America's Obsession with the Untamed West* (Lawrence: University Press of Kansas, 2007), 207.
25. Kenneth B. Ragsdale, *Centennial '36: The Year America Discovered Texas* (College Station: Texas A&M University Press, 1987), 208 (1st quotation), 211 (2nd quotation). See also Jerry Flemmons, *Amon: The Life of Amon Carter, Sr. of Texas* (Austin: Jenkins Publishing Company, 1978), 299–301; Caleb Pirtle, *Fort Worth: The Civilized West* (Tulsa, OK: Continental Heritage Press, 1980), 131; Gaylon Polatti, "The Magic City and the Frontier," *Legacies: A History Journal for Dallas and North Central Texas* 11, no. 1 (Spring 1999): 38; Jones, *Billy Rose Presents . . . Casa Mañana*, 16; Ty Cashion, *The New Frontier: A Contemporary History of Fort Worth & Tarrant County* (San Antonio: Historical Publishing Network, 2006), 76, 131.
26. Buenger, "Texas and the South," 312. Western states in general received more funding from New Deal programs than did other states. For a discussion of how federal funding influenced the American West during the Great Depression, see Gerald D. Nash, *The Federal Landscape: An Economic History of the Twentieth Century West* (Tucson: University of Arizona Press, 1999), 21–39; and Richard Lowitt, *The New Deal and the West* (Bloomington: Indiana University Press, 1984).
27. Richard Slotkin, *Gunfighter Nation: The Myth of the Frontier in Twentieth-Century America* (New York: Atheneum, 1992), 5; Robert V. Hine and John Mack Faragher, *The American West: A New Interpretive History* (New Haven: Yale University Press, 2000), 475.
28. Slotkin, *Gunfighter Nation*, 10–11 (quotation on 11).
29. Henry Nash Smith, *Virgin Land: The American West as Symbol and Myth* (Cambridge, MA: Harvard University Press, 1970), 55–61.
30. John G. Cawelti, *The Six-Gun Mystique* (Bowling Green, OH: Bowling Green University Popular Press, 1984), 31.
31. See Richard White, "Frederick Jackson Turner and Buffalo Bill," in

The Frontier in American Culture, ed. James R. Grossman (Berkeley: University Press of California, 1994), 7–9, 11.

32. White, "Frederick Jackson Turner and Buffalo Bill," 27–39.
33. Paul Reddin, *Wild West Shows* (Urbana and Chicago: University of Illinois Press, 1999), 121.
34. For an overview of frontier anxiety beginning in the 1890s, see Johnson, *Hunger for the Wild*, 204–37.
35. Smith, *Virgin Land*, 3–4.
36. Hine and Faragher, *The American West*, 495. See also G. Edward White, *The Eastern Establishment and the Western Experience: The West of Frederic Remington, Theodore Roosevelt, and Owen Wister* (New Haven: Yale University Press, 1968).
37. Cawelti, *The Six-Gun Mystique*, 93; Richard Etulain, "Origins of the Western," *Journal of Popular Culture* 5, no. 4 (1972): 800–801.
38. Kristine Fredriksson, *American Rodeo: From Buffalo Bill to Big Business* (College Station: Texas A&M University Press, 1985), 10.
39. Anne M. Butler, "Selling the Popular Myth," in *The Oxford History of the American West* ed. Clyde A. Milner, Carol A. O'Connor, and Martha A. Sandweiss (New York: Oxford University Press, 1994; paperback edition, 1996), 791.
40. Cawelti, *The Six-Gun Mystique*, 32.
41. Richard W. Etulain, *Western Films: A Brief History* (Manhattan, KS: Sunflower University Press, 1983; second printing, 1988), 3.
42. Don Graham, "Lone Star Cinema: A Century of Texas in the Movies," in *Twentieth-Century Texas: A Social and Cultural History*, ed. John W. Storey and Mary L. Kelly (Denton: University of North Texas Press, 2008), 246–47.
43. Pendleton, Oregon, selected a frontier theme to replace their Fourth of July celebration because of the potential appeal and profits of the Old West. See Renee M. Laegreid, *Riding Pretty: Rodeo Royalty in the American West* (Lincoln: University of Nebraska Press, 2006), 22–23. For a good discussion of how companies have capitalized on the American West in the advertising of their products, see Elliot West, "Selling the Myth: Western Images in Advertising," *Montana: The Magazine of Western History* 46, no. 2 (Summer 1996): 36–49.
44. See David M. Wrobel, *The End of American Exceptionalism: Frontier Anxiety from the Old West to the New Deal* (Lawrence: University Press of Kansas, 1993), 122–42.
45. See Don Graham, *Cowboys and Cadillacs: How Hollywood Looks at Texas* (Austin: Texas Monthly Press, 1983), 109–16.
46. Michael Steiner, "Frontierland as Tomorrowland: Walt Disney and the Architectural Packaging of the Mythic West," *Montana: The Magazine of Western History* 48, no. 1 (Spring 1998): 11. See also John M. Findlay,

Magic Lands: Western Cityscapes and American Culture after 1940 (Berkeley: University of California Press, paperback edition, 1993), 67–69.

47. See Lynn Sally, "Luna Park's Fantasy World and Dreamland's White City: Fire Spectacles at Coney Island as Elemental Performativity," in *The Themed Space: Locating Culture, Nation, and Self*, ed. Scott A. Lukas (Lanham, MD: Lexington Books, 2007), 39–55.
48. David Lowenthal, "The Past as a Theme Park," in *Theme Park Landscapes: Antecedents and Variations*, ed. Terence Young and Robert Riley (Washington, DC: Dumbarton Oaks Research Library, 2002), 11.
49. Terence Young, "Grounding the Myth—Theme Park Landscapes in an Era of Commerce and Nationalism," in Young and Riley, eds., *Theme Park Landscapes*, 4.
50. For studies of Disneyland's western themed environment, see Steiner, "Frontierland as Tomorrowland," 2–17; and Richard Francaviglia, "Walt Disney's Frontierland as an Allegorical Map of the American West," *Western Historical Quarterly* 30, no. 2 (Summer 1999): 155–82.
51. William T. Anderson, "Wall Drug—South Dakota's Tourist Emporium," *American West* 22, no. 2 (March/April 1985): 72–76.
52. Matthew F. Bokovoy, *The San Diego World's Fairs and Southwestern Memory, 1880–1940* (Albuquerque: University of New Mexico Press, 2005), 196–97.
53. Young, "Grounding the Myth," 1.
54. For a treatment of the Frontier Centennial after its opening on July 18, the major productions, and the subsequent seasons as the Frontier Fiesta, see Jones, *Billy Rose Presents . . . Casa Mañana*, especially chapters 5–8. For research addressing the technical achievements of Rose's Casa Mañana, see Annie O. Cleveland and M. Barrett Cleveland, "Fort Worth for Entertainment: Billy Rose's Casa Mañana (1936–1939)," *Theatre Design & Technology* 44, no. 1 (Winter 2008): 25–40. For an interesting discussion of the early radio broadcasts of Rose's *Jumbo*, see Geoffrey Block, "'Bigger Than a Show—Better Than a Circus': The Broadway Musical, Radio, and Billy Rose's *Jumbo*," *The Musical Quarterly* 89, no. 2–3 (Summer–Fall 2006): 164–98.

Chapter 1

1. Ragsdale, *Centennial '36*, 3–4 (quotation on 4). Quote taken from Theodore H. Price, "What Texas Has to Advertise and How to Advertise It," *Commerce and Finance*, November 5, 1923.
2. Robert W. Rydell, *All the World's a Fair: Visions of Empire at American International Expositions, 1876–1916* (Chicago: University of Chicago Press, 1984), 73.
3. Lawrence W. Levine, "American Culture and the Great Depression,"

The Yale Review 74, no. 2 (January 1985): 198.

4. Randolph B. Campbell, *Gone to Texas: A History of the Lone Star State* (New York: Oxford University Press, 2003), 378, 384.
5. Ragsdale, *Centennial '36*, 32.
6. See Robert W. Rydell, *World of Fairs: The Century-of-Progress Expositions* (Chicago: University of Chicago Press, 1993), 8–10 (quotation on 9).
7. Minutes of the Texas Centennial Commission in Session, 2–4.
8. See Proposal Form No. 1, Program of Requirements for the Competition for the Central Exposition of the Texas Centennial, in Minutes of the Texas Centennial Commission, 6.
9. Minutes of the Texas Centennial Commission, 7.
10. Ragsdale, *Centennial '36*, 49–52; Clarence R. Wharton to Amon G. Carter, August 23, 1934, Box 198, Folder 1 "Texas Centennial Commission, 1931–1934," Carter Papers.
11. Ragsdale, *Centennial '36*, 47–49.
12. Studies evaluating the competition for the host city often minimize or omit Fort Worth's bid. See Ragsdale, *Centennial '36*, 46; Jones, *Billy Rose Presents . . . Casa Mañana*, 3–4; Lois Gray, "History of the Fort Worth Frontier Centennial" (MA thesis, Texas Christian University, 1938), 27.
13. James M. North Jr. to S. H. McCarty, June 1, 1934, Box 198, Folder 1 "Texas Centennial Commission, 1931–1934," Carter Papers. Carter served on the Centennial Commission since December 1931 but failed to attend many of the organization's meetings. See Will H. Mayes to Amon G. Carter, June 2, 1934; Secretary of Amon Carter to Will H. Mayes, June 4, 1934; Lowry Martin to Amon Carter, July 13, 1934; and Amon Carter to Lowry Martin, July 14, 1934; Secretary of Mr. Carter to Lowry Martin, July 24, 1934, Box 198, Folder 1 "Texas Centennial Commission, 1931–1934," Carter Papers.
14. Prior to the host city race, James M. North Jr. mentioned the development of a Fort Worth movement to seek a joint Dallas-Fort Worth bid. James M. North Jr. to S. H. McCarty, June 1, 1934. Moreover, commenting on the selection of Dallas as the centennial host city, Mrs. C. C. Peters, vice chairman of the Tarrant County Advisory Board to the Texas Centennial Commission, stated, "I wish, of course, that Fort Worth and Dallas could have made a joint bid." "Exposition in North Texas Seen as Aid to Fort Worth," *Fort Worth Star-Telegram*, September 10, 1934, 2.
15. "Recommendations on Centennial Due," *Fort Worth Star-Telegram*, August 30, 1934, 4.
16. See Fort Worth City Council Meeting Minutes, Office of the City Secretary, Fort Worth, Texas.
17. For a detailed discussion of the selection process, see Ragsdale,

Centennial '36, 54–58.

18. Ragsdale, *Centennial '36*, 58. For a detailed description of the Dallas proposal, see "Dallas Shows Reasons Why This City Should Get Texas Centennial," *Dallas Morning News*, September 7, 1934, Section 2, 1.
19. Minutes of the Texas Centennial Commission, September 7, 1934, 3, Box 198, Folder "Texas Centennial Commission, 1931–1934," Carter Papers; Ragsdale, *Centennial '36*, 58.
20. Minutes of the Texas Centennial Commission, September 8, 1934, 6, Box 198, Folder "Texas Centennial Commission, 1931–1934," Carter Papers.
21. Ragsdale, *Centennial '36*, 58.
22. Minutes of the Texas Centennial Commission, September 8, 1934, 6.
23. Ragsdale, *Centennial '36*, 58.
24. Ragsdale, *Centennial '36*, 59.
25. "Exposition in North Texas Seen as Aid to Fort Worth," *Fort Worth Star-Telegram*, September 10, 1934, 2.
26. Flemmons, *Amon: The Life of Amon Carter*, 299.
27. "Dallas Gets the Centennial," *Fort Worth Star-Telegram*, September 12, 1934, 6.
28. See General and Special Laws of the State of Texas, Forty-Fourth Legislature, Regular Session (Austin, 1935), 1: 427–37; "Centennial Bill Signed by Governor," *Fort Worth Star-Telegram*, May 8, 1935, 1–2.
29. Advisory Board of Texas Historians "Bulletin No. 1," June 10, 1935, 1, Box 2B149, Folder "Reports to Commission of Control for Texas Centennial Celebrations, June 1935–June 1937," James Frank Dobie Papers, Center for American History, University of Texas, Austin, Texas (hereafter cited as CAH).
30. Ragsdale, *Centennial '36*, 98–99. For a more detailed overview of the Advisory Board of Texas Historians, see Jeffery Mason Hancock, "Preservation of Texas Heritage in the 1936 Centennial" (MA thesis, University of Texas, 1963), 17–21.
31. For a history of the early years of the Fort Worth stockyards, see J'Nell L. Pate, *Livestock Legacy: The Fort Worth Stockyards, 1887–1987* (College Station: Texas A&M University Press, 1988), especially chapters 1 and 2.
32. Clay Reynolds, *A Hundred Years of Heroes: A History of the Southwestern Exposition and Livestock Show* (Fort Worth: Texas Christian University Press, 1995), 8–10.
33. Ibid., 10, 26, 33.
34. Ibid., 30–31, 39, 58.
35. Ibid., 23, 45, 50, 54–55, 57.
36. Ibid., uncited quotation on 60.
37. Ibid., 71, 85–56, 92.
38. Talbert, *Cowtown-Metropolis*, 4, 35–37.

39. Pate, *Livestock Legacy*, 121.
40. Reynolds, *A Hundred Years of Heroes*, 84–85, 129.
41. Ibid., 130.
42. Ibid., 129, 141–42.
43. Ibid., 108–9, 142–43, 149–50, 157.
44. Ibid., 18, 28, 42, 68–69, 77 (quotation).
45. Ibid., 105, 136–37, 140.
46. The title "Battle of Cow Pens" played on "Battle of Cowpens" of the American Revolution, which took place in South Carolina on January 17, 1781. See Allan R. Millett and Peter Maslowski, *For the Common Defense: A Military History of the United States of America*, revised and expanded ed. (New York: The Free Press, 1994), 75–76.
47. Reynolds, *A Hundred Years of Heroes*, 68.
48. Ibid., 68, 88, 90 (quotation).
49. Jordan, *Trails to Texas*, 23.
50. Reynolds, *A Hundred Years of Heroes*, 18–19, 31, 40.
51. Ibid., 72.
52. Ibid., 77, 109, 111 (quotation).
53. Etulain, *Western Films*, 3.
54. Reddin, *Wild West Shows*, 181; Fredriksson, *American Rodeo*, 21 (quotation).
55. Reynolds, *A Hundred Years of Heroes*, 87, 111, 118, 131.
56. See Southwestern Exposition and Fat Stock Show, Rodeo and Horse Show, Souvenir Program, 1929, 47, 49; Southwestern Exposition and Fat Stock Show, Rodeo and Horse Show, Souvenir Program, 1934, 45, 47, Southwestern Exposition & Fat Stock Show Programs, Box 1, Fort Worth Public Library Archives (FTWPLA).
57. Southwestern Exposition and Fat Stock Show, Rodeo and Horse Show, Souvenir Program, 1929, 3.
58. Southwestern Exposition and Fat Stock Show, Rodeo and Horse Show, Souvenir Program, 1928, 60, Box 2, "State and Local History," Folder II, 2:14 "Fort Worth Stock Show Rodeo—Programs—1908–1931," Mary Daggett Papers, FTWPLA.
59. Southwestern Exposition and Fat Stock Show, Rodeo and Horse Show, Souvenir Program, 1928, 26.
60. Reynolds, *A Hundred Years of Heroes*, 143, 159 (quotation).
61. Ibid., 157, 162.
62. Ibid., 164 (quotation), 165, 168.
63. Exposition and Fat Stock Show, Rodeo and Horse Show, Souvenir Program, 1936, 7, Southwestern Exposition & Fat Stock Show Programs, Box 1, FTWPLA.
64. Reynolds, *A Hundred Years of Heroes*, 36, 170–72.
65. Ibid., 127.

66. Southwestern Exposition and Fat Stock Show, Rodeo and Horse Show, Souvenir Program, 1935, 30, Box 28, Folder 43 "Research Regarding the Stock Show Around 1935, undated," Clay Reynolds Papers, 1895–2002, Southwest Collection/Special Collections Library, Texas Tech University, Lubbock, Texas (cited hereafter as SWC).
67. "More Pleas Made for Allotment of Centennial Cash," *Dallas Morning News*, October 24, 1934, 3.
68. Amon G. Carter to Harold L. Ickes, May 9, 1935, Box 174, Folder "Southwestern Exposition & Fat Stock Show, 1935," Carter Papers.
69. Harold L. Ickes to Amon G. Carter, May 20, 1935, Box 174, Folder "Southwestern Exposition & Fat Stock Show, 1935," Carter Papers.
70. Amon G. Carter to Van Zandt Jarvis, February 11, 1937, Box 110, Folder "J-Miscellaneous, 1936–1940," Carter Papers.
71. Harold L. Ickes to Amon G. Carter, May 20, 1935.
72. Amon G. Carter to Van Zandt Jarvis, February 11, 1937; see "PWA Grant of $900,000 to be Sought," *Fort Worth Star-Telegram*, May 30, 1935, 1–2.
73. See Advisory Board of Texas Historians "Bulletin No. 2," June 18–19, 1935; and Advisory Board of Texas Historians "Bulletin No. 3," July 1–2, 1935, Box 2B149, Folder "Reports to Commission of Control for Texas Centennial Celebrations, June 1935–June 1937, Dobie Papers. "Texas Centennial Historical Advisors Plan State Survey," *Fort Worth Star-Telegram*, July 2, 1935, 9.
74. Minutes of the meeting of the Advisory Board of Texas Historians, July 8, 1935, 1, Box 2B149, Folder "Reports to Commission of Control for Texas Centennial Celebrations, June 1935–June 1937, Dobie Papers.
75. "Presentation by the City of Fort Worth to The Centennial Advisory Board of Texas Historians," cover, 6, Box 198, Folder "Texas Centennial Commission [Republic of Texas], 1935–1937," Carter Papers.
76. Byron C. Utecht, "Both State Boards Will Co-Operate," *Fort Worth Star-Telegram*, July 9, 1935, 1–2.
77. "Presentation by the City of Fort Worth to The Centennial Advisory Board of Texas Historians," 2 (1st quotation), 3 (2nd quotation).
78. Ibid., 1, 3 (quotation).
79. Ibid., 5.
80. Ibid., 4–5.
81. Ibid., 4, 15, 17–22.
82. See ibid., 4.
83. Byron C. Utecht, "Both State Boards Will Co-Operate," *Fort Worth Star-Telegram*, July 9, 1935, 1–2.
84. Byron C. Utecht, "Huge Livestock Show Is Visioned for Fort Worth," *Fort Worth Star-Telegram*, July 21, 1935, 1–2; James M. North Jr. to Ted Dealey, July 26, 1935, Box 198, Folder "Texas Centennial Commission

[Republic of Texas], 1935–1937," Carter Papers.

85. Byron C. Utecht, "Huge Livestock Show Is Visioned for Fort Worth," *Fort Worth Star-Telegram*, July 21, 1935, 1–2.
86. "Resolution of the Commission of Control for Texas Centennial Celebrations," July 20, 1935, Box 174, Folder "Southwestern Exposition and Fat Stock Show, 1935," Carter Papers.
87. Ragsdale, *Centennial '36*, 77–79.
88. Amon G. Carter to Fritz Lanham, July 12, 1935, Box 198, Folder "Texas Centennial Commission [Republic of Texas], 1935–1937," Carter Papers.
89. Van Zandt Jarvis, Amon G. Carter, John B. Davis, "Application by City of Fort Worth to the United States Centennial Commission for an appropriation," circa July 1935, Box 28, Folder 44 "Research Regarding the Stock Show Around 1936, Undated," Reynolds Papers.
90. William M. Thornton, "$250,000 Is Presented to Fort Worth to Hold 1936 Live Stock Show," *Dallas Morning News*, July 21, 1935, 1, 4.
91. Byron C. Utecht, "Huge Livestock Show Is Visioned for Fort Worth," *Fort Worth Star-Telegram*, July 21, 1935, 1–2.
92. "Dobie Concerned at Allotment of State Commission," *Dallas Morning News*, July 21, 1935, 1, 4.
93. "Advisory Board to Allot Markers for Centennial," *Dallas Morning News*, August 1, 1935, 2.
94. "Vandenberge Deplores Act of Commission," *Victoria Advocate*, July 23, 1935, 1, 3.
95. "Senator Is Indignant," *Dallas Morning News*, July 21, 1935, 4.
96. "More Objections Lodged to Grant for Stock Show," *Dallas Morning News*, July 24, 1935, 3.
97. See "Presentation by the City of Fort Worth to The Centennial Advisory Board of Texas Historians," 3; Amon G. Carter to Fritz Lanham, July 12, 1935, Box 198, Folder "Texas Centennial Commission [Republic of Texas], 1935–1937," (quotation), Carter Papers.
98. William M. Thornton, "$250,000 Is Presented to Fort Worth to Hold 1936 Livestock Show," *Dallas Morning News*, July 21, 1936, 1, 4.
99. William M. Thornton, "More Industries Would Share in Centennial Fund," *Dallas Morning News*, July 23, 1935, 1, 12.
100. James M. North Jr. to Ted Dealey, July 26, 1935, Box 198, Folder "Texas Centennial Commission [Republic of Texas], 1935–1937," Carter Papers.
101. "Tender Hearts in Dallas," *Fort Worth Star-Telegram*, July 28, 1935, "Oil, Editorial, Classifieds," 4.
102. "250,000 For Fort Worth Is Included," *Fort Worth Star-Telegram*, August 18, 1935, 1–2.
103. "Centennial Fund Appeal Is Repeated," *Fort Worth Star-Telegram*,

August 17, 1935, 1–2.

104. "Monnig Will Head Show Bond Drive," *Fort Worth Star-Telegram*, August 17, 1935, 1–2.

105. "Committee for Centennial Stock Show Bonds Named," *Fort Worth Star-Telegram*, August 18, 1935, 1–2.

106. "Many to Speak for Bond," *Fort Worth Star-Telegram*, August 22, 1935, 9.

107. "30,000 Entertained by Magnolia Business Men," *Fort Worth Star-Telegram*, August 31, 1935, 1–2.

108. In a telegram to Harry L. Hopkins, Amon Carter claimed, "Our two main arguments were forty-five percent grants from PWA and opportunity of solving local unemployment problem by giving work directly to two thousand men and a year's employment to every skilled and semi-skilled worker now idle in city." Amon G. Carter to Harry L. Hopkins, September 5, 1935, Box 174, Folder "Southwestern Exposition & Fat Stock Show," Carter Papers.

109. "Organized Labor for Bonds," *Fort Worth Star-Telegram*, August 23, 1935, 9.

110. "Building Council for All of Bonds," *Fort Worth Star-Telegram*, August 30, 1935, 1.

111. See "Bond Election Rallies Set," *Fort Worth Star-Telegram*, August 27, 1935, 9; "4 Rallies for Bonds to Be Held Tonight," *Fort Worth Star-Telegram*, August 29, 1935, 9.

112. "Women to Aid in Drive for Bond Issues," *Fort Worth Star-Telegram*, August 30, 1935, 9, 15.

113. "Tour of Show Sites Is Made," *Fort Worth Star-Telegram*, August 23, 1935, 9.

114. "Urge Decision on Stock Show," *Fort Worth Star-Telegram*, August 27, 1935, 9.

115. "N. Side Opens Drive Tonight," *Fort Worth Star-Telegram*, August 28, 1935, 9.

116. On August 28, 1935, the City Council voted unanimously to adopt a resolution indicating that only after the bond issue successfully passed would the council then hold a special meeting to select a site. See Fort Worth City Council Meeting Minutes, August 28, 1935, 128.

117. "9 Speak at Marine Park Bond Rally," *Fort Worth Star-Telegram*, August 29, 1935, 9; "N. Side Mass Meeting on Bonds Set for Monday," *Fort Worth Star-Telegram*, August 30, 1935, 9.

118. "North Side Asks Council To 'Get on Dotted Line,'" *Fort Worth Star-Telegram*, August 31, 1935, 1–2.

119. "Council to Consider All Show Sites," *Fort Worth Star-Telegram*, August 30, 1935, 1.

120. "Show Bonds Cause Rally Enthusiasm," *Fort Worth Star-Telegram*,

August 28, 1935, 9.

121. "A View All Should Take," *Fort Worth Star-Telegram*, August 29, 1935, 6.
122. "Only Regular Fee Involved If Show Site Option Closed," *Fort Worth Star-Telegram*, August 31, 1935, 3.
123. "Bond Election Votes by Boxes," *Fort Worth Star-Telegram*, September 4, 1935, 2.
124. "Centennial Hall Among 1,908 WPA Projects Refused," *Dallas Morning News*, September 10, 1935, 1, 3.
125. Amon G. Carter to Harry L. Hopkins, September 5, 1935, Box 174, Folder "Southwestern Exposition & Fat Stock Show," Carter Papers.
126. Preston M. Geren to Amon G. Carter, September 9, 1935, Box 174, Folder "Southwestern Exposition & Fat Stock Show," Carter Papers.
127. Harold Ickes to Amon G. Carter, September 27, 1935 and Amon G. Carter to Harold Ickes, September 28, 1935, Box 174, Folder "Southwestern Exposition & Fat Stock Show," Carter Papers.
128. Van Zandt Jarvis and William Monnig to Harold Ickes and Horatio M. Hackett, September 30, 1935; John B. Collier and Jack H. Hott to Harold Ickes and Horatio M. Hackett, September 30, 1935; T. B. Yarbrough to Horatio M. Hackett, October 9, 1935, Box 174, Folder "Southwestern Exposition & Fat Stock Show," Carter Papers.
129. Fort Worth City Council Meeting Minutes, September 23, 1935, 147; Fort Worth City Council, "Resolution," [circa] October 23, 1935, Folder "October 1935," Council Proceedings, FTWPLA.
130. Flemmons, *Amon: The Life of Amon Carter*, 300–301. Unfortunately, a search of the Amon G. Carter Papers turned up no sources documenting the story as told by Flemmons. In a 1937 letter to Van Zandt Jarvis, Carter briefly recounted the campaign to finance the construction of the centennial stock show facilities and speaking of Roosevelt noted, "We went to Washington and found that Secretary Ickes had not approved this part of our program. Some of our friends interceded with the President and obtained his consent." Amon G. Carter to Van Zandt Jarvis, February 11, 1937.
131. Amon G. Carter to Van Zandt Jarvis, February 11, 1937; Fort Worth City Council Meeting Minutes, January 2, 1936, 186–87. For a detailed discussion of the requirements and negotiations for the PWA loan/grant, see Gray, "History of the Fort Worth Frontier Centennial," 29–36.
132. The Centennial Building Site Committee included: T. J. Harrell, William Monnig, Jerome C. Martin, and Arthur Brown. Gray, "History of the Fort Worth Frontier Centennial," 46.
133. For summarized list of sites see Gray, "History of the Fort Worth Frontier Centennial," 50–51.
134. Gray, "History of the Fort Worth Frontier Centennial," 52. Apparently,

the City Secretary's Office maintained a now non-extant file titled "Selection of Site for the Fort Worth Centennial Exposition and Fat Stock Show" containing the petitions.

135. Fort Worth City Council Meeting Minutes, November 8, 1935, 160.
136. Gray, "History of the Fort Worth Frontier Centennial," 54–55.
137. Fort Worth City Council Meeting Minutes, November 13, 1935, 166; Fort Worth City Council Meeting Minutes, November 14, 1935, 167, 168.
138. Fort Worth City Council Meeting Minutes, November 6, 1935, 152.
139. "Possibility of New Site for Show," *Fort Worth Star-Telegram*, November 23, 1935, 1.
140. "Council Will Take Up Show Plant Issue," *Fort Worth Star-Telegram*, November 28, 1935, 9.
141. Baylor B. Brown to W. J. Hammond and Murphy, November 26, 1935, Box 28, Folder 43 "Research Regarding the Stock Show Around 1935, Undated," Reynolds Papers.
142. Fort Worth City Council Meeting Minutes, November 27, 1935, 173.
143. Baylor B. Brown, "Comparison of North Side Site and Van Zandt Site for Centennial Livestock Exposition," November 26, 1935, Box 28 F. 43 "Research Regarding the Stock Show Around 1935, Undated," Reynolds Papers.
144. Ibid.
145. "What We Voted For," *Fort Worth Star-Telegram*, December 9, 1935, 6.
146. See Fort Worth Association of Commerce, promotional pamphlet [no title], 1929; *Fort Worth, 1929* (no publication date), Box 21, Folder 45, Fort Worth Chamber of Commerce Papers, TCU/SC.
147. Fort Worth City Council Meeting Minutes, December 3, 1935, 173.
148. See Fort Worth City Council Meeting Minutes, December 13, 1935, 182; Fort Worth City Council Meeting Minutes, December 18, 1935, 183.
149. In her study of Fort Worth's centennial celebration, written only two years after the celebration transpired, Gray describes the Southwest Exhibition and Fat Stock Show as the "forerunner" of the centennial and devotes a whole chapter to the origins of the stock show. See Gray, "History of the Fort Worth Frontier Centennial," 1–25. Kenneth B. Ragsdale's study of the Texas state centennial devotes two chapters to Fort Worth's centennial but mentions Fort Worth's stock show only once in passing. See Ragsdale, *Centennial '36*, 10. Finally, Jan Jones's book-length study of Fort Worth's centennial and subsequent incarnations fails to mention the Fort Worth stock show. See Jones, *Billy Rose Presents . . . Casa Mañana*.

Chapter 2

1. In June 1935, Judge R. C. Crane, president of the West Texas Historical Association, developed a map defining West Texas for the Advisory Board of Texas Historians. Crane used the 1873 tax exemption status of Texas counties on the frontier to define the eastern border of West Texas. This definition established a dividing line running north to south on approximately the ninety-eighth meridian. See map insert in R. C. Crane Sr., "The Claims of West Texas to Recognition by Historians," *The West Texas Historical Association Year Book* 12 (July 1936): 11–33, map insert 16–17. More recently, scholars have used characteristics such as lack of population and lands devoted to ranching and pasture to define West Texas. According to this paradigm, Fort Worth also lies outside West Texas. See Tom Crum, "West Texas," *The West Texas Historical Association Year Book* 76 (October 2000): 16–32. West Texas historian Glen Ely argues that West Texas begins with the one hundredth meridian, where rainfall drops below twenty inches annually. Ely, *Where the West Begins*, 14, 16. Still others, primarily residents of Fort Worth, persist in defining Fort Worth as a West Texas city. See Mike Cochran and John Lumpkin, *West Texas: A Portrait of Its People and Their Raw and Wondrous Land* (Lubbock: Texas Tech University Press, 1999), x–xii, 116–21. In the present study, I use Crane's 1935 definition of West Texas as a guide for labeling counties or cities as part of that region.
2. West Texas Chamber of Commerce Administrative Office, "History of West Texas Chamber of Commerce," Box 71, Folder "History 1929–1986," West Texas Chamber of Commerce Records, 1893–1937 & undated, SWC.
3. For a brief history of the Chamber of Commerce, see "Twelve Years of Achievement," *West Texas Today* 11 (May 1930): 5–13.
4. Flemmons, *Amon: The Life of Amon Carter*, 59–61.
5. Amon G. Carter to Van Zandt Jarvis, February 11, 1937.
6. Scholars have paid limited attention to West Texas's participation in the Texas State Centennial. Kenneth B. Ragsdale addresses some of the relevant issues in *Centennial '36*. In his study of historical preservation as a result of the Texas State Centennial, Jeffery Mason Hancock fails to identify the eastern bias in the state's memorialization efforts. See Hancock, "Preservation of Texas Heritage in the 1936 Centennial." Texas State Senator Ben G. Oneal recounted his experiences lobbying for West Texas and the restoration of Fort Belknap as part of the centennial in a presentation before the West Texas Historical Association in 1953. See Ben G. Oneal, "A Brief Story of the Restoration of Fort Belknap," *West Texas Historical Association Year Book* 29 (October 1953): 105–14.
7. Ragsdale, *Centennial '36*, 21–22.

8. According to *The Texas Weekly*, the campaign included "the cooperation of some seventy-five daily newspapers and several hundred weeklies." See "For Sake of the Record," *The Texas Weekly*, October 1, 1932, 6. For examples of campaign messages, see Texas Centennial Commission, *Commemorating A Hundred Years of Texas History* (Austin, 1934), 13.
9. Peter Molyneaux, "Do Texans Really Revere Their Past?" *The Texas Weekly*, July 23, 1932, 5.
10. Ragsdale, *Centennial '36*, 23–24.
11. The position of the West Texas Chamber did not become public knowledge until September, when its assistant manager sent a copy of the statement to Peter Molyneaux of *The Texas Weekly* on September 19, 1932. A search of the papers of the West Texas Chamber of Commerce turned up no copies of the statement. See Peter Molyneaux, "West Texas Chamber's Blunder," *The Texas Weekly*, September 24, 1932, 4.
12. Molyneaux, "West Texas Chamber's Blunder," 4.
13. Peter Molyneaux, "The Centennial Amendment Again," *The Texas Weekly*, October 15, 1936, 4. Molyneaux includes additional excerpts from the statement when quoting from a letter from Wilber Hawk, president of the West Texas Chamber of Commerce.
14. For a detailed discussion of the crusade in favor of the passage of the amendment, including efforts of Peter Molyneaux to cover the battle within the pages of *The Texas Weekly*, see, Ragsdale, *Centennial '36*, 26–29.
15. Molyneaux, "Do Texans Really Revere Their Past?", 5.
16. Molyneaux, "West Texas Chamber's Blunder," 4.
17. *The Texas Weekly* included excerpts from editorials commenting on the amendment debate. See "The Economic Aspect," *The Texas Weekly*, September 24, 1932, 6; "Views of Our Views," *The Texas Weekly*, October 1, 1932, 11.
18. Excerpts from the *Fort Worth Star-Telegram* printed in "Views of Our Views," October 1, 1932, 11 and "Views of Our Views," *The Texas Weekly*, October 8, 1932, 11.
19. Excerpts from the *Brownwood Banner-Bulletin* printed in "Views of Our Views," October 8, 1932, 11.
20. Excerpts from *The San Antonio Express* printed in "The Centennial Amendment," *The Texas Weekly*, October 15, 1932, 12.
21. Excerpts from the *Riesel Rustler* printed in "The Centennial Amendment," 11.
22. Excerpts from the *Corpus Christi Caller* printed in "Views of Our Views," October 1, 1932, 11.
23. "The Centennial Amendment," 11.
24. "View of Our Views," October 8, 1932, 11.
25. Excerpts from the *Moore County News* printed in "Views of Our Views,"

October 1, 1932, 11.

26. For excerpts of Hawk's letter to Molyneaux, see Peter Molyneaux, "The Centennial Amendment Again," *The Texas Weekly*, October 15, 1932, 4. For excerpts of Hawk's rebuttal appearing in *West Texas Today*, see "West Texas Chamber Reiterates Opinion on State Centennial," *Dallas Morning News*, October 9, 1932, 7.
27. See Ely, *Where the West Begins*, 31–34.
28. Ragsdale, *Centennial '36*, 8–9.
29. For a roster of the Governing Board of One Hundred, see Texas Centennial Commission, *Commemorating A Hundred Years of Texas History*, 34–35.
30. Ibid., 10. The West Texas towns represented include Amarillo, Wichita Falls, and San Angelo.
31. Journal of the Senate of Texas, 4th Session, 43rd Legislature, 32.
32. Ragsdale, *Centennial '36*, 29.
33. For a list of the members of the commission and Executive Committee, see Texas Centennial Commission, *Commemorating A Hundred Years of Texas History*, 15, 16.
34. For a list of the leadership of the advisory board, see ibid., 17.
35. *Journal of the Senate of Texas*, 4th Session, 43 Legislature, 32–33.
36. Ibid.
37. Oneal, "A Brief Story of the Restoration of Fort Belknap," 109.
38. Amendments nos. 1 and 3 of Senate Bill 4 are included in Sections 4 and 5 of House Bill No. 11. See General and Special Laws of the State of Texas Passed by the 44th Legislature, 431–32.
39. Advisory Board of Texas Historians, "Bulletin No. 1," 2.
40. Calculating the total requests for allocations from West Texas counties and cities is problematic. A report produced in September 1935 documenting the total requests for funds does not agree with the reports generated at the time of the hearings in June, July, and August 1935. See Advisory Board of Texas Historians "Bulletin No. 2" and "Bulletin No. 3," Box 2B149, Folder "Reports to Commission of Control for Texas Centennial Celebrations, June 1935–June 1937, and Advisory Board of Texas Historians, [untitled], report of proposals, September 20, 1935, Box 2B149, Folder "Recommended Historical Markers or Land Marks by County, September 20, 1935," James Frank Dobie Papers, CAH.
41. William M. Thornton, "West Texas' Past Is Described to Historical Board," *Dallas Morning News*, July 3, 1935, 2.
42. Crane, "The Claims of West Texas to Recognition by Historians," 11, 31.
43. See Nash, *The Federal Landscape*, 3–20.
44. Crane, "The Claims of West Texas to Recognition by Historians," 31, 32.

45. "The Plainsman Says," *The Evening Journal* (Lubbock), July 16, 1935, 6.
46. Boyce House, "Centennial Is Refused Help," *Fort Worth Star-Telegram*, August 18, 1935, 12.
47. W. A. Jackson, "West Texas and the Centennial: They've Snubbed Us, as Usual—How Long, O Lord, Must We Submit?" *West Texas Today* 16, no. 7 (September 1935): 9.
48. J. Frank Dobie to L. W. Kemp, September 11, 1935, cited in Hancock, "Preservation of Texas Heritage in the 1936 Centennial," 24.
49. For a detailed discussion of the differing approaches to the memorialization of the historic sites within the Advisory Board of Texas Historians and the minority and majority reports, see Hancock, "Preservation of Texas Heritage in the 1936 Centennial," 21–35. For a firsthand description of Dobie's approach to memorialization, see J. Frank Dobie, Minority Report of the Advisory Board of Texas Historians to the Commission of Control for Texas Centennial Celebrations (Austin, 1935), 7–10.
50. The original state centennial appropriations bill granted $575,000 for local centennial memorials. Although the Commission of Control granted Fort Worth $250,000, the federal appropriation of a like amount negated the disposal of these funds for Fort Worth returning the amount to $575,000. The commission also granted both Goliad and Gonzales $50,000 bringing the allotment for all other local memorials to $475,000. After a federal allotment for the centennial, the state added an additional $200,000. Thus, the Advisory Board of Texas Historians made their recommendation based upon a total allotment of $675,000. See William M. Thornton, "Centennial Board Again Overrides Advisers' Request," *Dallas Morning News*, September 5, 1935, 13. J. Frank Dobie's Minority Report made recommendations based on a budget exceeding the allotment by nearly $100,000.
51. Neither the minority nor the majority report organized its recommendations according to east and west regions within the state. My calculations of Dobie's allocations for West Texas towns and counties are based on a comparison of the allotments in the minority report and R. C. Crane's definition of West Texas as provided in his July 2, 1935, address to the Advisory Board of Texas Historians. See Dobie, Minority Report of the Advisory Board of Texas Historians, 2–6.
52. For the recommendations of the Majority Report see William M. Thornton, "Historical Board Splits on Use of Centennial Fund," *Dallas Morning News*, October 8, 1935, 1, 2.
53. See Advisory Board of Texas Historians "Bulletin No. 2," 2; "Historical Board Hears Pleas for Centennial Cash," *Dallas Morning News*, June 19, 1935, 3.
54. Dobie, Minority Report, 6; "Historical Board Splits on Use of

Centennial Fund," *Dallas Morning News*, October 8, 1935, 1, 2.

55. The members of the Commission of Control for Texas Centennial Celebrations included: Chairman, Lieutenant Governor Walter F. Woodul, Houston; Speaker of the House Coke R. Stevenson, Junction; Karl Hoblizelle, Dallas; former governor Pat M. Neff, Waco; John Boyle, San Antonio; Joseph V. Vandenberge, Victoria; General John A. Hulen, Fort Worth; John K. Beretta, San Antonio; and James A. Elkins, Houston. Wallace Perry of El Paso was appointed to fill the position originally occupied by John Boyle. See Ragsdale, *Centennial '36*, 98, n1.
56. Wallace Perry to Amon G. Carter, October 12, 1935, Box 198, Folder "Texas Centennial Commission [Republic of Texas], 1935–1937," Carter Papers.
57. "El Paso Share in Centennial Ridiculed," *Fort Worth Star-Telegram*, evening edition, October 18, 1935, 13.
58. See Harold Schoen, *Monuments Erected by the State of Texas to Commemorate the Centenary of Texas Independence* (Austin: Commission of Control for Texas Centennial Celebrations, 1938), 21.
59. See Advisory Board of Texas Historians "Bulletin No. 2," 2; "5,000,000 Sought, $550,000 Available For '36 Centennial," *Dallas Morning News*, June 20, 1935, 2.
60. "WILL WEST TEXAS HAVE ANY PART IN THE TEXAS CENTENNIAL?" n.d., Box 10, Folder 5, Holden Papers. Although the origins and date of this document are unknown, because it illustrates the region encompassed by the "West Texas Regional Application" and is included with William Holden's correspondence about the West Texas regional application for a centennial museum in Lubbock, it is a reasonable assumption that A. B. Davis used this document to illustrate his points at the meeting with the advisory board.
61. William M. Thornton, "Over $5,000,000 Sought to Mark Historic Spots," *Dallas Morning News*, July 31, 1935, 1, 9.
62. See Advisory Board of Texas Historians, [untitled], report of proposals, September 20, 1935.
63. Louis W. Kemp to William C. Holden, October 3, 1935, Box 10, Folder 15, Holden Papers.
64. Ibid.
65. William C. Holden to R. C. Crane, October 8, 1935, Box 10, Folder 15, Holden Papers.
66. Ibid.
67. See William C. Holden to R. C. Crane, October 8, 1935; William C. Holden to Clifford B. Jones, October 9, 1935; William C. Holden to Claude Denham, October 12, 1935, Box 10, Folder 15, Holden Papers.
68. Oneal, "A Brief Story of the Restoration of Fort Belknap," 112–14.
69. V. Z. Rogers to William C. Holden, November 1, 1935, Box 10, Folder

15, Holden Papers.

70. "$50,000 Asked for Museum," *Fort Worth Star-Telegram*, October 18, 1935, 2.
71. Ibid.
72. William C. Holden to Walter Woodul, October 22, 1935, Box 10, Folder 15, Holden Papers; Schoen, *Monuments Erected by the State of Texas*, 26.
73. See William C. Holden to Walter Woodul, October 22, 1935; William C. Holden to John K. Beretta, October 24, 1935, Box 10, Folder 15, Holden Papers.
74. Ragsdale, *Centennial '36*, 112.
75. "Yesterday, Or Tomorrow?" *West Texas Today* 16, no. 9 (November 1935): 8.
76. Ibid.
77. Ibid.
78. Light Townsend Cummins, "History, Memory, and Rebranding Texas as Western for the 1936 Centennial," in *This Corner of Canaan: Essays on Texas in Honor of Randolph B. Campbell*, eds. Richard B. McCaslin, Donald E. Chipman, and Andrew J. Torget (Denton: University of North Texas, 2013), 37–57. See also Buenger, *The Path to a Modern South*, 258, and Cantrell, "The Bones of Stephen F. Austin," 148.

Chapter 3

1. On December 26, 1936, the Fort Worth City Council organized the Board of Control to "plan entertainment and supervise the financing" of the centennial. At the time of its organization, the Board of Control included John N. Sparks, Van Zandt Jarvis, William L. Pier, T. J. Harrell, Marvin D. Evans, J. M. North Jr., Seward Sheldon, E. H. Winton, J. C. Martin, O. B. Sellers, and William Monnig. See Fort Worth City Council, Meeting Minutes, December 26, 1935, 185. James F. Pollock replaced Seward Sheldon after Sheldon relocated to another city. Gray, "History of the Fort Worth Frontier Centennial," 39. Amon G. Carter's name is conspicuously absent from the Board of Control. He subsequently explained to his daughter that he and the *Fort Worth-Star Telegram* were represented by J. M. North Jr. See Amon G. Carter to Mrs. Harry R. Kay (Bertice Carter), April 15, 1936, Box 113, Folder "Kay, Bertice Carter (Speck)," Carter Papers.
2. "Centennial Stock Show Is Organized," *Fort Worth Star-Telegram*, January 4, 1936, Second Section, 1. See also "Centennial Livestock Show Board Will Meet," *Fort Worth Star-Telegram*, January 10, 1936, Second Section, 1.
3. "Urges More Attention Be Given Stock Show," *Fort Worth Star-Telegram*, February 21, 1936, 3.
4. J. M. North Jr. to R. C. Crane, January 7, 1936, Box 13, Folder 4, Papers

of R. C. Crane Sr., SWC.

5. "Centennial Livestock Exposition's Control Board Maps Program," *Fort Worth Star-Telegram*, January 11, 1936, 1–2.
6. Robert W. Rydell, John E. Findling, and Kimberly D. Pelle, *Fair America: World's Fairs in the United States* (Washington, DC: Smithsonian Institution Press, 2000), 86–87.
7. "Expect Show to Bring Two Million Here," *Fort Worth Star-Telegram*, January 18, 1936, 1–2.
8. "June 6–Nov. 29 Centennial, Having $15,000,000 Plant, Expected to Draw 12,000,000," *Dallas Morning News*, November 28, 1935, 7.
9. "Centennial Livestock Exposition's Control Board Maps Program," *Fort Worth Star-Telegram*, January 11, 1936, 1–2.
10. "Expect Show to Bring Two Million Here," *Fort Worth Star-Telegram*, January 18, 1936, 1–2.
11. "Centennial Livestock Exposition's Control Board Maps Program," *Fort Worth Star-Telegram*, January 11, 1936, 1–2; "Board of Control Sets June 6 for Opening of Frontier Centennial," *Fort Worth Star-Telegram*, February 11, 1936, 1–2.
12. "Livestock Structure Plans Ready," *Centennial News* 1, no. 7 (October 19, 1935): 4.
13. "Work is Started on All but One of Major Halls," *Centennial News* 1, no. 14 (December 7, 1935): 2.
14. "Expo to Get Fine Cattle," *Centennial News* 1, no. 9 (November 2, 1935): 4.
15. Amon G. Carter to John Nance Garner, September 25, 1935, Box 174, Folder "Southwestern Exposition and Fat Stock Show, 1935," Carter Papers.
16. "Opportunity a Threat," *Fort Worth Star-Telegram*, January 18, 1936, 6.
17. "Frontier Show Bonds Backed," *Fort Worth Press*, January 18, 1936, 1–2.
18. Quote from "Expect Show to Bring Two Million Here," *Fort Worth Star-Telegram*, January 18, 1936, 1–2; "Centennial Livestock Exposition's Control Board Maps Program," *Fort Worth Star-Telegram*, January 11, 1936, 1–2.
19. "Centennial Livestock Exposition's Control Board Maps Program," *Fort Worth Star-Telegram*, January 11, 1936, 1–2.
20. Reddin, *Wild West Shows*, 181.
21. Ibid., 183.
22. "Centennial Livestock Exposition's Control Board Maps Program," *Fort Worth Star-Telegram*, January 11, 1936, 1–2.
23. "Women's Club Offers Support to Group," *Fort Worth Star-Telegram*, January 4, 1936, 9. See Anna Shelton and Mattie Ingram to Fort Worth City Council, January 10, 1936, Folder "January 1936," Fort Worth City Council, Proceedings, FTWPLA.

24. The charter of The Woman's Club of Fort Worth is reproduced in Marion Day Mullins, *A History of The Woman's Club of Fort Worth, 1923–1973* (published privately), 11–13, copy held at the Tarrant County Archives, Fort Worth, Texas (hereafter cited as TCA).
25. Elizabeth Miller, *The Woman's Club of Fort Worth: The First Twenty-Five Years, 1923–1948* (published privately, 1959), 19; Angela Boswell, "From Farm to Future: Women's Journey through Twentieth-Century Texas," in *Twentieth-Century Texas: A Social and Cultural History* ed. John W. Storey and Mary L. Kelley (Denton: University of North Texas Press, 2008), 114–15, 122. See also Judith N. McArthur, *Creating the New Woman: The Rise of Southern Women's Progressive Culture in Texas, 1893–1918* (Urbana and Chicago: University of Illinois Press, 1998).
26. For more information on Anna Shelton, see Mullins, *A History of The Women's Club of Fort Worth*, 22–25.
27. Edith Alderman Guedry, "'Who Says Women Putter?' Not This Texas Frontier Centennial Body of 500," *Fort Worth Press*, January 27, 1936, 6.
28. "Women to Band for Centennial," *Fort Worth Star-Telegram*, January 24, 1936, 20.
29. Edith Alderman Guedry, "'Who Says Women Putter?' Not This Texas Frontier Centennial Body of 500," *Fort Worth Press*, January 27, 1936, 6; "Women Launch Mammoth Plans for Centennial; Will Set Up Museum," *Fort Worth Press*, March 9, 1936, 8.
30. "Women Launch Mammoth Plans for Centennial; Will Set Up Museum," *Fort Worth Press*, March 9, 1936, 8.
31. "Which Best Portrays Frontier Days," *Fort Worth Star-Telegram*, January 25, 1936, 1.
32. "Ideas on Costumes for Show Asked," *Fort Worth Star-Telegram*, January 30, 1936, 10.
33. C. L. Douglas, "Chic Gown of Frontier Days Served for All Occasions," *Fort Worth Press*, February 15, 1936, 8; C. L. Douglas, "A Ride, Eh? Well, Milady, Copy Styles During Expo," *Fort Worth Press*, February 20, 1936, 2.
34. "Paisley Suggested as Show Costume," *Fort Worth Star-Telegram*, February 10, 1936, 4.
35. "Women Urged Not to Adopt Freakish Frontier Costumes," *Fort Worth Star-Telegram*, February 23, 1936, 8.
36. "Sunbonnets Are Not Likely to Set Centennial Style," *Fort Worth Star-Telegram*, January 25, 1936, 1.
37. "And It Cost Less Than $1," *Fort Worth Star-Telegram*, February 16, 1936, 3.
38. "Centennial Costume Urged Entirely of Texas Products," *Fort Worth Star-Telegram*, February 16, 1936, 3.
39. "Ideal Costume for Show is Offered by Gladewater Women," *Fort Worth*

Star-Telegram, February 8, 1936, 8.

40. "Split Bonnets Urged at Show," *Fort Worth Star-Telegram*, January 27, 1936, 12.
41. "Sunbonnets Are Not Likely to Set Centennial Style," *Fort Worth Star-Telegram*, January 25, 1936, 1.
42. "White Costumes Urged for Wear at Centennial," *Fort Worth Star-Telegram*, February 14, 1936, 15.
43. "On Costuming TFC," *Fort Worth Star-Telegram*, February 26, 1936, 6.
44. "Women's Group to Discuss Costumes," *Fort Worth Press*, February 27, 1936, 6.
45. "Frontier Show Dress to Vary," *Fort Worth Star-Telegram*, February 29, 1936, 9.
46. "Women and the Frontier Centennial," *Fort Worth Star-Telegram*, February 5, 1936, 6. See also "Centennial Plea Made to Rotarians by Monnig," *Fort Worth Star-Telegram*, January 18, 1936, 8; "Harrell Will Speak On Centennial Plans," *Fort Worth Star-Telegram*, February 19, 1936, 9; "Urges More Attention Be Given Stock Show," *Fort Worth Star-Telegram*, February 21, 1936, 3; Group Hears Talk On Show," *Fort Worth Star-Telegram*, February 21, 1936, 9. For an example of rhetoric used to sell the centennial to Fort Worth citizens, see *Fort Worth Frontier Centennial,* A Statement by William Monnig, Chairman of the Board of Control, 1936, Box 3, Folder 46, Tarrant County Historical Society Records, FTWPLA.
47. "Women Launch Mammoth Plans for Centennial; Will Set Up Museum," *Fort Worth Press*, March 9, 1936, 8.
48. "5,000 Women Expected to Aid Frontier Centennial," *Fort Worth Star-Telegram*, February 4, 1936, 9; "Name Groups for Centennial," *Fort Worth Star-Telegram*, February 9, 1936, 4; "Guide Chart for Use of Patriotic Societies Applicable to Each Period, 1819–1936," n.d., Folder "Fort Worth Frontier Centennial, Historical Research Committee—Miscellaneous—1936," Box 2 "State and Local History," Series II, Mary Daggett Lake Papers, FTWPLA.
49. "Women's Frontier Body Will Search County for History," *Fort Worth Star-Telegram*, March 6, 1936, 9.
50. Women's organizations that oversaw research for specific historical periods include Mary Isham Keith, Six Flags, and Fort Worth chapters of the Daughters of the American Revolution; Catholic Daughters of the Americas; United States Daughters of 1812; United Daughters of the Confederacy; Daughters of Union Veterans; National Society of New England Women; United Spanish American War Veterans Women's Auxiliary; and Disabled American Veterans of World War Auxiliary. See "Period Research Committee, Patriotic Organization Allotments," n.d., Folder "Fort Worth Frontier Centennial, Historical

Research Committee—Miscellaneous—1936, Box 2 "State and Local History," Series II, Lake Papers. Other women's organizations that aided the Historical Research Committee include the Colonial Dames of America, the National Society of the Colonial Dames of America, the United States Daughters of 1812, the American Legion Auxiliary of Bothwell Kane Post, the American War Mothers, and the Veterans of Foreign Wars Auxiliary. See "Name Groups for Centennial," *Fort Worth Star-Telegram*, February 9, 1936, 4.

51. "Van Zandt Home to Be Restored at Show Site," *Fort Worth Star-Telegram*, February 13, 1936, 9; Dora Davenport Jones, *The History of the Julia Jackson Chapter #141, United Daughters of the Confederacy: Fort Worth, Texas, 1897–1976* (Fort Worth: Kwik-Kopy Printing Center, 1976), 70. A copy is available at the TCA.
52. The Julia Jackson Chapter of the UDC and Major K. M. Van Zandt, himself, launched several unsuccessful campaigns to build a monument to the memory of Confederate soldiers. In 1933, the Julia Jackson Chapter placed a bronze tablet in the new Fort Worth Federal Post Office. Interestingly, the dedication of the marker was held on the 68th anniversary of the ending of the Civil War and commemorated the bravery of southern women during Reconstruction. See Jones, *The History of the Julia Jackson Chapter #141*, 42–51.
53. Jones, *The History of the Julia Jackson Chapter #141*, 66–67.
54. Ibid., 68, 70.
55. "Van Zandt Home to Be Restored at Show Site," *Fort Worth Star-Telegram*, February 13, 1936, 9.
56. "Centennial Plans Heard," *Fort Worth Star-Telegram*, February 7, 1936, 9.
57. J. B. Davis to Margaret McLean, June 2, 1936. A transcription of the letter is published in Jones, *The History of the Julia Jackson Chapter #141*, 68, 71.
58. "Frontier Show Group Meets," *Fort Worth Star-Telegram*, February 7, 1936, 14.
59. "Plan Museum," *Fort Worth Press*, February 26, 1936, 6.
60. "Women Launch Mammoth Plans for Centennial; Will Set Up Museum," *Fort Worth Press*, March 9, 1936, 8.
61. "Women Determined Culture Will Have Day During Show," *Fort Worth Star-Telegram*, March 7, 1936, 9.
62. Ibid. This article inaccurately labeled the opera "Life in a Mission."
63. For a detailed discussion of Venth's life and contribution to the development of the fine arts in Texas, see Gary Dan Gibbs, "Carl Venth (1860–1938): Texas's Master Musician: His Life, His Music, His Influence" (PhD diss., Austin, University of Texas, 1990); Carl Venth, *My Memories* (San Antonio, TX: Alamo Printing, 1939), in Box 1, Folder

"Book, 'My Memories' by Carl Venth," Carl Venth Papers, FTWPLA.

64. "Women Determined Culture Will Have Day During Show," *Fort Worth Star-Telegram*, March 7, 1936, 9.
65. Gibbs, "Carl Venth (1860–1938)," 205.
66. See "Old Ranch House for Texas Ranger Headquarters," *Centennial News* 1, no. 12 (November 23, 1935): 3; "Sheriffs of Texas Planning to Build Court Replica," *Centennial News* 1 no. 17-A (December 28, 1935): 4.
67. Bokovoy, *The San Diego World's Fairs*, 165, 210.
68. Cheryl R. Ganz, *The 1933 Chicago World's Fair: A Century of Progress* (Urbana and Chicago: University of Illinois Press, 2008), 34.
69. "Frontier Days to Be Revived," *Fort Worth Press*, January 11, 1936, special insert, "A Greater Fort Worth in 1936," 8.
70. "Frontier Bonds Backed," *Fort Worth Press*, January 18, 1936, 1–2.
71. "Council Asks for Pioneer Village Plan," *Fort Worth Star-Telegram*, January 25, 1936, 1–2; "Show Control to Be Shared by City, Board," *Fort Worth Press*, January 25, 1936, 1–2.
72. C. L. Douglas, "Community Will Revive Memories Among Pioneers Visiting Here," *Fort Worth Press*, January 24, 1936, 8.
73. J. M. North Jr. to R. C. Crane, January 14, 1936, Folder 3, Box 3, Crane Papers.
74. R. C. Crane to J. M. North Jr., January 20, 1936, Folder 3, Box 13, Crane Papers.
75. C. L. Douglas, "Community Will Revive Memories Among Pioneers Visiting Here," *Fort Worth Press*, January 24, 1936, 8.
76. J. M. North Jr. to R. C. Crane, January 14, 1936.
77. "Now for the Frontier Centennial," *Fort Worth Star-Telegram*, January 30, 1936, 6.
78. "A Big Job Ahead," *Fort Worth Press*, February 6, 1936, 4.
79. "Centennial Plans Heard," *Fort Worth Star-Telegram*, February 7, 1936, 9. Opened in 1889 as a vehicle to advertise Fort Worth and the products of Texas, the Spring Palace—an oriental-style pavilion—housed exhibits from many of the surrounding counties. See Sandra L. Myres, "Fort Worth, 1870–1900," *Southwestern Historical Quarterly* 72, no. 2 (October 1968): 204–5.
80. "Centennial Plans Heard," Fort Worth *Star-Telegram*, February 7, 1936, 9.
81. McArthur, *Creating the New Woman*, 3.
82. "Replica of Old Fort Worth Takes Shape on Drawing Board," *Fort Worth Press*, February 11, 1936, 1.
83. "Centennial Board to Continue Plans Today," *Fort Worth Star-Telegram*, February 13, 1936, 1–2.
84. "Council to Get Building Plans," *Fort Worth Star-Telegram*, February

12, 1936, 1–2.

85. "Here's How Centennial Buildings are to be Arranged on Van Zandt Site," *Fort Worth Press*, February 13, 1936, 3. This article contains the proposed layout created by Pelich, Bush, and Hoelscher.
86. "Negroes Will Open Own Show June 15," *Fort Worth Star-Telegram*, June 3, 1936, 2.
87. "Centennial Board to Continue Plans Today," *Fort Worth Star-Telegram*, February 13, 1936, 1–2.
88. "Show Building Plans to Davis," *Fort Worth Press*, February 15, 1936, 5.
89. "How Old Fort Worth Will Live Over Again at Texas Frontier Exposition," February 18, 1936, 3. See also "These Replicas of Frontier Buildings Will be Scene of Colorful Centennial Pageantry," *Fort Worth Star-Telegram*, evening edition, February 18, 1936, 4.
90. "West Texas to Create Exhibit," *Fort Worth Star-Telegram*, February 23, 1936, 1–2; "Half Million Frontier Show Fund Sought," *Fort Worth Press*, February 26, 1936, 1.
91. J. M. North Jr. to R. C. Crane, January 7, 1936, Crane Papers.
92. "Expos in Texas to Emphasize Opportunities," *Fort Worth Press*, January 31, 1936, 19.
93. For example, see "West Texas to 'Steal Show,'" *Fort Worth Star-Telegram*, January 15, 1936, 11.
94. "Texas Frontier Centennial," *Fort Worth Star Telegram*, January 16, 1936, 6.
95. "Plan Museum," *Fort Worth Press*, February 26, 1936, 6.
96. "Frontier Show Clubs Planned," *Fort Worth Star-Telegram*, March 7, 1936, 3; "Back Plan for W. Texas All States Centennial Club," *Fort Worth Star-Telegram*, March 8, 1936, 8.
97. "Tourists Will Invite West Texans to Show," *Fort Worth Star-Telegram*, March 5, 1936, 9.
98. "Booster Trip Schedule to West Texas Is Set," *Fort Worth Star-Telegram*, March 6, 1936, 13; "70 Show Trippers Are Off Today to Invite Texas," *Fort Worth Star-Telegram*, March 9, 1936, 12.
99. "Bandeen Praises Plans for Show," *Fort Worth Star-Telegram*, January 29, 1936, 2.
100. Byron C. Utecht, "Show Praised by Officials," *Fort Worth Star-Telegram*, February 13, 1936, 1–2.
101. "West Texas Booms Livestock Show," *Fort Worth Press*, January 7, 1936, 7.
102. Minutes of Executive Board Meeting West Texas Chamber of Commerce, February 21, 1936, 2, Box 17, "West Texas Chamber of Commerce, Internal Affairs," West Texas Chamber of Commerce Records, 1918–1968, SWC. See also "Cotton to be Main Feature," *Fort Worth Star-Telegram*, January 16, 1936, 1–2; "Area Plans for Centennial," *Fort*

Worth Star-Telegram, January 24, 1936, 2.

103. "W.T.C.C. to Talk," *Fort Worth Star-Telegram*, February 21, 1936, 19.
104. "West Texas Will Have Exhibit Here," *Fort Worth Star-Telegram*, February 22, 1936, 9.
105. "Will Confer on WTCC Exhibit," *Fort Worth Press*, February 25, 1936, 1.
106. Ibid.
107. "West Texans Plan Exhibit," *Fort Worth Press*, February 22, 1936, 2.
108. "West Texas and Fort Worth," *Fort Worth Star-Telegram*, February 24, 1936, 6.
109. "West Texas Group Named to Plan $66,000 Frontier Show Exhibit," *Fort Worth Star-Telegram*, March 4, 1936, 10.
110. Tracey Jean Boisseau, "Once Again in Chicago: Revisioning Women As Workers at the Chicago Woman's World's Fairs of 1925–1928," *Women's History Review* 18, no. 2 (April 2009): 265–66. See also Boisseau, "White Queens at the Chicago World's Fair, 1893: New Womanhood in the Service of Class, Race, and Nation," *Gender & History* 12, no. 1 (April 2000): 33–81.
111. Rydell, *World of Fairs*, 117, 140.
112. Kenneth B. Ragsdale's study of the Texas State Centennial does not indicate that women's clubs local or otherwise participated in the planning of the central exposition in Dallas. See Ragsdale, *Centennial '36*. A recent article by Light T. Cummins suggests that in addition to commodified sex objects, women did make important contributions to the celebrations as artists, sculptors, and photographers. See Light Townsend Cummins, "From the Midway to the Hall of State at Fair Park: Two Competing Views of Women at the Dallas Celebration of 1936," *Southwestern Historical Quarterly* 64, no. 3 (January 2011): 225–51. There is some evidence that the state centennial attempted to marshal the aid of local women's clubs to help with city beautification, compiling local history, collecting Texas history books for schools, and organizing a grassroots advertising campaign. See Frank N. Watson to W. A. Webb, November 9, 1935, Box 159, Folder "Prom: Women's Club Participation," Texas Centennial Central Exposition in Dallas Collection, Dallas Historical Society, Dallas, Texas. See also A Centennial Message to Women's Clubs, Written by Elithe Hamilton Beal, Dallas, Texas, Folder "Undated Speeches, Maus 13—Pages 41," Box 151, Texas Centennial Central Exposition in Dallas Collection.

Chapter 4

1. "Billy Rose, Who Put New York on Edge of Seat, Signs to Stage Frontier Show," *Fort Worth Press*, March 9, 1936, 1, 14; "Work on Show Awaiting Rose," *Fort Worth Star-Telegram*, March 10, 1936, 1, 2.

2. "No. 1 Showman of America Signs to Stage Frontier Show," *Fort Worth Press*, March 9, 1934, 14.
3. "Billy Rose, Who Put New York on Edge of Seat, Signs to Stage Frontier Show," *Fort Worth Press*, March 9, 1936, 1, 14.
4. Ibid.; "Billy Rose, 'Jumbo' Producer, Will Present Giant Spectacle for Fort Worth's Centennial," *Dallas Morning News*, March 10, 1936, 4.
5. "Centennial Livestock Exposition's Control Board Maps Program," *Fort Worth Star-Telegram*, January 11, 1936, 1–2.
6. "Council Asks for Pioneer Village Plan," *Fort Worth Star-Telegram*, January 25, 1936, 1–2; "Here's How Centennial Buildings Are to Be Arranged On Van Zandt Site," *Fort Worth Press*, February 13, 1936, 3; "How Old Fort Worth Will Live Over Again At Texas Frontier Exposition," *Fort Worth Press*, February 18, 1936, 3; J. M. North Jr. to R. C. Crane, January 14, 1936, R. C. Crane Sr. Papers.
7. "Show Control to Be Shared by City, Board," *Fort Worth Press*, January 25, 1936, 1–2.
8. J. M. North Jr. to George H. Dern, February 17, 1936, Box 89, Folder 6, "Frontier Centennial," Carter Papers.
9. "Frontier Show Bonds Backed," *Fort Worth Press*, January 18, 1936, 1–2; "Here's How Centennial Buildings Are to Be Arranged On Van Zandt Site," *Fort Worth Press*, February 13, 1936, 3.
10. "Frontier Days to Be Revived," *Fort Worth Press*, January 11, 1936, special insert, "A Greater Fort Worth in 1936," 8.
11. Dave Hall, "Merchant Sees Humming City," *Fort Worth Press*, January 11, 1936, special insert "A Greater Fort Worth in 1936," 6; "Show Board Must Speed Up Work to Pen Expo June 6," *Fort Worth Press*, February 11, 1936, 1.
12. "Show Board Must Speed Up Work to Pen Expo June 6," *Fort Worth Press*, February 11, 1936, 1.
13. "Now for The Frontier Centennial," *Fort Worth Star-Telegram*, January 30, 1936, 6; "TFC's Potential Visitors," *Fort Worth Star-Telegram*, February 7, 1936, 6.
14. "Way Cleared for Show by Bond Victory," *Fort Worth Press*, January 29, 1936, 1–2.
15. See "West Texas to 'Steal Show,'" *Fort Worth Star-Telegram*, January 15, 1936, 11; "Bandeen Praises Plans for Show," *Fort Worth Star-Telegram*, January 29, 1936, 2; Byron C. Utecht, "Show Praised by Officials," *Fort Worth Star-Telegram*, February 13, 1936, 1–2.
16. *Texas Centennial Celebrations: Centennial Year Calendar* (Dallas, 1936), Box 4-16/117, "Texas Centennial Materials: Pamphlets and Printed Materials," Texas Centennial Collection, Texas State Archives (TSA). Texas Centennial advertisements, including depictions of Fort Worth's western-themed celebration, were published in papers throughout

the nation. See "You'll See it All in Texas," *World Herald* (Omaha, Nebraska), May 3, 1936, 14E; "More for your Vacation Money See Texas," *The Kansas City Star*, April 19, 1936; "This Year's Star Vacation Attractions!" *The Seattle Sunday Times*, April 5, 1936. Copies in folder "Advertisements from Newspapers," Box 4-16/98B, "Texas Centennial Commission—Correspondence," Texas Centennial Collection, TSA.

17. "Board of Control Sets June 6 Opening of Frontier Centennial," *Fort Worth Star-Telegram*, February 11, 1936, 1–2.
18. See Olmstead, "'Un-Southern,' 371–94.
19. Herbert De Shong, "Centennial Gets Nation-Wide Publicity on Cody Statue as Press Agent Chortles At Hoax," *Dallas Times-Herald*, March 1, 1936, Box 60, Folder "Cody, 'Buffalo Bill' Statue Controversy, 1936," Carter Papers.
20. B. H. Friedman, *Gertrude Vanderbilt Whitney* (New York: Doubleday, 1978), 459; Diana Rice, "Mrs. Whitney's Buffalo Bill," *The New York Times*, February 26, 1922, Special Features, 87.
21. "Against Narrowness, Mrs. Whitney's Cody Rides in Dallas," *The Art Digest*, June 1, 1936, 19.
22. Amon G. Carter to Walter Holbrook, February 26, 1936, Box 60, Folder "Cody, 'Buffalo Bill' Statue Controversy, 1936," Carter Papers.
23. Carter to Holbrook, February 26, 1936.
24. A copy of a list of addresses to which Carter sent the telegram can be found in Box 60, Folder "Cody, 'Buffalo Bill' Statue Controversy, 1936," Carter Papers.
25. Carter to Holbrook, February 26, 1936.
26. Reddin, *Wild West Shows*, 58–61.
27. See White, "Frederick Jackson Turner and Buffalo Bill," 7–9, 11.
28. Reddin, *Wild West Shows*, 121.
29. Carter to Holbrook, February 26, 1936.
30. "Pawnee Bill May Present Centennial Wild West Show," *Fort Worth Press*, February 26, 1936, 16. Reddin, *Wild West Shows*, 152–56.
31. Glenn Shirley, *Pawnee Bill: A Biography of Major Gordon W. Lillie* (Albuquerque: University of New Mexico Press, 1958), 227–37 (quotation on 227).
32. "Rufus LeMaire Dies; Ft. Worth Cinema Figure," *Fort Worth Star-Telegram*, December 4, 1950, 1, 4.
33. Block, "'Bigger Than a Show—Better Than a Circus," 183–86.
34. Nelson, *"Only a Paper Moon": The Theatre of Billy Rose*. Ann Arbor, MI: UMI Research Press, 1985; reprint 1987), 11–12.
35. Quote from Billy Rose, *Wine, Women and Words* (New York: Simon and Schuster, 1946), 14; Maurice Zolotow, "The Fabulous Billy Rose," *Collier's*, March 1, 1947, 54. See also Barbara W. Grossman, *Funny Woman: The Life and Times of Fanny Brice* (Bloomington and

Indianapolis: Indiana University Press, 1991), 192.

36. Maurice Zolotow, "The Fabulous Billy Rose," *Collier's*, March 1, 1947, 54.
37. Nelson, *"Only a Paper Moon,"* 13–20.
38. Ibid., 21.
39. Ibid., 22–24. See also Susan Waggoner, *Nightclub Nights: Art, Legend, and Style, 1920–1960* (New York: Rizzoli: 2001), 44–45.
40. Nelson, *"Only a Paper Moon,"* 25.
41. Maurice Zolotow, "The Fabulous Billy Rose," *Collier's*, March 1, 1947, 55; Nelson, *"Only a Paper Moon,"* 28.
42. Quotation extracted from Maurice Zolotow, *Billy Rose of Broadway*, unpublished manuscript, 1945, published in Nelson, *"Only a Paper Moon,"* 30.
43. Block, "'Bigger Than a Show—Better Than a Circus,'" 175.
44. Nelson, *"Only a Paper Moon,"* 31.
45. Nelson, *"Only a Paper Moon,"* 31–34.
46. Nelson, *"Only a Paper Moon,"* 36.
47. Ibid.
48. Ibid., 31–32.
49. Block, "'Bigger Than a Show—Better Than a Circus,'" 164; Maurice Zolotow, "The Fabulous Billy Rose," *Collier's*, March 1, 1947, 56.
50. Block, "'Bigger Than a Show—Better Than a Circus,'" 168.
51. Nelson, *"Only a Paper Moon,"* 45.
52. Ibid., 45–46.
53. "Producer, Director Predicts Huge Centennial Crowds," *Fort Worth Press*, March 6, 1936, 1, 8.
54. Quotation from a March 3, 1936 letter from Billy Rose to Richard Maney; quoted in Nelson, *"Only a Paper Moon,"* 48.
55. Amon G. Carter to Jock Whitney, March 4, 1936, Box 89, Folder "Frontier Centennial," Carter Papers.
56. Nelson, *"Only a Paper Moon,"* 48.
57. Carter to Whitney, March 4, 1936.
58. Ibid.
59. Nelson, *"Only a Paper Moon,"* and Jones in *Billy Rose Presents . . . Casa Mañana* base their discussion of Fort Worth's hiring of Rose primarily on an unpublished biography authored by Maurice Zolotow titled *Billy Rose of Broadway*. In a four-part series, Zolotow published portions of the larger work in *Collier's*. See Zolotow, "The Fabulous Billy Rose," *Collier's*, February 15, 1947, 11–13, 81–84; February 22, 1947, 18–19, 83–87; March 1, 1947, 20, 54–56; March 8, 1947, 44, 52–56. Ragsdale's *Centennial '36* rests upon Flemmons, *Amon: The Life of Amon Carter*. The omission of references and the quoting of conversations that likely went unrecorded undermine the reliability of Zolotow's

and Flemmons's work. Other less than credible works describing Rose's work in Fort Worth are Polly Rose Gottlieb, *The Nine Lives of Billy Rose* (New York: Crown Publishers, 1968), 105–16, and Earl Conrad, *Billy Rose: Manhattan Primitive* (Cleveland: World Publishing, 1968), 105–9.

60. Nelson, *"Only a Paper Moon,"* 48.
61. Zolotow, "The Fabulous Billy Rose," *Collier's*, March 8, 1947, 44.
62. Ibid., 44–45 (quotation on 45).
63. Ibid., 45; Jones, *Billy Rose Presents . . . Casa Mañana*, 24.
64. Zolotow, "The Fabulous Billy Rose," *Collier's*, March 8, 1947, 52.
65. Quotation taken from Zolotow, Billy Rose of Broadway quoted in Jones, *Billy Rose Presents . . . Casa Mañana*, 24.
66. Nelson, *"Only a Paper Moon,"* 50.
67. Zolotow, "The Fabulous Billy Rose," *Collier's*, March 8, 1947, 52.
68. Rose, *Wine, Women and Words*, 18.
69. "Teamwork for Centennial Urged," *Fort Worth Star-Telegram*, February 4, 1936, 5.
70. "City Is Told It Can 'Steal Show' At Expo," *Fort Worth Press*, February 6, 1936, 10.
71. "Frontier Show Draws Praise," *Fort Worth Star-Telegram*, February 9, 1936, 9.
72. "Teamwork for Centennial Urged," *Fort Worth Star-Telegram*, February 4, 1936, 5.
73. James M. North Jr. to George H. Dern, February 17, 1936, Box 89, Folder "Frontier Centennial," Carter Papers.
74. "So All Over Texas," *The Texas Weekly*, February 22, 1936, 3.
75. "The City of Fort Worth," *Variety*, March 11, 1936, 38. For a copy of the ad appearing in both *Billboard* and *Variety*, see Box 89, Folder "Frontier Centennial," Carter Papers.
76. Arthur L. Kramer to William Monnig, March 19, 1936, Box 89, Folder "Frontier Centennial," Carter Papers.
77. William Monnig to Arthur L. Kramer, n.d., Box 89, Folder "Frontier Centennial," Carter Papers.
78. Louis W. Kemp to W. H. Kershaw, March 16, 1936, Box 60, Folder "Cody, 'Buffalo Bill' Statue Controversy," 1936, Carter Papers.
79. Quotation taken from Zolotow, *Billy Rose of Broadway*, published in Jones in *Billy Rose Presents . . . Casa Mañana*, 24.

Chapter 5

1. Joseph Mitchell, "Rose Maps an Ambitious Program," *Fort Worth Press*, March 10, 1936, 1–2; A. H. Montford Jr., "Billy Rose is Back More Enthusiastic Than Ever," *Fort Worth Star-Telegram*, March 14, 1936, 1–2.
2. Joseph Mitchell, "Rose Maps an Ambitious Program," *Fort Worth Press*,

March 10, 1936, 1–2; Jack Gordon, "Billy Rose Picks a Beauty, But That's Only Beginning," *Fort Worth Press*, March 17, 1936, 10.

3. Joseph Mitchell, "Rose Maps an Ambitious Program," *Fort Worth Press*, March 10, 1936, 1–2; "2 Big Spectacles Planned for Frontier Centennial," *Fort Worth Press*, March 18, 1936, 2.
4. 2 Big Spectacles Planned for Frontier Centennial," *Fort Worth Press*, March 18, 1936, 2.
5. Quotation taken from Maurice Zolotow, *Billy Rose of Broadway*, quoted in Jones, *Billy Rose Presents . . . Casa Mañana*, 24. Zolotow used a similar quote in his article titled "The Fabulous Bill Rose," *Colliers*, March 8, 1947, 44.
6. Joseph Mitchell, "Rose Maps an Ambitious Program," *Fort Worth Press*, March 10, 1936, 1–2; A. H. Montford Jr. "Billy Rose is Back More Enthusiastic Than Ever," *Fort Worth Star-Telegram*, March 14, 1936, 1–2.
7. Once composed of over twenty committees, by April the Women's Division contained only twelve in all. They included committees assigned to the museum, historical research, fine arts, pilgrimage, publicity, centennial in the schools, speaker's bureau, street signs, suggestions, civic clean-up and beautification, hospitality, and the All-States Club. See "Clubwomen Plan Good Will Trips," *Fort Worth Press*, April 15, 1936, 3.
8. "Frontier Show Clubs to Form," *Fort Worth Star-Telegram*, March 17, 1936, 3. See also "All-States Club Session Becomes International," *Fort Worth Star-Telegram*, March 18, 1936, 9.
9. "All-State Club Parley Called," *Fort Worth Star-Telegram*, March 29, 1936, 10; "Adopted Texans Urged to Enroll in State Groups," *Fort Worth Star-Telegram*, March 26, 1936, 13; "States Club Banquet Set," *Fort Worth Star-Telegram*, April 23, 1936, 9; "Show Boosters Write Letters," *Fort Worth Press*, May 8, 1936, 12.
10. "State Clubs Will Invite Governors," *Fort Worth Press*, April 15, 1936; "Show Boosters Write Letters," *Fort Worth Press*, May 8, 1936, 1; "42 Governors to Get Frontier Show Bids," *Fort Worth Press*, May 13, 1936, 1; "Plan Special Days for Frontier Show," *Fort Worth Press*, May 21, 1936, 3.
11. "Frontier Exposition to Draw Governors to Fort Worth from Coast-to-Coast," *Fort Worth Press*, June 6, 1936, 3.
12. "All-States Club to be Separate Unit," *Fort Worth Star-Telegram*, April 21, 1936, 9.
13. "Women to Hear of Show Plans," *Fort Worth Star-Telegram*, May 3, 1936, 3. See "Clubwomen Plan Tours for Expo," *Fort Worth Press*, April 14, 1936, 1; "Clubwomen Plan Good Will Trips," *Fort Worth Press*, April 15, 1936, 3; "'Frontier' Boosters Plan First Trip," *Fort Worth Press*,

May 8, 1936, 3.

14. See "Women Will Make Trip to Boost Show," *Fort Worth Star-Telegram*, May 13, 1936, 20; "Women Start Goodwill Tour," *Fort Worth Press*, May 14, 1936, 5; "Women Start Planning Their Second Junket," *Fort Worth Press*, May 15, 1936, 6; "Women Make Good Will Tour for Centennial," *Fort Worth Star-Telegram*, May 15, 1936, 9; "68 Women Boosters Leaving Tomorrow," *Fort Worth Press*, May 21, 1936, 3; "Bridgeport to Hear of Frontier Show," *Fort Worth Star-Telegram*, May 30, 1936, 9.
15. "Fort Worth's Campaign of Friendliness Gains Ground," *Fort Worth Press*, April 13, 1936, 7.
16. See "Pinwheel Avenue," Frontier Centennial Postcards, TCA.
17. "Flag Prizes Received for Centennial Contest," *Fort Worth Press*, March 16, 1936, 9.
18. "Ninth Business Women's Week," *Fort Worth Star-Telegram*, March 18, 1936, 6; "Beautification Program is Adopted by P. T. A., Kiwanis, Garden Club Members," *Fort Worth Star-Telegram*, March 13, 1936, 13; "Women Press Cleanup Drive," *Fort Worth Star-Telegram*, March 22, 1936, 3.
19. "Centennial Pilgrimage Announced," *Fort Worth Press*, March 12, 1936, 6; "Arrival of Tourists from North Forces Sightseeing Tours into Early Start," *Fort Worth Star-Telegram*, June 17, 1936, 9; "Second Bus Tour of City Held Today," *Fort Worth Press*, June 16, 1936, 8; "Seeing Fort Worth Points of Interest Treat to Visitors," *Fort Worth Star-Telegram*, July 9, 1936, 3.
20. "Committee Named to Study Details of Van Zandt Home," *Fort Worth Star-Telegram*, May 13, 1936, 9.
21. "Restoration of Old Van Zandt Home Is Interesting Project," *Fort Worth Star-Telegram*, July 12, 1936, "Society & Clubs," 6; Edith Alderman Guedry, "Stage Coach Road Passed [*sic*]; Van Zandt Home; Being Restored for Centennial," *Fort Worth Press*, June 19, 1936, 14. For the custodianship of the local chapters of the DRT and the UDC, see Margaret McLean to J. S. Morris, June 26, 1936, Box 6, Folder 19, "Van Zandt Cottage," United Daughters of the Confederacy, Julia Jackson Chapter, 1897–1969, Collection, FTWPLA.
22. "Old Van Zandt Homestead Party is Set," *Fort Worth Star-Telegram*, July 16, 1936, 10.
23. "Women Told How to Aid Centennial," *Fort Worth Star-Telegram*, March 25, 1936, 1–2; "Women Rally to Centennial," *Fort Worth Press*, March 25, 1936, 1.
24. "Women Told How to Aid Centennial," *Fort Worth Star-Telegram*, March 25, 1936, 1–2.
25. "Group Hears Reports on Space for Exhibitions," *Fort Worth Star-Telegram*, May 8, 1936, 10.

26. "Women Told How to Aid Centennial," *Fort Worth Star-Telegram*, March 25, 1936, 1–2.
27. "Village Street Plans are Told," *Fort Worth Star-Telegram*, May 1, 1936, 9.
28. For an overview of the materials exhibited in the museum, see Edith Alderman Guedry," Rare Relics Arrive Now Every Day for Museum to be in Frontier Building," *Fort Worth Press*, June 4, 1936, 6; Pauline Naylor, "Frontier Museum is being Stocked with Treasures of Pioneers," *Fort Worth Star-Telegram*, June 14, 1936, "Society & Clubs," 9; Pauline Naylor, "Texas Got National Publicity Century Ago, Museum Shows," *Fort Worth Star-Telegram*, June 28, 1936, "Society & Clubs," 5; "To Exhibit Old Hand-Carved Set," *Fort Worth Press*, July 17, 1936, 13; and "Baby Bag of Porcupine Quills, Necklace of Human Finger Bones on Exhibit," *Fort Worth Press*, July 17, 1936, 15. At the last minute, an exhibit featuring relics from Mexico collected by Mrs. Glover Johnson was added to the exhibits. See "Museum Exhibits Will Be Ready for Opening July 18," *Fort Worth Star-Telegram*, July 7, 1936, 18.
29. See Pauline Naylor, "1,000 Volumes for Frontier Show Library are Assured," *Fort Worth Star-Telegram*, June 7, 1936, "Society & Clubs," 7; Pauline Naylor, "Frontier Museum is Being Stocked with Treasures of Pioneers," *Fort Worth Star-Telegram*, June 14, 1936, "Society & Clubs," 9; "Frontier Museum to House 600 Old Manuscripts, Maps, Documents about Texas," *Fort Worth Press*, July 17, 1936, 16.
30. Sallie Blythe Mummert, "Art on Exhibit," *Fort Worth Star-Telegram*, July 5, 1936, "Radio, Art, Stage," 8. See also "Art Exhibit Depicts Days of Frontier," *Fort Worth Press*, July 17, 1936, 15.
31. "Women Busy at the Frontier Centennial have Bucked Up Against Numerous Problems," *Fort Worth Press*, July 14, 1936, 6. See also "Population Boom Hits Frontier Show Grounds—Staff Moves In," *Fort Worth Star-Telegram*, June 28, 1936, 1, 4. Flemmons, *Amon: The Life of Amon Carter*, 306 (quotation).
32. See Pauline Naylor, "Frontier Museum is being Stocked with Treasures of Pioneers," *Fort Worth Star-Telegram*, June 14, 1936, "Society & Clubs," 9.
33. See "Billy Rose to Set Up Office," *Fort Worth Press*, March 10, 1936, 1–2.
34. Mary Wynn, "Was Billy Rose Stormed by Girls? No, He Wasn't," *Fort Worth Star-Telegram*, March 15, 1936, 2.
35. Jack Gordon, "Billy Rose Picks a Beauty. But That's Only Beginning," *Fort Worth Press*, March 17, 1936, 10.
36. "Billy Rose to Fly After New Ideas," *Fort Worth Star-Telegram*, March 21, 1936, 10.
37. Jack Gordon, "It's Plucky Beauty Who Dares Sharp Eyes and Tongue of Little Barnum," *Fort Worth Press*, March 23, 1936, 8.

38. Joe Cooper, "Rose Qualifies as Show Judge; Splits Sheep from Goats," *Fort Worth Star-Telegram*, March 23, 1936, 2. For a photograph of the auditions, see "Girls, Can You Strut? If You Are Looking for Job with Billy Rose, You Had Better Not Shuffle Along," *Fort Worth Press*, March 23, 1936, 5.
39. "Towns Planning Contests to Pick Frontier Belles," *Fort Worth Star-Telegram*, April 12, 1936, 1, 4; "60 Towns Stage Beauty Contests," *Fort Worth Star-Telegram*, April 23, 1936, 2.
40. See "Colorado, Texas, Will Pick Beauty for Fort Worth Frontier Show," *Fort Worth Star-Telegram*, April 18, 1936, 1, 2; "60 Beauties in Haskell County Enter Contest for Sweetheart," *Fort Worth Star-Telegram*, April 21, 1936, 1; "Miss Lexington of Texas Chosen at Gonzales for Frontier Contest," *Fort Worth Star-Telegram*, April 24, 1936, 1; "Graham to Pick Frontier Belle," *Fort Worth Star-Telegram*, April 26, 1936, 1; "Frontier Belle to be Picked May 8 in Hamilton Area for District Trip," *Fort Worth Star-Telegram*, April 27, 1936, 1; "McKinney Invites Beauties to Enter," *Fort Worth Star-Telegram*, April 30, 1936, 1; "Three Towns Pick Beauties," *Fort Worth Star-Telegram*, May 10, 1936, 10; "Lions Club Beauty is Coleman Winner," *Fort Worth Star-Telegram*, May 12, 1936, 2; "Stephenville Beauty Named," *Fort Worth Star-Telegram*, May 14, 1936, 2; "30 in Centennial Beauty Contest at Eastland May 30," *Fort Worth Star-Telegram*, May 17, 1936, 9; "Midland Beauty Picked on Birthday," *Fort Worth Star-Telegram*, May 19, 1936, 1; "Beauty Picking Due Saturday," *Fort Worth Star-Telegram*, May 24, 1936, 9; "Texas Selects Many Beauties," *Fort Worth Star-Telegram*, May 28, 1936, 1.
41. See "Wouldn't She Get Your Vote? *Fort Worth Press*, April 22, 1936, 1; "These Girls Enter Frontier Beauty Contest," *Fort Worth Press*, April 28, 1936, 5; "34th-May be 1st," *Fort Worth Press*, May 15, 1936, 1; "Now How'd You Pick 'Miss Fort Worth'?" *Fort Worth Press*, May 20, 1936, 1; "Goes a'Gunning for Beauty Title," *Fort Worth Press*, May 22, 1936, 1; "Seeks to be Fort Worth's Sweetheart," *Fort Worth Star-Telegram*, May 8, 1936, 7; "Wants to be Sweetheart," *Fort Worth Star-Telegram*, May 10, 1936, 10; "She Would be Queen There," *Fort Worth Star-Telegram*, May 12, 1936, 8; "Did You Notice the Wagon," *Fort Worth Star-Telegram*, May 14, 1936, 19; "Oh, for Life of a Judge," *Fort Worth Star-Telegram*, May 16, 1936, 16; and "To Appear at Follies Revue," *Fort Worth Star-Telegram*, May 22, 1936, 11.
42. "Beauty Picking Due Saturday," *Fort Worth Star-Telegram*, May 24, 1936, 9; "Friends Hail Beauty Winner," *Fort Worth Press*, May 27, 1936, 3.
43. "Beauty Picking Due Saturday," *Fort Worth Star-Telegram*, May 24, 1936, 9.
44. Mary Wynn, "Borger Beauty Captures Sweetheart Title," *Fort Worth*

Star-Telegram, May 31, 1936, 1, 4; "They're Texas' Three Fairest Ladies!" *Fort Worth Press*, June 1, 1936, 1.

45. Brenda Foley, *Undressed for Success: Beauty Contestants and Exotic Dancers as Merchants of Morality* (New York: Palgrave Macmillan, 2005), 46–49 (quotation on 47). See also Lois W. Banner, *American Beauty* (New York: Alfred Knopf, 1983), 66–70. For more on Ziegfeld and burlesque see Robert C. Allen, *Horrible Prettiness: Burlesque and American Culture* (Chapel Hill: University of North Carolina Press, 1991), 243–46.
46. Mary Crutcher, "Frontier Show's Marked Success in Finding Natural Beauties in Texas Opens New Era in the Show World," *Fort Worth Press*, June 2, 1936, 2 (quotation); Laegreid, *Riding Pretty*, 100–101.
47. Mary Crutcher, "Frontier Show's Marked Success in Finding Natural Beauties in Texas Opens New Era in the Show World," *Fort Worth Press*, June 2, 1936, 2.
48. "Faye Cotton, True Daughter of Texas, is Fond of Guns," *Fort Worth Press*, June 4, 1936, 3.
49. Edith Alderman Guedry, "Texas Sweetheart No. 1 is Good Reading Because She Dares to be Herself," *Fort Worth Press*, June 8, 1936, 6.
50. "Texas Sweetheart is Sure Judges Wrong," *Fort Worth Star-Telegram*, June 1, 1936, 1–2.
51. In the establishment of the first successful modeling agency in 1923, John Powers made "modeling acceptable to women (and to men) by connecting it with 'naturalness' and the 'all-American way.' His 'girls,' he said, came from the best homes and the best finishing schools; none walked in the 'mincing artificial manner' of the ordinary actress-model; and none wore 'excessive makeup.' His 'girls' were 'typical American girls, pretty, healthy, vivacious, and self-reliant.'" William Leach, *Land of Desire: Merchants, Power, and the Rise of a New American Culture* (New York: Pantheon Books, 1993), 310.
52. "Rose Show Girls and Boys Arrive," *Fort Worth Star-Telegram*, June 7, 1936, 4; "Frontier Dancers at Work," *Fort Worth Star-Telegram*, June 7, 1936, "Sports & Amusements," 8.
53. For example, see "New York Show Girls Begin Rehearsal for Parts in Exposition," *Fort Worth Press*, June 8, 1936, 3; "Rehearse for Frontier Show Follies," *Fort Worth Star-Telegram*, June 9, 1936, 9.
54. "Women's Division of Show Seeks to House Chorines," *Fort Worth Star-Telegram*, June 21, 1936, 3.
55. "17 Young Beauties in Cast of 'Jumbo' Live by Rules Like Those of Convent," *Fort Worth Star-Telegram*, June 26, 1936, 9.
56. "'Inferno' Roars Tonight; Show Girls on Part Pay; Who Said Fried Chicken?" *Fort Worth Press*, June 11, 1936, 11.
57. Jack Gordon, "Billy's Amusement Fantasy Makes Our Head Swim," *Fort Worth Press*, March 9, 1936, 1.

58. Jack Gordon, "It's Plucky Beauty Who Dares Sharp Eyes and Tongue of Little Barnum," *Fort Worth Press*, March 23, 1936, 8.
59. Ernie Pyle, "About Billy Rose: 'A Broadway Spellbinder Talks Three Hours,' Says Ernie Pile, 'And Sells Himself to Texans for $100,000,'" *Fort Worth Press*, March 31, 1936, 1–2.
60. Lloyd Lewis, *It Takes All Kinds* (New York: Books for Libraries Press, 1974; 1947 repr.), 204.
61. Waggoner, *Nightclub Nights*, 11–15, 43.
62. Nelson, *"Only a Paper Moon,"* 23, 25.
63. Jack Gordon, "Billy's Amusement Fantasy Makes Our Head Swim," *Fort Worth Press*, March 9, 1936, 1.
64. Ganz, *The 1933 Chicago World's Fair*, 14.
65. Lisa Krissoff Boehm, "The Fair and the Fan Dancer: A Century of Progress and Chicago's Image," *Chicago History* 27, no. 2 (July 1998): 54–55.
66. Ganz, *The 1933 Chicago World's Fair*, 14.
67. See Boehm, "The Fair and the Fan Dancer," 42–52.
68. Bokovoy, *The San Diego World's Fairs*, 196.
69. Gray, "History of the Fort Worth Frontier Centennial," 88. See also Southwestern Exposition and Fat Stock Show, Souvenir Annual, 1935, 1, Box 1, Southwestern Exposition and Fat Stock Show Programs, FTWPLA; "Rainbeau Garden!" Advertisement, *Fort Worth Star-Telegram*, March 15, 1935, 10.
70. "Beauty of San Diego Nudist Colony 'Gets' Texas Centennial Concessions Director," *Fort Worth Star-Telegram*, August 21, 1935, 1.
71. "Texas Rangerettes Greet Visitors to Exposition," *Centennial News*, December 7, 1935, 3.
72. William Monnig to Arthur L. Kramer, n.d.; "Sally Rand's Boss is Ready to Spend $250,000 at Fair," *Dallas Morning News*, March 17, 1936, 10; "'Streets of Paris' Seen for Centennial," *Dallas Morning News*, March 27, 1936, 14.
73. See Holly Knox, *Sally Rand: From Film to Fans* (Bend, OR: Maverick Publications, 1988), 1–18. See also Studs Terkel, *Hard Times: An Oral History of the Great Depression* (New York: Pantheon Books, 1970), 169.
74. For a discussion of Rand's appearance in San Diego, see Bokovoy, *The San Diego World's Fairs*, 219–21.
75. "Sally Rand: 'Frontier Show Needs Some Sex Appeal,'" *Fort Worth Press*, April 8, 1936, 2. See also Bess Stephenson, "Sally to Use Electricity in Dance to Shock 'Em," *Fort Worth Star-Telegram*, April 8, 1936, 1–2.
76. "Billy Rose, 'Now a Texan,' Tells Jumbo Works of Frontier Show's Magnitude," *Fort Worth Press*, April 21, 1936, 1.
77. Ibid.
78. "Ned Alvord Has Arrived, Folks!" *Fort Worth Press*, April 14, 1936, 1.

79. Nelson, *"Only a Paper Moon,"* 19, 30.
80. A. H. Montford Jr., "Alvord Arrives Full of Enthusiasm for Centennial Promotional Duties," *Fort Worth Star-Telegram*, April 14, 1936, 5.
81. "Show Ads Will Cover 9 States," *Fort Worth Star-Telegram*, June 10, 1936, 3.
82. Apparently, the first drawing of "a girl in an abbreviated costume atop a bucking bronc" came from Mrs. Pauline Belew of Fort Worth. The official version, which received much wider distribution, came from Jewel Brannon Parker, a local artist. See "Stickers Will Advertise Frontier Show," *Fort Worth Star-Telegram*, April 23, 1936, 9; "How're They Going to Stay Away?" *Fort Worth Press*, May 5, 1936, 3.
83. Laegreid, *Riding Pretty*, 98–101.
84. Reynolds, *A Hundred Years of Heroes*, 188.
85. "How're They Going to Stay Away?" *Fort Worth Press*, May 5, 1936, 3.
86. For example, see *Bulletin of the Tarrant County Medical Society* 9, no 3 (June 1936), 8–9.
87. The *Oxford Dictionary* defines whoopee as "wild celebration and merry-making" and the phrase "make whoopee" as "celebrate wildly" or "have sexual intercourse." See *Oxford Dictionary of Current English*, 2001, 3d ed., "Whoopee," ed. Catherine Soanes.
88. "Aviators to Barnstorm and Advertise Show Here," *Fort Worth Star-Telegram*, May 7, 1936, 1. To promote the show's sex appeal, Rose unsuccessfully attempted to obtain a zeppelin from Hitler's Germany to fly fifty showgirls from New York to Fort Worth. See Amon G. Carter to James R. Record, April 8, 1936, Box 89, Folder "Frontier Centennial," Carter Papers.
89. "Frontier Centennial News on Radio Program for Tonight," *Fort Worth Star-Telegram*, May 22, 1936, 19.
90. "Permit Issued at Dallas for Giant Sign Pointing Way to Frontier Show," *Fort Worth Star-Telegram*, June 3, 1936, 1; "Giant 'Whoopee' Sign Clears Its Last Big Hurdle," *Fort Worth Star-Telegram*, June 10, 1936, 22.
91. Jones, *Billy Rose Presents . . . Casa Mañana*, 49. "Giant 'Whoopee' Sign Clears Its Last Big Hurdle," *Fort Worth Star-Telegram*, June 10, 1936, 22.
92. "West Texas, Fort Worth and Dallas Join Hands for Centennial Shows," *Fort Worth Star-Telegram*, May 13, 1936, 1–2.
93. Richard Maney, *Fanfare: The Confessions of a Press Agent* (New York: Harper & Brothers, 1957), 165.
94. Billy Rose to Amon G. Carter, June 3, 1936, Box 89, Folder "Frontier Centennial," Carter Papers.
95. See Owen P. White, "Texas Roundup," *Collier's*, May 30, 1936, 21, 64–65; Stanley Walker, "Texas Range: A Sketch of Violent Texas and

Its Two Rival Fairs," *Vogue*, June 1, 1936, 66–67, 108; "Texas Fiesta: Lone Star Land's Centenary; Southwest in Gala Mood for Parties," *The Literary Digest*, June 6, 1936, 32; "The Lone Star Rise and Shines," *Business Week*, June 6, 1936, 17–18, 20; "Bluebonnet Boldness," *Time*, June 8, 1936, 11–13; "Ft. Worth Starts Thinkin' Dallas' Gal Stuff Beat 'Em to the Punch," *Variety*, June 17, 1936, 1, 63; "Fort Worth Festival," *Architectural Forum*, September 1936, 9, 39.

96. Owen P. White, "Texas Roundup," *Collier's*, May 30, 1936, 65.
97. Amon G. Carter to Mr. Maxwell, n.d., Box 89, Folder "Frontier Centennial," Carter Papers.
98. Stanley Walker, "Texas Range: A Sketch of Violent Texas and Its Two Rival Fairs," *Vogue*, June 1, 1936, 66–67; Amon G. Carter to Condé Nast, n.d., Box 220, Folder "Walker, Stanley [*Vogue* article on Texas Centennial]," Carter Papers.
99. Billy Rose to Amon G. Carter, June 3, 1936, Carter Papers.
100. Mike Dillon, "March of Time, The," in *Encyclopedia of American Journalism*, ed. Stephen L. Vaughn (New York: Routledge, 2008), 292–93.
101. Jack Gordon, "Here's Preview of That 'March of Time' Reel on Fort Worth-Dallas Feud," *Fort Worth Press*, June 18, 1936, 12.
102. *The March of Time* (newsreel), "The Battle of a Centennial" (originally aired June 1936), Archives, Amon Carter Museum, Fort Worth, Texas.
103. Billy Rose to Amon G. Carter, June 15, 1936, Box 89, Folder "Frontier Centennial," Carter Papers.
104. Rose, *Wine, Women and Words*, 14; Maurice Zolotow, "The Fabulous Billy Rose," *Collier's*, March 1, 1947, 54.
105. Ernie Pyle, "'Whoopee' Aspect of Show Causes a Few Doubts Here," *Fort Worth Press*, June 3, 1936, 8.
106. *Wild and Whoo-pee!: Fort Worth Frontier Centennial*, 1936, TCU/SC. By April 1936, Frontier Centennial letterhead reflected the new title of the celebration. See Billy Rose to Amon G. Carter, April 13, 1936, Box 116, Folder "Lanham, Fritze, 1926–1947," Carter Papers.
107. With a few exceptions, the *Fort Worth Star-Telegram* did not cover those protesting the immorality of the entertainment featured at the Frontier Centennial.
108. "Church Hits Type of Show Fixed by Rose," *Fort Worth Press*, May 22, 1936, 1.
109. "'Show to be Decent—But,' Says Monnig," *Fort Worth Press*, May 23, 1936, 1.
110. "Billy Rose Welcomes Baptist Probe of Frontier Show; Warns 'Publicity Seekers,'" *Fort Worth Press*, May 26, 1936, 1.
111. Ibid.
112. "Baptist Committee Holds Closed Session with Rose," *Fort Worth*

Star-Telegram, June 2, 1936, 9.

113. "Billy Rose Welcomes Baptist Probe of Frontier Show; Warns 'Publicity Seekers,'" *Fort Worth Press*, May 26, 1936, 1; "Pastors Slap at Plans for Frontier Expo," *Fort Worth Press*, June 8, 1936, 1.
114. "Women Ask Dignified Literature on Show," *Fort Worth Star-Telegram*, evening edition, May 16, 1936, clipping in *Frontier Centennial Scrapbook*, Volume II, TCU/SC. The request also coincided with the need for promotional literature for distribution as part of the centennial tours of Fort Worth initiated by the Pilgrimage Committee of the Women's Division. "What if You are Asked to Point Out Beauty Spots?" *Fort Worth Star-Telegram*, May 21, 1936, 9.
115. "Typically Western?" *Fort Worth Press*, May 18, 1936, 4.
116. Hugh Abercrombie Anderson, *Out Without My Rubbers: The Memoirs of John Murray Anderson* (New York: Library Publishers, 1954), 164.
117. "Part of 'Educational' Exhibit at Coliseum Tonight," *Fort Worth Star-Telegram*, March 22, 1936, 8.
118. "Recognize Her with Her Clothes On? *Fort Worth Star-Telegram*, April 8, 1936, 1.
119. "Picking Dancers No Job for Man with High Blood Pressure," *Fort Worth Star-Telegram*, April 28, 1936, 9.
120. "No Fair Peeping! 2 Youths Nabbed as Follies Cavort," *Fort Worth Star-Telegram*, June 10, 1936, 1.
121. "Billy Rose on Smut," *Fort Worth Press*, June 3, 1936, 4.
122. Edith Alderman Guedry, [title missing], *Fort Worth Press*, June 10, 1936, 8.
123. C. V. Dunn, "Gospel is Remedy for immorality," *Fort Worth Press*, July 6, 1936, 4; C. V. Dunn, "Says Nude Shows at Exposition Defile State's Name," *Fort Worth Press*, June 15, 1936, 4.
124. Bokovoy, *The San Diego World's Fairs*, 196.
125. The General Ministers Association also produced a resolution censuring the Frontier Centennial ad campaign. See "Billy Rose Welcomes Baptist Probe of Frontier Show; Warns 'Publicity Seekers,'" *Fort Worth Press*, May 26, 1936, 1; "Rose Will Answer Public's Queries," *Fort Worth Press*, June 2, 1936, 8.
126. Jack Gordon, "Smut Just Not Good Business Says Maestro," *Fort Worth Press*, June 3, 1936, 8.
127. "Billy Rose Welcomes Baptist Probe of Frontier Show; Warns 'Publicity Seekers,'" *Fort Worth Press*, May 26, 1936, 1.
128. Barry Hankins, *God's Rascal: J. Frank Norris & the Beginnings of Southern Fundamentalism* (Lexington: University Press of Kentucky, 1996), 2, 16, 90.
129. Pirtle, *Fort Worth: The Civilized West*, 131. Pirtle provides no citation for the story's origin.

130. "Show Ads Will Cover 9 States," *Fort Worth Star-Telegram*, June 10, 1936, 3.
131. "The Fort Worth Frontier Centennial," *Fort Worth Star-Telegram*, June 7, 1936, 3.
132. "Advance in Price, Frontier," *Fort Worth Star-Telegram*, July 8, 1935, 3. Apparently, centennial planners never purchased ad space in the *Fort Worth Press* to promote the Frontier Centennial.
133. "Opens Saturday, Fort Worth Frontier Centennial," n.d., Box 7, Folder 40, Jary Collection.
134. *Fort Worth Frontier Centennial in the Capital of the Cattle Kings* (no publication data), Box 89, Folder "Frontier Centennial," Carter Papers. Other handbills also surfaced featuring the western element of the centennial, highlighting the recreated frontier village and characterizing Rose's *The Last Frontier* as "a rip-roaring colorful dramatization of the old west." See *Fort Worth Frontier Centennial a living, breathing recreation of the Old West* (no publication data), Box 89, Folder "Frontier Centennial," Carter Papers.
135. "Ft. Worth Starts Thinkin' Dallas' Gal Stuff Beat 'Em to the Punch," *Variety*, June 17, 1936, 1, 63. For example, the *Texas Centennial Review* reported in mid-June: "Details of this unique attraction have not been made known to the public but sponsors indicate that unlimited surprises are in store for visitors to this innovation in ranch life." *Texas Centennial Review* 1, no. 31 (June 17, 1936): 4.
136. "Bans Fans," *Fort Worth Press*, July 2, 1936, 3.
137. Anderson, *Out Without My Rubbers*, 164.
138. "Sally Rand Wears Bonnet, Gingham to Town," *Fort Worth Star-Telegram*, evening edition, n.d., "Frontier Centennial," Vertical File, FTWPLA.
139. Miller, *The Woman's Club of Fort Worth*, 19.
140. "Fan Dancer Is 'So Quaint,' Fort Worth Women Find," *Fort Worth Press*, July 1, 1936, 1, 10.
141. "Sally Rand Mounted to the Cabin," *Fort Worth Star-Telegram*, July 14, 1936, 8; "Sally Will Fan-Interest in Softball Here Tonight," *Fort Worth Press*, July 16, 1936, 10; ". . . Sally Rand Now Pitching!" *Fort Worth Star-Telegram*, July 15, 1936, 10; Ed Prell, "Sally Rand, Three Games Thrill Fans at Forest Park," *Fort Worth Star-Telegram*, July 17, 1936, 13.
142. "Clever Sally," *Fort Worth Star-Telegram*, July 2, 1936, 20.
143. "Bubble Dancer Show Booster," *Fort Worth Press*, July 9, 1936, 9.
144. "Darned Good Cook as Well as Fan-Tosser, the Sally Rand!" *Fort Worth Press*, July 10, 1936, 14.
145. "Sally Rand to Visit Austin, San Antonio," *Fort Worth Star-Telegram*, July 5, 1936, 7; "Grape Dane Due, Says Sally," *Fort Worth Star-Telegram*, July 7, 1936, 9.

146. "Jack Gordon, "Sally's Due With Fans! Dancer's Wit, Intellect Should Quiet All Alarm," *Fort Worth Press*, June 30, 1936, 7.
147. Edith Alderman Guedry, "Claire Ogden Davis here with Sally Rand Started Her Career in Fort Worth," *Fort Worth Press*, July 6, 1936, 6.
148. "Ft. Worth Starts Thinkin' Dallas' Gal Stuff Beat 'Em to the Punch," *Variety*, June 17, 1936, 1, 63.
149. "Sally Picks Nudies," *Fort Worth Star-Telegram*, July 9, 1936, 5.
150. "Costumers Get Sally's Cuties Ready," *Fort Worth Star-Telegram*, July 15, 1936, 5.
151. Rachel Shteir, *Striptease: The Untold History of the Girlie Show* (New York: Oxford University Press, 2004), 155.
152. M. Jordan, "Deplores Tendency Toward Nudity," *Fort Worth Press*, June 22, 1936, 4.
153. Edith Alderman Guedry, "Risqué Shows Take Floor; History, Science in Texas Fade into Dim Background," *Fort Worth Press*, June 24, 1936, 6.
154. Elizabeth Wright, "Are Standards for Women Changing? Reader Wonders," *Fort Worth Press*, July 14, 1936, 4.
155. "Typically Western?" *Fort Worth Press*, May 18, 1936, 4.
156. See *Bulletin of the Tarrant County Medical Society* 9, no. 3 (June 1936), cover.
157. Rydell, *World of Fairs*, 117.
158. See "Enters Contest," *Fort Worth Star-Telegram*, May 5, 1936, 5. This article identifies the Casa Mañana as Casa Diablo.

Chapter 6

1. "Frontier Grounds Viewed from Air Seem a Fairyland," *Fort Worth Star-Telegram*, June 8, 1936, 2.
2. Nelson, *"Only a Paper Moon,"* 8.
3. Rose, *Wine, Women and Words*, 18.
4. Gottlieb, *The Nine Lives of Billy Rose*, 109.
5. See "Little Barnum Becomes a Full-Fledged Officer," *Fort Worth Press*, April 28, 1936, 1; "Rose Dines in Jail, Gets Commission," *Fort Worth Star-Telegram*, April 28, 1936, 9; "Rose Gets Pistol to Back up Badge," *Fort Worth Star-Telegram*, May 5, 1936, 2.
6. See photo printed in Jones, *Billy Rose Presents . . . Casa Mañana*, 56.
7. "Billy Rose, 'Now a Texan,' Tells Jumbo Workers of Frontier Show's Magnitude," *Fort Worth Press*, April 21, 1936, 1.
8. "Fort Worth Festival," *Architectural Forum* 65, no. 3 (September 1936), 9.
9. "Frontiersman," *The American Magazine*, July 1936, 90.
10. Ernie Pyle, "About Billy Rose: 'A Broadway Spellbinder Talks Three Hours,' Says Ernie Pyle, 'And Sells Himself to Texans for $100,000," *Fort*

Worth Press, March 31, 1936, 1–2. Rose apparently spent some time in Texas in the 1920s. He worked as a stenographer in Wichita Falls, and at the Republican State Convention in San Antonio he made $1,000 selling typewritten copies of the proceedings, he had taken the preceding day in shorthand. See *Billy Rose Presents Frontier Fiesta*, Playbill, (Fort Worth, 1937), 2. Copy available at TCU/SC.

11. "Centennial Bond Issue Unanimously Indorsed," *Fort Worth Star-Telegram*, March 11, 1936, 1–2.
12. Amon G. Carter to Franklin Delano Roosevelt, April 13, 1936, Carter Papers.
13. See "Frontier Show to Have Texas Spirit," *Fort Worth Star-Telegram*, March 16, 1936, 4.
14. "'Big Four' Attractions of Frontier Show Visualized," *Fort Worth Press*, June 1, 1936, 1, 3.
15. "Gotta Slogan?" *Fort Worth Press*, April 15, 1936, 1.
16. See "What Our Readers Say," *Fort Worth Press*, April 20, 1936, 4; "What Our Readers Say," *Fort Worth Press*, April 28, 1936, 4.
17. Zolotow, *Collier's*, March 8, 1947, 52.
18. See Joseph Mitchell, "Rose Maps an Ambitious Program," *Fort Worth Press*, March 10, 1936, 1–2.
19. *Texas Centennial Celebrations, Centennial Year Calendar*, 1936, "Texas Centennial Materials Pamphlets & Printed Materials" Box 4-16/117, TSA.
20. "Stock Show Friday Night," *Fort Worth Star-Telegram*, March 11, 1936, 6. See also "The Spirit of Fort Worth," *Fort Worth Star-Telegram*, March 12, 1936, 6.
21. "Advance Sales of Tickets Indicate Attendance Will Exceed 300,000," *Fort Worth Star-Telegram*, March 13, 1936, 1.
22. "Broncs and Men from Cow Tails Still Show Feature," *Fort Worth Press*, March 13, 1936, 3.
23. A. H. Montford Jr., "Billy Rose Is Back More Enthusiastic than Ever," *Fort Worth Star-Telegram*, March 14, 1936, 1–2.
24. "Billy Rose to Fly after New Ideas," *Fort Worth Star-Telegram*, March 21, 1936, 10.
25. Ibid.
26. Bokovoy, *The San Diego World's Fairs*, 196–97.
27. Rydell, *All the World's a Fair*, 63, 65.
28. Ibid., 88.
29. Ibid., 2.
30. Bokovoy, *The San Diego World's Fairs*, 114.
31. Rydell, *World of Fairs*, 9.
32. Quotation from promotional materials cited in Rydell, *World of Fairs*, 104.

33. Bokovoy, *The San Diego World's Fairs*, 173.
34. Amon G. Carter to Harry L. Hopkins, September 5, 1935, Box 174, Folder "Southwestern Exposition & Fat Stock Show," Carter Papers.
35. "Full Speed Ahead," *Fort Worth Star-Telegram*, January 23, 1936, 4; "What We Voted For," *Fort Worth Star-Telegram*, December 9, 1935, 6.
36. "Frontier Show Plans Pushed," *Fort Worth Press*, February 3, 1936, 1–2; "Frontier Show Already Fascinating Spectacle with Amazing Growth," *Fort Worth Star-Telegram*, May 15, 1936, 9. Cohen, *Cowtown Moderne*, 122.
37. Cohen, *Cowtown Moderne*, 124 (quotation), 126, 132; Amon G. Carter to Dan Moran, April 17, 1936, Box 89, Folder "Frontier Centennial," Carter Papers.
38. Cohen, *Cowtown Moderne*, 126–28.
39. Ibid., 125–26. See also Fort Worth City Council, Meeting Minutes, July 22, 1936, 285.
40. Cohen, *Cowtown Moderne*, 129.
41. Gray, "History of the Fort Worth Frontier Centennial," 71. Hammond initially asked S. P. Ziegler, the head of TCU's Art Department, to compose the designs. On March 17, 1936, the Fort Worth City Council reviewed his sketches (Fort Worth City Council, Meeting Minutes, March 17, 1936, 215). Apparently, Hammond or the City Council passed on these designs in favor of those of Kenneth Gale. Cohen erroneously suggests that the friezes were the work of Herman Koeppe, Wyatt C. Hedrick's chief designer. *Cowtown Moderne*, 124–26.
42. Delbert Willis, "Shanty Town Residents Gladly Move Out to Make Way for Centennial," *Fort Worth Press*, April 14, 1936, 18.
43. "Break Earth for Frontier Centennial," *Fort Worth Star-Telegram*, March 11, 1936, 1–2. Amon G. Carter orchestrated the event. He arranged for the placement of a podium and sent out 300 personal invitations. Amon G. Carter to Jack H. Hott, March 7, 1936, Box 6, Folder "Correspondence, 1934–1936," Carter Papers.
44. "Hammers Ring as Work Starts on Frontier Show," *Fort Worth Press*, March 11, 1936, 1–2.
45. "Expo Construction is Started Early," *Fort Worth Press*, March 25, 1936, 1. Lack of funding resulted in the omission of the Casino and Agricultural Exhibit Building and Manufacture's Exhibit Building from the facilities. See "2 More Show Structures Are Planned," *Fort Worth Star-Telegram*, June 25, 1936, 1; Gray, "History of the Fort Worth Frontier Centennial," 69.
46. Wyatt C. Hedrick and Elmer G. Withers Architectural Company Incorporated to City of Fort Worth, March 31, 1936, Box 1, Folder "April 1936, folder 3 of 3," Fort Worth City Council, Council Proceedings, FTWPLA.

47. Cohen, *Cowtown Moderne*, 129–30. The City Council subsequently adopted a resolution to call the building the Will Rogers Memorial Coliseum several days later on September 23, 1936. Fort Worth City Council, Meeting Minutes, September 23, 1936, 318. Amon Carter referred to the coliseum as the Will Rogers Memorial Coliseum as early as April 1936. See Amon G. Carter to Dan Moran, April 17, 1936, Box 89, Folder "Frontier Centennial," Carter Papers.
48. Cohen, *Cowtown Moderne*, 132.
49. "Now for the Frontier Centennial," *Fort Worth Star-Telegram*, January 30, 1936, 6.
50. "Centennial Livestock Exposition's Control Board Maps Program," *Fort Worth Star-Telegram*, January 11, 1936, 1–2.
51. "Frontier Show to Pay, Will Not Be Pageant, Says Rose," *Fort Worth Star-Telegram*, March 19, 1936, 8.
52. See Amon G. Carter to William Cameron, March 13, 1936, Box 89, Folder "Frontier Centennial," Carter Papers.
53. "New York Columnist Breaks Out in Rhetorical Rash over Billy Rose's Fort Worth Plans," *Fort Worth Star-Telegram*, March 27, 1936, 11.
54. "Lonely Hearts to Get Chance to be Less Lonely When Frontier Centennial Opens," *Fort Worth Star-Telegram*, March 24, 1936, 7.
55. "Show Board Meets with Billy Rose," *Fort Worth Star-Telegram*, April 5, 1936, 8.
56. "Fort Worth Festival," *Architectural Forum* 65 no. 3 (September 1936), 9.
57. "Work to Start Next Week on Frontier Show," *Fort Worth Press*, March 23, 1936, 7; "Lonely Hearts to Get Chance to be Less Lonely When Frontier Centennial Opens," *Fort Worth Star-Telegram*, March 24, 1936, 7; "Women Told How to Aid Centennial," *Fort Worth Star-Telegram*, March 25, 1936, 1–2; "Two 'Old-Time' Buildings to Feature Show," *Fort Worth Press*, March 26, 1936, 2.
58. "Here's First Sketch of Centennial 'Frontier City,'" *Fort Worth Press*, March 26, 1936, 2.
59. Bess Stephenson, "Centennial Show Sketch Plans Ready," *Fort Worth Star-Telegram*, March 26, 1936, 1–2.
60. Centennial officials contracted construction of the Casa Mañana for $150,000. "Plans Ready on Two Buildings," *Fort Worth Star-Telegram*, April 2, 1936, 20. Although judged safe for occupation, the quickly constructed redwood buildings of the Frontier City did not meet the typical safety standards set by the city. See "Frontier City Contract Let," *Fort Worth Press*, April 1, 1936, 1, 9; L. G. Larson to G. D. Fairtrace, May 19, 1936, Box 1, Folder "May 1936," Fort Worth City Council, Council Proceedings.
61. Bess Stephenson, "Centennial Show Sketch Plans Ready," *Fort Worth Star-Telegram*, March 26, 1936, 1–2; "Frontier Centennial Will Be Riot

of Color," *Fort Worth Star-Telegram*, April 12, 1936, 1, 4; "Frontier City Contract Let," *Fort Worth Press*, April 1, 1936, 1, 9.

62. "Frontier Show Almost Ready," *Fort Worth Star-Telegram*, July 3, 1936, 9.
63. "Frontier City Contract Let," *Fort Worth Press*, April 1, 1936, 1, 9.
64. "Paul Whitman's Orchestra Signed for 6 Weeks' Stay at Frontier Show," *Fort Worth Star-Telegram*, April 7, 1936, 1–2; Show Dance Hall's Name Is Changed to Pioneer Palace," *Fort Worth Star-Telegram*, May 3, 1936, 2. See also "Casa Mañana—House of Tomorrow—Rapidly Becomes House of Today," *Fort Worth Press*, May 23, 1936, 1.
65. "Centennial Show Sketch Plans Ready," *Fort Worth Star-Telegram*, March 26, 1936, 1–2; "'Jumbo' Will Be Here for Centennial," *Fort Worth Star-Telegram*, April 10, 1936, 1–2; "Here's Where 'Jumbo' Will Be Housed for Summer," *Fort Worth Star-Telegram*, April 12, 1936, 1.
66. "'Jumbo Will Be Here for Centennial," *Fort Worth Star-Telegram*, April 10, 1936, 1–2.
67. "Paul Whiteman's Orchestra Signed for 6 Weeks' Stay at Frontier Show," *Fort Worth Star-Telegram*, April 7, 1936, 1–2; "Frontier Centennial Will Be Riot of Color," *Fort Worth Star-Telegram*, April 12, 1936, 1, 4.
68. "Centennial Show Sketch Plans Ready," *Fort Worth Star-Telegram*, March 26, 1936, 1–2; "Western Show Stage is Large," *Fort Worth Star-Telegram*, May 6, 1936, 1; "'Last Frontier' Stage to Be Like This," *Fort Worth Star-Telegram*, May 20, 1936, 10.
69. "Western Show Stage is Large," *Fort Worth Star-Telegram*, May 6, 1936, 1.
70. "Rose Plans 'Honky Tonk' Entertainment Palace," *Fort Worth Press*, April 7, 1936, 16; "Jumbo Will Be Here for Centennial," *Fort Worth Star-Telegram*, April 10, 1936, 16.
71. "Show Palace Contract Let," *Fort Worth Press*, May 5, 1936, 1; "Frontier Centennial Will Be Riot of Color," *Fort Worth Star-Telegram*, April 12, 1936, 1, 4.
72. See "Fort Worth Festival," *Architectural Forum* 65, no. 3 (September 1936), 9.
73. "Billy Rose Is Back with Ideas of Zeppelin Size," *Fort Worth Star-Telegram*, April 4, 1936, 16; "Here's First Sketch of Centennial 'Frontier City,'" *Fort Worth Press*, March 26, 1936, 2; "Centennial Show Sketch Plans Ready," *Fort Worth Star-Telegram*, March 26, 1936, 1–2. Apparently, the excavation of the foundation and the laying of sewer and water lines for the Opery House had already commenced before the building was scrapped. See "Skyline at Frontier Centennial Grounds Shapes Up as Roofing Work is Rushed," *Fort Worth Star-Telegram*, May 16, 1936, 3.
74. "'Airplanes' Will Roar Around 250-Foot Tower to Thrill Frontier Show

Crowds," *Fort Worth Press*, April 29, 1936, 3.

75. "Sale of Frontier Show Tickets at Bargain Rates to be Begun Monday," *Fort Worth Star-Telegram*, May 29, 1936, 1–2. See also "Here's Some More Actors Who'll Be in Centennial Show," *Fort Worth Star-Telegram*, July 1, 1936, 8.
76. In his study of the theming of Six Flags Over Texas theme park, Richard Francaviglia suggests that the first use of the symbols of the six nations to govern Texas used on grounds of the Texas State Centennial in 1936 represented the first "amusement-oriented environment to use the six flags theme." See Richard Francaviglia, "Texas History in Texas Theme Parks: Six Flags Over Texas Revisited," *Legacies: A History Journal for Dallas and North Texas* 7 (Fall 1995): 34–43 (quotation on 35). I would argue that since the Texas State Centennial focused on education rather than entertainment and only drew upon the themes as ornamentation rather cultivating specific organizational or architectural themes, the Frontier Centennial represents the first use of the six flags theme for entertainment purposes.
77. "Westex Centennial Exhibit Plan Broadened with Main Showing at Fort Worth's Frontier Centennial," *West Texas Today* 17, no. 1 (March 1936): 7; "All West Texas Rally at Frontier Show is Urged," *Fort Worth Star-Telegram*, March 14, 1936, 3.
78. "Westex Centennial Exhibit Plan Broadened with Main Showing at Fort Worth's Frontier Centennial," *West Texas Today* 17, no. 1 (March 1936): 7.
79. "West Texas Exhibits Start is Asked," *Fort Worth Star-Telegram*, March 17, 1936, 9; "Big Spring Man to Draw Plans," *Fort Worth Star-Telegram*, March 19, 1936, 4.
80. "Old Railroad Station Replica to Be at Show," *Fort Worth Star-Telegram*, April 25, 1936, 1–2; "Railroad Station Replica at Show Nears Completion," *Fort Worth Star-Telegram*, May 27, 1936, 3.
81. "Pioneer Railway Station at Show Will Be Completed," *Fort Worth Star-Telegram*, May 28, 1936, 9; "Old T. P. Equipment Rebuilt for Exhibits in Centennial," *Fort Worth Star-Telegram*, May 31, 1936, 10.
82. See "1,000 at Work on WTCC Show," *Fort Worth Star-Telegram*, May 17, 1936, 7; Ella Daggett, "Pinwheels and Pioneers," 28–29, typescript, Folder "II: 2:11 Fort Worth Frontier Centennial—Typescript by Ella Daggett—1936," Box 2, Series 11, Lake Papers. For an architectural rendering of the interior and exterior of the West Texas Chamber of Commerce building, see D. A. Bandeen, "Who'd Like to be an Ethiopian? West Texas to Get its Story Told at the Frontier Centennial," *West Texas Today* 17, no. 3 (May 1936): 28.
83. Cawelti, *The Six-Gun Mystique*, 28–29.
84. "Tomorrow in Fort Worth," *Fort Worth Star-Telegram*, July 17, 1936, 6.

85. Harold Brown, "Well, Sir, We'll Amble Over to Cactus Ike's Bar and a More Dilapidated Structure You've Never Seen; When Last Nail's Driven It'll Be a He Man's Stomping Ground," *Fort Worth Press*, June 3, 1936, 1, 8.
86. See "C. L. Douglas, "Frontier Show Village Scene Merits Praise," *Fort Worth Press*, June 24, 1936, 7; "What Our Readers Say," *Fort Worth Press*, June 17, 1936, 4.
87. See "Village Street Plans are Told," *Fort Worth Star-Telegram*, May 1, 1936, 9; "Show Sites Allocated to Women," *Fort Worth Press*, May 5, 1936, 6; Edith Alderman Guedry, "Rare Relics Arrive Now Every Day for Museum to be in Frontier Building," *Fort Worth Press*, June 4, 1936, 6.
88. "Village Street Plans are Told," *Fort Worth Star-Telegram*, May 1, 1936, 9; see also Daggett, "Pinwheels and Pioneers," 3, 16, 18–19, 22.
89. Ernie Pyle, "'Big Four' Attractions of Frontier Show Visualized," *Fort Worth Press*, June 1, 1936, 1.
90. Daggett, "Pinwheels and Pioneers," 3, 23; "Show to Have Early Texas 'Main Street,'" *Fort Worth Press*, April 13, 1936, 1. For a copy of the mock frontier paper, see *The Frontier City Weekly Star*, Folder "July 5, 1936–July 29, 1936," Box 322 (6), Carter Papers.
91. See *Jumbo*, playbill, Fort Worth, 1936, Folder 2, Jane Wiggins Gudgeon York Collection, TCA.
92. See Billy Rose to Amon G. Carter, April 13, 1936, Box 116, Folder "Lanham, Fritz, 1926–1947," Carter Papers.
93. Ragsdale, *Centennial '36*, 246–47.
94. Van Zandt Jarvis, untitled document, May 1936, Box 163, Folder "Roosevelt, Franklin D., 1934–1936," Carter Papers.
95. For details regarding the purpose of the president's trip to Texas, see "Roosevelt to Stay Here June 12 and Part of 13th," *Fort Worth Star-Telegram*, May 28, 1936, 8.
96. "Fort Worth Set to Hail Roosevelt," *Fort Worth Star-Telegram*, June 12, 1936, 1–2; "Route to Be Followed by President Roosevelt and Party," *Fort Worth Star-Telegram*, June 12, 1936, 2; "'Wonderful,' Says President on Viewing Show Grounds," *Fort Worth Star-Telegram*, June 13, 1936, 1 (quotation). For a photograph of Carter instructing Roosevelt, see "President Finds Much of Interest as He Inspects Frontier Centennial Site," *Fort Worth Star-Telegram*, June 13, 1936, 9.
97. David M. Wrobel, *Promised Lands: Promotion, Memory, and the Creation of the American West* (Lawrence: University Press of Kansas, 2002), 122.

Epilogue

1. Jones, *Billy Rose Presents . . . Casa Mañana*, 77, 94; Rose, *Wine, Women*

and *Words*, 21–22.

2. Jones, *Billy Rose Presents . . . Casa Mañana*, 94.
3. Ibid., 80, 96–97. See also Amon G. Carter to Walter A. Jones, August 21, 1936, Box 110, Folder "J-Miscellaneous, 1936–1940," Carter Papers.
4. Jones, *Billy Rose Presents . . . Casa Mañana*, 86, 99.
5. J. Frank Norris, quoted in Jones, *Billy Rose Presents . . . Casa Mañana*, 98.
6. After the show opened, a solitary complaint about Rand's performance came from a Reverend Joe Scheumack. See Fort Worth City Council, Meeting Minutes, August 5, 1936, 290. Jones, *Billy Rose Presents . . . Casa Mañana*, 132–33.
7. Jones, *Billy Rose Presents . . . Casa Mañana*, 103; Ragsdale, *Centennial '36*, 294.
8. Report of the Texas Centennial Livestock and Frontier Days Exposition, Inc., March 11, 193[7], in Lois Gray, "History of the Fort Worth Centennial," appendix.
9. Amon G. Carter to Billy Rose, November 14, 1936, Box 163, Folder "Billy Rose, 1936–1939," Carter Papers.
10. "The Story of West Texas at the Frontier Centennial; Permanency of Exhibit Now Under Consideration," *West Texas Today* 17 no. 9 (November 1936): 3–4.
11. Rose, quoted in Jones, *Billy Rose Presents . . . Casa Mañana*, 107.
12. James F. Pollock to Frank L. McNeny, April 5, 1937; James F. Pollock to Frank N. Watson, April 6, 1937 (quotation); Frank N. Watson to James F. Pollock, April 10, 1937, Box 15, Folder "Ft. Worth Frontier Fiesta," Texas Centennial Central Exposition in Dallas Collection.
13. Jones, *Billy Rose Presents . . . Casa Mañana*, 108–9.
14. *Billy Rose Presents Frontier Fiesta*, Fort Worth, 1937.
15. Jones, *Billy Rose Presents . . . Casa Mañana*, 121–23.
16. Ibid., 133.
17. Ibid., 109–10, 114, 116.
18. Nelson, *"Only a Paper Moon,"* 63–64.
19. Ibid., 65.
20. Ibid., 69–70, 74.
21. Howard A. Flanigan to Amon G. Carter, July 30, 1936, Box 125, Folder "N-Miscellaneous, 1936–1939," Carter Papers.
22. Nelson, *"Only a Paper Moon,"* 81, 83, 86–87.
23. Amon G. Carter to Van Zandt Jarvis, February 11, 1937, box 110, folder "J-Miscellaneous, 1936–1940," Carter Papers.
24. Reynolds, *A Hundred Years of Heroes*, 210–11.
25. Ibid., 218–19.
26. Ella Daggett, "Pinwheels and Pioneers."
27. E. Clyde Whitlock, "The Night Isn't Young but Memory Beautiful—the

Frontier Centennial," *Fort Worth Star-Telegram*, 1946, copy in "Frontier Centennial," vertical file, FTWPLA.

28. *Fort Worth Fiesta-Cade: A Century in Review* (Fort Worth, 1949), Box 7, Folder 32, Jary Collection.
29. "City Urged to Forego Nude for History," [unknown newspaper], January 14, 1941, Box 3, Folder 32, "FW Centennial, Clippings, 1941, Tarrant County Historical Society, TCA.
30. Miller, *The Woman's Club of Fort Worth*, 19.
31. Jack Gordon, "Stars from Casa of 1939 sought," *Fort Worth Star-Telegram*, evening edition, April 27, 1981, 6B.
32. "Turn an Eyesore into a Park," *Fort Worth Press*, November 14, 1946, 15.
33. Jones, *Billy Rose Presents . . . Casa Mañana*, 159.
34. "In 1936, an Office Was Here," *Fort Worth Press*, July 16, 1961, 23A.
35. "Guests expected from afar for reunion of showgirls," clipping from box 8, folder 2, Jary Collection.
36. Jack Gordon, "Stars from Casa of 1939 sought," *Fort Worth Star-Telegram*, evening edition, April 27, 1981, 6B; Jack Gordon, "He Couldn't Hope for a Better Tipper," *Fort Worth Star-Telegram*, evening edition, June 8, 1981, 6B.
37. See Perry Stewart, "The Summer of Their Lives," *Fort Worth Star-Telegram*, April 12, 2001, Theaters—Casa Mañana—Texas Centennial, folder 2, vertical files, TCA.
38. See Talbert, *Cowtown-Metropolis*.
39. See Pirtle, *Fort Worth: The Civilized West*.
40. Ty Cashion, *The New Frontier*, cover.
41. See Fort Worth Clearing House Association advertisement in *Billy Rose Presents Frontier Fiesta* (Fort Worth, 1937), 5, and Fort Worth Chamber of Commerce advertisement in *West Texas Today* 30, no. 9 (November 1949), 1.
42. M. Jeffrey Hardwick, *Mall Maker: Victor Gruen, Architect of an American Dream* (Philadelphia: University of Pennsylvania Press, 2004), 169–92. See Victor Gruen Associates, *A Greater Fort Worth Tomorrow* (Greater Fort Worth Planning Committee, 1956).
43. Renee M. Laegreid, "Faux-Low Pop: Urban Cowboys and the Inversion of High-Pop," Metropoli e Nuovi Consumi Culturali: Performance urbane dell'identita, *Annali del Dispartimento di Science della Comunicazione dell'Universita degli Studi de Teramo* 4, no. 1 (October 2009): 86.
44. See Peter Cawley, "Fort Worth Rides Again," *Historic Preservation* 31, no. 1 (January–February 1980): 10–16.
45. See *Fort Worth: City of Cowboys and Culture* (Fort Worth Convention & Visitors Bureau, n.d.); *Fort Worth: Cultural District* (no publication data). Both pamphlets in the possession of the author.

46. See press release, "Amon Carter Museum Adds "of American Art" to Its Name," August 2, 2010, copy in possession of the author. For a history of the evolution of the Amon Carter Museum, see Bart C. Pointer, "Culture in Cowtown: The Amon Carter Museum," *East Texas Historical Journal* 39, no. 2 (2001): 40–46.

BIBLIOGRAPHY

ARCHIVAL AND MANUSCRIPT COLLECTIONS

Carter, Amon G. Papers. Special Collections, Mary Couts Burnett Library, Texas Christian University, Fort Worth, Texas.

Crane, R. C., Sr. Papers. Southwest Collection/Special Collections Library Archives, Texas Tech University, Lubbock, Texas.

Daggett, Mary. Papers. Fort Worth Public Library Archives, Fort Worth, Texas.

Dobie, James Frank. Papers. Center for American History, University of Texas, Austin, Texas.

Fort Worth Chamber of Commerce Papers. Special Collections, Mary Couts Burnett Library, Box 21, Folder 45. Texas Christian University, Fort Worth, Texas.

Fort Worth City Council Meeting Minutes. Office of the City Secretary, Fort Worth, Texas.

Fort Worth City Council Proceedings. Fort Worth Public Library Archives, Fort Worth, Texas.

"Frontier Centennial," Vertical Files. Fort Worth Public Library Archives, Fort Worth, Texas.

Frontier Centennial Scrapbooks. Special Collections, Mary Couts Burnett Library, Texas Christian University, Fort Worth, Texas.

Jary, William E. Collection. Special Collections, University of Texas at Arlington, Arlington, Texas.

The March of Time (newsreel). "The Battle of a Centennial" (originally aired June 1936). Amon Carter Museum Library, Fort Worth, Texas.

Reynolds, Clay. Papers, 1895–2002. Southwest Collection/ Special Collections Library, Texas Tech University, Lubbock, Texas.

Southwestern Exposition & Fat Stock Show Programs. Fort Worth Public Library Archives, Fort Worth, Texas.

Tarrant County Historical Society Records. Fort Worth Public Library Archives, Fort Worth, Texas.

Texas Centennial Central Exposition in Dallas Collection. Dallas Historical Society, Dallas, Texas.

United Daughters of the Confederacy, Julia Jackson Chapter, 1897–1969, Collection. Fort Worth Public Library Archives, Fort Worth, Texas.

Venth, Carl. Papers. Fort Worth Public Library Archives, Fort Worth, Texas.

West Texas Chamber of Commerce Records, 1893–1937 & undated. Southwest Collection/Special Collections, Texas Tech University, Lubbock, Texas.

York, Jane Wiggins Gudgeon. Collection. Tarrant County Archives, Fort Worth, Texas.

GOVERNMENT DOCUMENTS AND PUBLICATIONS

Dobie, J. Frank. Minority Report of the Advisory Board of Texas Historians to the Commission of Control for Texas Centennial Celebrations. Austin, 1935.

General and Special Laws of the State of Texas Passed by the 44th Legislature, Austin 1935.

Journal of the Senate of Texas, 4th Session, 43rd Legislature. Austin, 1935.

Schoen, Harold. *Monuments Erected by the State of Texas to Commemorate the Centenary of Texas Independence.* Austin: Commission of Control for Texas Centennial Celebrations, 1938.

Texas Centennial Commission. *Commemorating A Hundred Years of Texas History.* Austin, 1934.

PAMPHLETS, PLAYBILLS, SOUVENIR PUBLICATIONS

Billy Rose Presents Casa Mañana. Playbill, Fort Worth, 1936.

Billy Rose Presents Frontier Fiesta. Playbill, Fort Worth, 1937.

Billy Rose Presents The Last Frontier. Playbill, Fort Worth, 1936.

By Greyhound to Greater Texas and Pan-American Exposition and Frontier Fiesta. (No publication data.)

Davidson, Nelson. *Pencil Trails: Fort Worth Frontier Centennial.* Dealey and Lowe, 1936.

Diamond Jubilee Committee. *Diamond Jubilee.* Fort Worth: Claud Gross Co., 1923.

Fort Worth Amusement Center of the Southwest. (No publication data.)

Fort Worth Association of Commerce. Promotional pamphlet (no title), 1929.

Fort Worth Chamber of Commerce. "Fort Worth, 1929." (No publication data.)

Fort Worth: City of Cowboys and Culture. Fort Worth Convention & Visitors Bureau n.d..

Fort Worth: Cultural District. (No publication data.)

Fort Worth Fiesta-Cade: A Century in Review. Fort Worth, 1949.

Fort Worth Frontier Centennial. A Statement by William Monnig, Chairman of the Board of Control. 1936.

Fort Worth Frontier Centennial: A living, breathing recreation of the Old West. (No publication data.)

Fort Worth Frontier Centennial in the Capital of the Cattle Kings. (No publication data.)

Fort Worth Frontier Fiesta. (No publication data.)

Frontier City Weekly Star. 1936.

Jumbo. Playbill, Fort Worth, 1936.

Texas Centennial Celebrations: Centennial Year Calendar. Dallas, 1936.

Victor Gruen Associates. *A Greater Fort Worth Tomorrow.* Greater Fort Worth Planning Committee, 1956.

The Westerner. Playbill, Fort Worth, 1940.

Wild and Whoo-Pee: Fort Worth Frontier. Fort Worth, 1936.

ARTICLES AND BOOK CHAPTERS

Anderson, William T. "Wall Drug—South Dakota's Tourist Emporium." *American West* 22, no. 2 (March/April 1985): 72–76.

Block, Geoffrey. "'Bigger Than a Show—Better Than a Circus': The Broadway Musical, Radio, and Billy Rose's *Jumbo*." *The Musical Quarterly* 89, no. 2–3 (Summer–Fall 2006): 164–98.

Boehm, Lisa Krissoff. "The Fair and the Fan Dancer: A Century of Progress and Chicago's Image." *Chicago History* 27, no. 2 (July 1998): 42–55.

Boisseau, Tracey Jean. "Once Again in Chicago: Revisioning Women As Workers at the Chicago Woman's World's Fairs of 1925–1928." *Women's History Review* 18, no. 2 (April 2009): 265–91.

———. "White Queens at the Chicago World's Fair, 1893: New Womanhood in the Service of Class, Race, and Nation." *Gender & History* 12, no. 1 (April 2000): 33–81.

Boswell, Angela. "From Farm to Future: Women's Journey through Twentieth-Century Texas." In *Twentieth-Century Texas: A Social and Cultural History*, edited by John W. Storey and Mary L. Kelley, 105–34. Denton: University of North Texas Press, 2008.

Brundage, W. Fitzhugh. "No Deed but Memory." In *Where These Memories Grow: History, Memory, and Southern Identity*, edited by W. Fitzhugh Brundage, 1–28. Chapel Hill: University of North Carolina Press, 2000.

Buenger, Walter L. "Texas and the South." *Southwestern Historical Quarterly* 103, no. 3 (January 2000): 309–24.

Buenger, Walter L, and Robert A. Calvert. "The Shelf Life of Truth in Texas." In *Texas Through Time: Evolving Interpretations*, edited by Walter L. Buenger and Robert A. Calvert, ix–xxxv. College Station: Texas A&M University Press, 1991.

Butler, Anne M. "Selling the Popular Myth." In *The Oxford History of the American West*, edited by Clyde A. Milner, Carol A. O'Connor, and Martha A. Sandweiss, 771–801. New York:

Oxford University Press; 1994 (1996 paperback edition).

Cantrell, Gregg. "The Bones of Stephen F. Austin: History and Memory in Progressive-Era Texas." *Southwestern Historical Quarterly* 108, no. 2 (October 2004): 145–78.

Cleveland, Annie O., and M. Barrett Cleveland. "Fort Worth for Entertainment: Billy Rose's Casa Mañana (1936–1939)." *Theatre Design & Technology* 44, no. 1 (Winter 2008): 25–40.

Confino, Alon. "Collective Memory and Cultural History: Problems of Method." *The American Historical Review* 102, no. 5 (December 1997): 1386–1403.

Crane, R. C., Sr. "The Claims of West Texas to Recognition by Historians." *The West Texas Historical Association Year Book* 12 (July 1936): 11–33.

Crum, Tom. "West Texas." *The West Texas Historical Association Year Book* 76 (October 2000): 16–32.

Cummins, Light Townsend. "From the Midway to the Hall of State at Fair Park: Two Competing Views of Women at the Dallas Celebration of 1936." *Southwestern Historical Quarterly* 64, no. 3 (January 2011): 225–51.

———. "History, Memory, and Rebranding Texas as Western for the 1936 Centennial." In *This Corner of Canaan: Essays on Texas in Honor of Randolph B. Campbell*, edited by Richard B. McCaslin, Donald E. Chipman, and Andrew J. Torget, 37–57. Denton: University of North Texas, 2013.

Dillon, Mike. "March of Time, The." In *Encyclopedia of American Journalism*, edited by Stephen L. Vaughn, 292–93. New York: Routledge, 2008.

Etulain, Richard. "Origins of the Western." *Journal of Popular Culture* 5, no. 4 (1972): 799–805.

Francaviglia, Richard. "Walt Disney's Frontierland as an Allegorical Map of the American West." *Western Historical Quarterly* 30, no. 2 (Summer 1999): 155–82.

———. "Texas History in Texas Theme Parks: Six Flags Over Texas Revisited." *Legacies: A History Journal for Dallas and North Texas* 7 (Fall 1995): 34–43.

Gedi, Noa, and Yigal Elam. "Collective Memory—What Is It?"

History & Memory 8, no. 1 (Spring/Summer 1996): 30–50.

Graham, Don "Lone Star Cinema: A Century of Texas in the Movies." In *Twentieth-Century Texas: A Social and Cultural History*, edited by John W. Storey and Mary L. Kelly, 245–66. Denton: University of North Texas Press, 2008.

Hooks, Michael Q. "The Role of Promoters in Urban Rivalry: The Dallas-Fort Worth Experience, 1870–1910." *Red River Valley Historical Review* 7, no. 2 (Spring 1982): 4–16.

Kansteiner, Wulf. "Finding Meaning in Memory: A Methodological Critique of Collective Memory Studies." *History and Theory* 41, no. 2 (May 2002): 179–97.

Laegreid, Renee M. "Faux-Low Pop: Urban Cowboys and the Inversion of High-Pop." Metropoli e Nuovi Consumi Culturali: Performance urbane dell'identita. *Annali del Dispartimento di Science della Comunicazione dell'Universita degli Studi de Teramo* 4, no. 1 (October 2009): 73–88.

Levine, Lawrence W. "American Culture and the Great Depression." *The Yale Review* 74, no. 2 (January 1985): 196–223.

Lowenthal, David. "The Past as a Theme Park." In *Theme Park Landscapes: Antecedents and Variations*, edited by Terence Young and Robert Riley, 11–23. Washington, DC: Dumbarton Oaks Research Library, 2002.

Manning, Frank E. "Cosmos and Chaos: Celebration in the Modern World." In *The Celebration of Society: Perspectives on Contemporary Cultural Performance*, edited by Frank E. Manning, 3–31. Bowling Green, OH: Bowling Green University Popular Press, 1983.

Myres, Sandra L. "Fort Worth, 1870–1900." *Southwestern Historical Quarterly* 72, no. 2 (October 1968): 200–206.

Olmstead, Jacob W. "'Un-Southern': Buffalo Bill, The Texas State Centennial, and Texas's Western Turn." *Southwestern Historical Quarterly* 122, no. 4 (April 2019): 371–94.

Oneal, Ben G. "A Brief Story of the Restoration of Fort Belknap." *West Texas Historical Association Year Book* 29 (October 1953): 105–14.

Polatti, Gaylon. "The Magic City and the Frontier." *Legacies: A History Journal for Dallas and North Central Texas* 11, no. 1 (Spring 1999): 37–39.

Sally, Lynn. "Luna Park's Fantasy World and Dreamland's White City: Fire Spectacles at Coney Island as Elemental Performativity." In *The Themed Space: Locating Culture, Nation, and Self*, edited by Scott A. Lukas, 39–55. Lanham, MD: Lexington Books, 2007.

Steiner, Michael. "Frontierland as Tomorrowland: Walt Disney and the Architectural Packaging of the Mythic West." *Montana: The Magazine of Western History* 48, no. 1 (Spring 1998): 2–17.

West, Elliot. "Selling the Myth: Western Images in Advertising." *Montana: The Magazine of Western History* 46, no. 2 (Summer 1996): 36–49.

White, Richard. "Frederick Jackson Turner and Buffalo Bill." In *The Frontier in American Culture*, edited by James R. Grossman, 6–65. Berkeley: University Press of California, 1994.

Young, Terence. "Grounding the Myth—Theme Park Landscapes in an Era of Commerce and Nationalism." In *Theme Park Landscapes: Antecedents and Variations*, edited by Terence Young and Robert Riley, 1–10. Washington, DC: Dumbarton Oaks Research Library, 2002.

BOOKS

Abbott, Carl. *Boosters and Businessmen: Popular Economic Thought and Urban Growth in the Antebellum Middle West.* Westport, CT: Greenwood Press, 1981.

Allen, Robert C. *Horrible Prettiness: Burlesque and American Culture.* Chapel Hill: University of North Carolina Press, 1991.

Anderson, Hugh Abercrombie. *Out Without My Rubbers: The Memoirs of John Murray Anderson*. New York: Library Publishers, 1954.

Banner, Lois W. *American Beauty.* New York: Alfred Knopf, 1983.

Barber, Alicia. *Reno's Big Gamble: Image and Reputation in the*

Biggest Little City. Lawrence: University Press of Kansas, 2008.

Barker, Evelyn. *A Texas Journey: The Centennial Photographs of Polly Smith*. Dallas: Dallas Historical Society, 2008.

Bokovoy, Matthew F. *The San Diego World's Fairs and Southwestern Memory, 1880–1940*. Albuquerque: University of New Mexico Press, 2005.

Buenger, Walter L. *The Path to a Modern South: Northeast Texas between Reconstruction and the Great Depression*. Austin: University of Texas Press, 2001.

Campbell, Randolph B. *Gone to Texas: A History of the Lone Star State*. New York: Oxford University Press, 2003.

Cashion, Ty. *The New Frontier: A Contemporary History of Fort Worth & Tarrant County*. San Antonio: Historical Publishing Network, 2006.

Cawelti, John G. *The Six-Gun Mystique*. Bowling Green, OH: Bowling Green University Popular Press, 1984.

Christensen, Bonnie. *Red Lodge and the Mythic West: Coal Miners to Cowboys*. Lawrence: University Press of Kansas, 2002.

Cochran, Mike, and John Lumpkin. *West Texas: A Portrait of Its People and Their Raw and Wondrous Land*. Lubbock: Texas Tech University Press, 1999.

Cohen, Judith Singer. *Cowtown Moderne: Art Deco Architecture of Fort Worth, Texas*. College Station: Texas A&M University Press, 1988.

Conrad, Earl. *Billy Rose: Manhattan Primitive*. Cleveland: World Publishing, 1968.

Ely, Glen Sample. *Where the West Begins: Debating Texas Identity*. Lubbock: Texas Tech University Press, 2011.

Etulain, Richard W. *Western Films: A Brief History*. Manhattan, KS: Sunflower University Press, 1983; second printing, 1988.

Findlay, John M. *Magic Lands: Western Cityscapes and American Culture after 1940*. Berkeley: University of California Press; 1992 (1993 paperback edition).

Flemmons, Jerry. *Amon: The Life of Amon Carter, Sr. of Texas*. Austin: Jenkins Publishing Company, 1978.

Foley, Brenda. *Undressed for Success: Beauty Contestants and*

Exotic Dancers as Merchants of Morality. New York: Palgrave Macmillan, 2005.

Fredriksson, Kristine. *American Rodeo: From Buffalo Bill to Big Business*. College Station: Texas A&M University Press, 1985.

Friedman, B. H. *Gertrude Vanderbilt Whitney*. New York: Doubleday, 1978.

Ganz, Cheryl R. *The 1933 Chicago World's Fair: A Century of Progress*. Urbana and Chicago: University of Illinois Press, 2008.

Gottlieb, Polly Rose. *The Nine Lives of Billy Rose*. New York: Crown Publishers, 1968.

Graham, Don. *Cowboys and Cadillacs: How Hollywood Looks at Texas*. Austin: Texas Monthly Press, 1983.

Grossman, Barbara W. *Funny Woman: The Life and Times of Fanny Brice*. Bloomington and Indianapolis: Indiana University Press, 1991.

Hankins, Barry. *God's Rascal: J. Frank Norris & the Beginnings of Southern Fundamentalism*. Lexington: University Press of Kentucky, 1996.

Hardwick, M. Jeffrey. *Mall Maker: Victor Gruen, Architect of an American Dream*. Philadelphia: University of Pennsylvania Press, 2004.

Hernández-Ehrisman, Laura. *Inventing the Fiesta City: Heritage and Carnival in San Antonio*. Albuquerque: University of New Mexico Press, 2008.

Hine, Robert V., and John Mack Faragher. *The American West: A New Interpretive History*. New Haven: Yale University Press, 2000.

Johnson, Michael L. *Hunger for the Wild: America's Obsession with the Untamed West*. Lawrence: University Press of Kansas, 2007.

Jones, Dora Davenport. *The History of the Julia Jackson Chapter #441, United Daughters of the Confederacy: Fort Worth, Texas, 1897–1976*. Fort Worth: Kwik-Kopy Printing Center, 1976.

Jones, Jan. *Billy Rose Presents . . . Casa Mañana*. Fort Worth: Texas Christian University Press, 1999.

Jordan, Terry G. *Trails to Texas: Southern Roots of Western Cattle*

Ranching. Lincoln: University of Nebraska Press, 1981.

Knight, Oliver. *Fort Worth: Outpost on the Trinity.* Norman: University of Oklahoma Press, 1953.

Knox, Holly. *Sally Rand: From Film to Fans.* Bend, OR: Maverick Publications, 1988.

Kropp, Phoebe S. *California Vieja: Culture and Memory in a Modern American Place.* Berkeley: University of California Press, 2006.

Laegreid, Renee M. *Riding Pretty: Rodeo Royalty in the American West.* Lincoln: University of Nebraska Press, 2006.

Leach, William. *Land of Desire: Merchants, Power, and the Rise of a New American Culture.* New York: Pantheon Books, 1993.

Lewis, Lloyd. *It Takes All Kinds.* New York: Books for Libraries Press, 1974 (1947 reprint).

Limerick, Patricia Nelson. *The Legacy of Conquest: The Unbroken Past of the American West.* New York: W.W. Norton, 1987.

Lowitt, Richard. *The New Deal and the West.* Bloomington: Indiana University Press, 1984.

Maney, Richard. *Fanfare: The Confessions of a Press Agent.* New York: Harper & Brothers, 1957.

McArthur, Judith N. *Creating the New Woman: The Rise of Southern Women's Progressive Culture in Texas, 1893–1918.* Urbana and Chicago: University of Illinois Press, 1998.

Miller, Elizabeth. *The Woman's Club of Fort Worth: The First Twenty-Five Years, 1923–1948.* Published privately, 1959.

Millett, Allan R., and Peter Maslowski. *For the Common Defense: A Military History of the United States of America*, revised and expanded ed. New York: The Free Press, 1994.

Mullins, Marion Day. *A History of The Woman's Club of Fort Worth, 1923–1973.* Published privately. Copy held at the Tarrant County Archives, Fort Worth, Texas.

Nash, Gerald D. *The Federal Landscape: An Economic History of the Twentieth Century West.* Tucson: University of Arizona Press, 1999.

Nelson, Stephen. *"Only a Paper Moon": The Theatre of Billy Rose.* Ann Arbor, MI: UMI Research Press, 1985; reprint 1987).

Pate, J'Nell L. *Livestock Legacy: The Fort Worth Stockyards, 1887–1987.* College Station: Texas A&M University Press, 1988.

Pirtle, Caleb. *Fort Worth: The Civilized West.* Tulsa, OK: Continental Heritage Press, 1980.

Pointer, Bart C. "Culture in Cowtown: The Amon Carter Museum." *East Texas Historical Journal* 39, no. 2 (2001): 40–46.

Ragsdale, Kenneth B. *Centennial '36: The Year America Discovered Texas.* College Station: Texas A&M University Press, 1987.

Reddin, Paul. *Wild West Shows.* Urbana and Chicago: University of Illinois Press, 1999.

Reynolds, Clay. *A Hundred Years of Heroes: A History of the Southwestern Exposition and Livestock Show.* Fort Worth: Texas Christian University Press, 1995.

Rose, Billy. *Wine, Women and Words.* New York: Simon and Schuster, 1946.

Rydell, Robert W. *All the World's a Fair: Visions of Empire at American International Expositions, 1876–1916.* Chicago: University of Chicago Press, 1984.

——— . *World of Fairs: The Century-of-Progress Expositions.* Chicago: University of Chicago Press, 1993.

Rydell, Robert W., John E. Findling, and Kimberly D. Pelle. *Fair America: World's Fairs in the United States.* Washington, DC: Smithsonian Institution Press, 2000.

Shirley, Glenn. *Pawnee Bill: A Biography of Major Gordon W. Lillie.* Albuquerque: University of New Mexico Press, 1958.

Shteir, Rachel. *Striptease: The Untold History of the Girlie Show.* New York: Oxford University Press, 2004.

Slotkin, Richard. *Gunfighter Nation: The Myth of the Frontier in Twentieth-Century America.* New York: Atheneum, 1992.

Smith, Henry Nash. *Virgin Land: The American West as Symbol and Myth.* Cambridge, MA: Harvard University Press, 1970.

Soanes, Catherine, ed. *Oxford Dictionary of Current English.* Oxford: Oxford University Press, 1993; third edition, 2001.

Talbert, Robert H. *Cowtown-Metropolis: Case Study of a City's Growth and Structure.* Fort Worth: Leo Potishman Foundation, Texas Christian University, 1956.

Terkel, Studs. *Hard Times: An Oral History of the Great Depression.* New York: Pantheon Books, 1970.

Van Zandt, Khleber Miller. *Force Without Fanfare: The Autobiography of K. M. Van Zandt.* Fort Worth: Texas Christian University Press, 1995 (reprint 1968).

Venth, Carl. *My Memories.* San Antonio: Alamo Printing, 1939.

Waggoner, Susan. *Nightclub Nights: Art, Legend, and Style, 1920–1960.* New York: Rizzoli: 2001.

Webb, Walter Prescott. *The Great Plains,* 1931. Reprint, New York: Ginn and Company, 1959.

Wilson, Chris. *The Myth of Santa Fe: Creating a Modern Regional Tradition.* Albuquerque: University of New Mexico Press, 1997.

White, G. Edward. *The Eastern Establishment and the Western Experience: The West of Frederic Remington, Theodore Roosevelt, and Owen Wister.* New Haven and London: Yale University Press, 1968.

Wrobel, David M. *Promised Lands: Promotion, Memory, and the Creation of the American West.* Lawrence: University Press of Kansas, 2002.

———. *The End of American Exceptionalism: Frontier Anxiety from the Old West to the New Deal.* Lawrence: University Press of Kansas, 1993.

THESES AND DISSERTATIONS

Gibbs, Gary Dan. "Carl Venth (1860–1938): Texas's Master Musician: His Life, His Music, His Influence." PhD diss., Austin: University of Texas, 1990.

Gray, Lois. "History of the Fort Worth Frontier Centennial." MA thesis, Texas Christian University, 1938.

Hancock, Jeffery Mason. "Preservation of Texas Heritage in the 1936 Centennial." MA thesis, University of Texas, 1963.

INDEX

Numbers in italics indicate images.

ABOUT THE AUTHOR

Photo courtesy of Leslie Nilsson

Jacob W. Olmstead is a curator of historic sites in the Church History Department of The Church of Jesus Christ of Latter-day Saints. In 2011, he received a PhD in American history from Texas Christian University, where he studied civic memory and identity in the American West. His research and writing have appeared in *BYU Studies*, *Journal of Mormon History*, *Southwestern Historical Quarterly*, and *Utah Historical Quarterly*.